PARADOXES OF POWER

 Mark A. Boyer, University of Connecticut, Series Editor

International Studies Intensives (ISI) is a book series that springs from the desire to keep students engaged in the world around them. Books in the series address a wide array of topics in the international studies field, all devoted to getting students involved in the ways in which international events affect their daily lives. ISI books focus on innovative topics and approaches to study that cover popular and scholarly debates and employ new methods for presenting theories and concepts to students and scholars alike. ISI books pack a lot of information into a small space—they are meant to offer an intensive introduction to subjects often left out of the curriculum. ISI books are relatively short, visually attractive, and affordably priced.

Editorial Board

Titles in the Series

Paradoxes of Power: U.S. Foreign Policy in a Changing World
edited by David Skidmore
The Rules of the Game: A Primer on International Relations
by Mark R. Amstutz
A Tale of Two Quagmires: Iraq, Vietnam, and the Hard Lessons of War
by Kenneth J. Campbell

PARADOXES OF POWER

U.S. Foreign Policy in a Changing World

edited by
David Skidmore

Paradigm Publishers
Boulder • London

Copyright © 2007 by Paradigm Publishers

Published in the United States by Paradigm Publishers, 3360 Mitchell Lane, Suite E, Boulder, CO 80301 USA.

Paradigm Publishers is the trade name of Birkenkamp & Company, LLC,
Dean Birkenkamp, President and Publisher.

Library of Congress Cataloging-in-Publication Data
Paradoxes of power : U.S. foreign policy in a changing world / edited by David Skidmore.
    p. cm. — (International studies intensives)
    Includes bibliographical references.
    ISBN 978-1-59451-402-9 (hardcover : alk. paper) — ISBN 978-1-59451-403-6 (pbk. : alk. paper)
    1. United States—Foreign relations—2001– 2. United States—Foreign relations—21st century. 3. World politics—21st century. 4. War on Terrorism, 2001– 5. Hegemony—United States. 6. Imperialism. 7. Unilateral acts (International law) 8. United States—Foreign relations—Public opinion. 9. United States—Foreign public opinion. I. Skidmore, David, 1958–
  E895.P37 2007
  327.73009'0511—dc22

                         2006035691

ISBN-13: 978-1-59451-402-9 (hardcover : alk. paper)
ISBN-10: 1-59451-402-X (hardcover : alk. paper)
ISBN-13: 978-1-59451-403-6 (pbk. : alk. paper)
ISBN-10: 1-59451-403-8 (pbk. : alk. paper)

Printed and bound in the United States of America on acid-free paper that meets the standards of the American National Standard for Permanence of Paper for Printed Library Materials.

Typeset by Mulberry Tree Enterprises.

11 10 09 08 07   1 2 3 4 5

Contents

Preface

This volume addresses the intersection of power and purpose as they relate to U.S. foreign policy in a changing world. The United States today possesses clear military superiority over its nearest rivals. America remains the central player in the world economy, with 5 percent of the world's population accounting for over one quarter of global output. The spread of American cultural symbols and fashions is reshaping societies the world over. In short, the United States is currently the world's sole superpower.

Yet power gives rise to a distinctive set of conundrums that lead to some paradoxical answers. How long before American dominance fades? To what purposes should American power be put? Should the United States seek to strengthen international institutions as lasting mechanisms for global cooperation? Or should America retain the freedom to act alone when its interests so dictate? Do other states and peoples view American hegemony in benign terms or does U.S. power inevitably prompt fear, distrust, and resentment? Does power ensure security or merely heighten the risks of entanglement abroad and growing vulnerability? In the end, what choices do Americans face in seeking to craft a more stable world order at a moment when the United States enjoys international supremacy of uncertain duration and consequence?

These questions have risen in salience since the tragic events of 9/11 and the commitment of U.S. military forces in Afghanistan and Iraq, and they have stimulated wide-ranging debate among knowledgeable observers over the basic contours of U.S. foreign and national security policy. This volume assembles some of the best essays written on these topics by a uniquely qualified set of authors. This book is aimed principally at students in courses on world politics and U.S. foreign policy, yet this collection should be of great interest to any citizen who seeks to better understand America's role in the world during a time of great challenges and changes.

Paradoxes of Power: U.S. Foreign Policy in a Changing World is distinguished by the following features:

- *Coherence:* The volume as a whole offers a coherent focus on the paradoxes of America's international power in a changing world. The book is organized in a logical progression. Part I examines the current configuration of global power and America's unique position within it. Part II explores debates over the notion of an emerging "American empire." Part III evaluates the relative merits of unilateralist and multilateralist approaches to U.S. foreign policy. Part IV describes public attitudes, both at home and abroad, toward U.S. foreign policy and the issues with which it deals. Finally, part V offers incisive commentaries on the war in Iraq and the war on terror as recent case studies in U.S. foreign and national security policy.

- *Diversity of Perspectives:* This volume features a broad array of opinions and perspectives on contemporary U.S. foreign policy. Three schools of thought—realism, democratic nationalism, and liberal institutionalism—are highlighted. Pieces representative of each school are distributed through the various sections of the book, providing students with a clearer sense of how divergent policy prescriptions arise from varying norms, assumptions, and historical understandings. Students gain a balanced view of the underlying ideas that drive debates over U.S. foreign policy.

- *Highly Qualified Authors:* The contributors to this volume include many of today's most respected and influential commentators on foreign affairs. The list of authors includes academic specialists from the fields of political science and history as well as nonacademic observers such as journalists, policy analysts, and current or former public officials.

- *Currency:* All of the selections included here postdate the terrible and momentous events of September 11, 2001. The book as a whole offers a multifaceted set of reflections on the altered circumstances of a post-9/11 world. Yet the pieces included here speak as well to broad questions of international structure, strategic choice, and normative preference that are likely to prove of lasting relevance in the years to come.

- *Context:* The book's editorial materials, including introductory and concluding chapters and the overviews preceding each major section, provide students with historical and conceptual context for understanding the policy debates represented here. The editorial commentaries highlight points of comparison among the contributions to the volume and offer suggested discussion questions.

- *Conciseness:* Each piece has been edited for the purposes of conciseness, relevance, and the elimination of redundancy. Students will be able to complete most individual readings in a single sitting. Judicious editing has also made it possible to offer a large range of selections in a compact volume.

In short, this book is intended to provide a lively and readable introduction to current debates over American power and purpose in world affairs. I would like to thank the authors and publishers who have kindly given permission to reprint the essays that appear here. My appreciation is also extended to the many anonymous reviewers whose helpful suggestions contributed to the book's final form.

Introduction

Over much of its early history, the United States was an also-ran in the game of great-power politics, preoccupied with the tasks of securing its independence, expanding its reach westward across the North American continent, and coping with the internal divisions over slavery that eventually led to civil war. Insulated by distance from the power struggles of Europe, the United States pursued a relatively isolationist foreign policy for more than a century. By the end of the nineteenth century, however, America's size and level of economic development surpassed those of Europe's leading nations. Even so, the United States eschewed international leadership during the first half of the twentieth century and served instead as the balancer in a system of multiple great powers. The United States intervened reluctantly and tardily in each of the two world wars, seeking principally to ensure that no single rival power consolidated control over the resources of Europe and East Asia.

Emerging victorious from World War II, the United States enjoyed unprecedented power and prestige. Finally rejecting its isolationist traditions, the United States moved decisively following the war toward an activist foreign policy designed to shape the international order along lines congenial to American interests and values. Yet with the emergence of the cold war, the United States faced a peer competitor, in the form of the Soviet Union, whose power served to balance, at least partially, that of the United States. American dominance thus faced real limits imposed by the reach of the Soviet empire.

With each shift in America's international position, as this thumbnail sketch suggests, U.S. policymakers faced the task of adapting U.S. foreign policy to account for emerging new realities in the balance of power. Isolationism best fit the needs of a relatively minor power that enjoyed the advantages of insularity in the nineteenth century. As an emerging great power in a multipolar system in the first half of the twentieth century, the United States came to play a balancing role in European and Asian contests of power. Under the bipolar conditions of the cold war, the United States devoted its now enormous resources to a global struggle to contain the power of its lone remaining rival.

ADAPTING TO CHANGE

With the end of the cold war and the collapse of the Soviet Union, America's position within the distribution of international power shifted yet again. The United States operated for the first time in an era of unipolarity. And although the United States now faces enemies with the capacity to impose costs on Americans, no potential rival state wields resources sufficient to effectively balance American power.

Enough time has passed to allow us to appreciate the challenges of this unique era and to frame the paradoxes U.S. policymakers face as the world system continues to change. The shocking events of September 11, 2001, the subsequent war on terrorism, and the controversial American decision to invade and occupy Iraq underline the reality that dominance does not easily translate into security or stability. The paradoxes of power raise a series of important questions:

- How great and how lasting is American dominance? By what calculations will other major powers choose between following American leadership and balancing against American power?
- Is the United States an imperial power? What lessons, if any, can the United States draw from the experience of past imperial or hegemonic powers?
- Does unipolarity lead inexorably to a unilateralist American foreign policy? What are the advantages and disadvantages, respectively, of unilateral versus multilateral approaches to U.S. foreign policy?
- How do Americans view their role in the world? In what ways does American political culture color the interests and values to which American power is put? How does the rest of the world view the United States and its foreign policies? Are the attitudes of other peoples toward the United States shaped more by who we are or what we do? Are favorable or unfavorable opinions about the United States

relatively stable or have they shifted in response to events? Does U.S. power necessarily breed resentment?

- How has U.S. foreign policy changed since 9/11? Is the Bush doctrine of preemptive warfare a major departure from past practice? Was the war to topple Saddam Hussein in Iraq a unique event or a harbinger of how the United States will deal with "rogue" states in the future? What lessons can be learned from the U.S. experience in the Iraq war and its aftermath?

The purpose of this volume is to explore these questions by exposing readers to the reflections offered by a well-qualified set of authors. Not surprisingly, opinions differ over each of the sets of questions listed above. A range of provocative viewpoints is therefore reflected in the readings included in this book. The collection is organized into five major sections, corresponding to the debating points listed above. Each section is accompanied by an editor's overview designed to provide context and highlight points of comparison. Discussion questions and lists of suggested readings are also provided.

PARADOXES OF POWER

Among observers and practitioners of U.S. foreign policy, responses to the challenges and opportunities of this new era are shaped by long-standing philosophies about the purposes and modalities of U.S. foreign policy. These contending worldviews or schools of thought intersect with the changed realities of international power to produce varied policy prescriptions. The principal axes of debate focus on two overarching questions: (1) Interests/Values: Should U.S. foreign policy focus narrowly on the promotion of U.S. interests as defined by economic and security needs? Or should the U.S. also seek to spread American values, such as democracy and individual liberty, to other societies? (2) Unilateralist/Multilateralist: Should the United States preserve the freedom to act alone in the promotion of its interests and values? Or should it work principally through multilateral institutions, accepting the constraints that participation in these institutions entails?

Debate over these questions does not necessarily yield either/or answers. Few would advocate the pursuit of values to the exclusion of interests or the reliance on international institutions without exception. Rather, we should think about these as choices along two continuums. Where one is located along each continuum is a matter of priority and emphasis. For instance, while some argue that the United States should act unilaterally when we can and multilaterally when we must, others instead advocate that the United States act multilaterally when we can and unilaterally when we must. Moreover, the two debates intersect in important ways. Two observers might agree that the United States should promote democracy and liberty abroad but disagree about whether the best way to accomplish this is through unilateral or multilateral means. In the end, of course, what matters most is not the abstract debate over contending principles but concrete policy choices that result from the application of these principles to actual foreign policy problems and cases.

Considering these two dimensions of debate, we can identify three contending schools of foreign policy thought into which many, though not all, of the readings that follow can be classified: realist, democratic nationalist, and liberal institutionalist. As a first step toward understanding the choices facing the United States in a changing era, it is worthwhile to provide a brief sketch of each of these three perspectives.

REALISM

Realists conceive of international politics as a struggle for power and security among self-interested states. Given the context of an anarchic international system, realists place little faith in the ability of international law and institutions to curb the ambitions of power-seeking states or to ensure that peace and cooperation triumph over war and conflict. From a realist standpoint, wise statespersons place the pursuit of national interests, conceived in terms of power, security, and economic might, ahead of the promotion of humanitarian or moral aims. Efforts to export a nation's political, religious, or cultural values abroad seldom succeed and often divert scarce national resources from more pressing priorities.

Though often criticized as out of step with the underlying moral character of American political culture, realists have nonetheless played a significant role in debates over U.S. foreign policy. In the 1930s, realist historian E. H. Carr authored a searing critique of the idealism that drove Woodrow Wilson's approach to peacemaking after World War II, pointing to the inability of the League of Nations and international disarmament efforts to curb the rising power and imperial ambitions of Germany and Japan during the interwar period. Following World War II, scholar Hans Morgenthau, diplomat George Kennan, and journalist Walter Lippmann called attention to the growing Soviet threat and warned against a return to the policies of appeasement and isolationism that had failed so spectacularly during the 1930s.

During the cold war, realists supported a strong military combined with vigorous efforts to deter or contain Soviet expansion. Realists looked with favor upon close U.S. relations with right-wing authoritarian regimes that shared America's aim of balancing Soviet power, even if this meant setting aside America's historic commitment to democratic values.

Yet it would be a mistake to characterize realists as warmongers. Realists view military strength as a means to discourage would-be aggressors, thus averting, whenever possible, the necessity of war and violence. Moreover, realists have often served among the foremost critics of military force as a means to promote the spread of U.S. values abroad in cases where genuine national interests are not at stake. George Kennan, for instance, coined the doctrine of containment as a means to balance the power of the Soviet Union, but he came to lament the crusading zeal with which the United States sought to universalize the fight against communism during the cold war. Kennan, Morgenthau, and other realists denounced the Vietnam War as an unwise and unnecessary intrusion of American force into the domestic politics of a country that played only a minor strategic role in the great power competition of the cold war. More recently, realist scholars such as Stephen Walt and John Mearsheimer publicly warned against the 2003 invasion of Iraq on the grounds that the threat posed by Saddam Hussein's regime had been overstated and could be more effectively countered through traditional deterrence.

Despite the threat of international terrorism, most realists view the post–cold war period as an era of relative strength and security for the United States. While realists differ over whether the present circumstances of unipolarity can last, they unite in agreeing that the most important priority for the United States at present is to prolong American dominance and closely monitor the rise of potential competitors, such as a growing China, a uniting Europe, and a reviving Russia, as well as the spread of weapons of mass destruction. From a realist standpoint, the United States must avoid two dangerous temptations: the naive illusion that American interests can best be secured through reliance upon the weak reed of multilateral institutions and the equally suspect faith that the unilateral exercise of U.S. power can remake the world in America's own image.

DEMOCRATIC NATIONALISM

Democratic nationalists share with realists a concern for preserving American dominance, a distrust of international institutions, and a preference for unilateralism in U.S. foreign policy. Yet they depart from realists in their approach to assessing and responding to external threats.

Realists adopt a largely disinterested view concerning the internal political, economic, and cultural character of potential friends and foes. What matters is a country's capacity to threaten the United States combined with a record of international behavior suggesting the intention to do so. How a state organizes its domestic order is largely irrelevant.

Democratic nationalists, on the other hand, believe that a country's internal order largely dictates its external behavior. Countries that share commitments to democracy, individual liberty, and a free-market economy can be counted as friends of the United States (despite occasional disagreements over specific issues) and responsible members of the international community. Threats to international order and to American interests tend to arise from two sources: rogue states that reject democracy, markets, liberty, and cultural pluralism and failed states that are too weak to prevent a society from sinking into poverty, chaos, and violence.

From such circumstances arise international aggression, transnational criminal networks, regional or global terrorism, and the proliferation of weapons of mass destruction. Seldom are international carrots and sticks sufficient to contain the negative external consequences where such conditions exist. Where this is the case, democratic nationalists argue that it becomes the responsibility of the United States—either alone or, where possible, in collaboration with other states—to seek a change of regime and impose a new and stable democratic order. The available tools for seeking regime change range from external pressures (e.g., economic sanctions, diplomatic isolation) to covert intervention (e.g., funding of opposition groups, disinformation campaigns, encouragement of coups d'états) to overt military force (e.g., targeted bombing, ground intervention, occupation).

During the cold war, realists were content to contain, where possible, the expansion of Soviet influence beyond existing boundaries. In the 1950s, however, democratic nationalists called for the "rollback" of communism from Eastern Europe and East Asia, a policy that was largely rejected by the Truman and Eisenhower administrations as likely to raise the risks of major-power war. Despite the urgings of General Douglas MacArthur, President Harry Truman passed up the opportunity to expand the Korean War to mainland China. Similarly, President Dwight Eisenhower declined to intervene in 1956 when Soviet tanks violently suppressed moves toward political reform in Hungary, a Soviet client state. Democratic nationalists were more successful in pushing an agenda of regime change during the 1980s, however, when President Ronald Reagan provided American financial assistance, weapons, and covert support to rebel groups fighting to overthrow socialist or communist governments in Nicaragua, Angola, and Afghanistan.

Democratic nationalists, sometimes labeled neoconservatives, also gained influence in the post-9/11 era when President George W. Bush touted the promotion of democracy among the rationales for seeking to weaken or overthrow a series of so-called rogue or failed states. The U.S. invasions of Afghanistan and Iraq were justified in part as mechanisms for installing more stable and peaceful democratic governments in those countries.

Along with Iraq, Bush has referred to the governments of Iran and North Korea as poles in an "axis of evil" that threatens international peace and the human rights of the peoples of these countries. While holding out the possibility of a diplomatic approach to dealing with U.S. concerns about the spread of weapons of mass destruction to Iran and North Korea, Bush has made no secret of his ultimate preference for regime change in both countries.

Likewise, the Bush administration has launched a high-profile initiative to promote democratic reform across the Middle East, with Iraq serving as a model for other countries of the region that remain encumbered by authoritarian regimes. These policies have been met with skepticism from traditionally nondemocratic but pro-American governments in the region and from U.S. allies in Europe, who fear that Bush's sweeping agenda of political reform will result in failure and instability.

LIBERAL INSTITUTIONALISM

Unlike realists and democratic nationalists, liberal institutionalists embrace an approach to U.S. foreign policy that is rooted in multilateralism, the deepening of international law, and sensitivity toward the imperatives of international interdependence. In these respects, liberal institutionalists share Woodrow Wilson's vision of U.S. power as an instrument for creating a more peaceful and cooperative world order centered upon strong international institutions and the spread of democracy. In contrast with democratic nationalists, however, who seek to promote liberty and democracy abroad through the threat or use of force against rogue states, liberal institutionalists prefer the use of carrots rather than sticks. Enticements such as foreign aid, economic interdependence, global treaties, and changing norms provide the principal means for drawing recalcitrant states into a cooperative international community.

These differing perspectives are well illustrated in terms of U.S. policy toward China. Both realists and democratic nationalists lean toward policies designed to contain and slow China's rapid economic and military growth, the former as a means to maintain a favorable balance of power and the latter out of disdain toward China's authoritarianism and political repression at home. Liberal institutionalists favor instead a policy of engagement, seeking to impress upon Chinese leaders the economic and political benefits of peaceful cooperation through multilateral mechanisms. Institutionalists hope to encourage gradual internal reform in China by exposing the Chinese people to liberal democratic ideas as China opens to the outside world. Liberal institutionalists argue that isolation and confrontation will only strengthen the Chinese government's worst authoritarian and militarist tendencies and raise the prospect of violence and conflict.

As this example suggests, liberal institutionalists emphasize the mutual gains to be had by states that work together to realize common aims. The liberal institutional perspective thus contrasts sharply with the realist perspective, which portrays international politics as a zero-sum game in which the struggle for power compels states to pursue relative gains in relations with one another. From a liberal point of view, international institutions play a key role in facilitating international cooperation and helping states to escape the ruinous consequences of unrestrained competition. Arms control treaties make participating states more secure by curtailing the dangerous and unrealizable pursuit of military dominance. Trade agreements lower the barriers to mutually profitable economic exchange. Environmental accords allow states to cope with global ecological challenges that no country could successfully manage alone. In general, international institutions enhance trust, transparency, policy coordination, and information sharing while establishing the rules necessary to manage the processes of interdependence in an era of economic, social, and cultural globalization.

Liberal institutionalists reject, however, the common criticism that their perspective is based upon unrealistically idealist or utopian premises. Indeed, liberals argue that the case for vigorous U.S. engagement in strong international institutions can be made in terms of a dispassionate and hardheaded analysis of American national interests. From its position of international dominance, the United States enjoys the ability to ensure that the rules and norms of the international institutional order reflect its own values and preferences. Multilateral institutions also pool the resources of many states, thus spreading the costs of maintaining international order. As a result, American-influenced institutions provide a more cost-effective means for influencing the behavior of participating states than the unilateral exercise of power. Since institutions tend to change slowly over time, locking in American-influenced rules and norms also provides some long-term guarantee for U.S. interests even in the event that U.S. power should wane in the future.

Liberal institutionalists point to the crucial role that U.S.-supported international institutions, such as the United Nations, the North Atlantic Treaty Organization, and various international economic agencies, played in cementing strong ties among Western states and winning the cold war in the half century following World War II. The recent unilateralist turn in U.S. foreign policy, by contrast, is viewed as a strategic error of the first order. By isolating itself from world opinion and rejecting a series of major international agreements over the past decade, the United States has undermined crucial alliance relationships and robbed itself of the ability to exert positive influence over an emerging post–cold war world order.

MAPPING THE DEBATE

These three perspectives help us to understand the parameters of debate over U.S. foreign policy. Nevertheless, even the best scheme for classifying foreign policy schools of thought can be misleading if applied too mechanically. A complex mixture of beliefs and values, material interests, changing international events, and domestic politics drives actual policy choices.

Under such pressures, policy consistency is a rare commodity in any presidential administration.

Even so, one can identify historical periods in which each of the foreign policy approaches identified in the previous sections of this introduction has played a dominant role. With his triangular approach to great-power relations with the Soviet Union and China, Richard Nixon was perhaps the most devoted practitioner of realism among recent U.S. presidents. Jimmy Carter and Bill Clinton, by contrast, began their presidencies as advocates of liberal institutionalism. Carter built his early foreign policies around the promotion of human rights while Clinton embraced a doctrine of "assertive multilateralism." In both cases, however, liberal institutionalist principles were gradually abandoned under the pressure of international events and domestic constraints. Ronald Reagan and George W. Bush (post-9/11) each pursued a vigorous brand of democratic nationalism. The Reagan Doctrine depended upon arms sales and covert intervention to bring down socialist and communist regimes in the third world while Bush's war on terrorists and rogue states led to policies of regime change in Afghanistan and Iraq.

These three perspectives are also reflected in the writings of foreign policy experts and intellectuals, as exemplified by many of the readings in this book. Not all of the authors in this collection can easily be classified as realist, democratic nationalist, or liberal institutionalist, and some adopt complex positions that overlap two or more categories. Still, we can identify most with a particular school of thought and locate areas of agreement and disagreement that correspond to the classification scheme I introduced earlier. Briefly, here is an overview of the debate as reflected in the readings that follow. More extensive summaries and comparisons of these selections can be found in the introductions that accompany each part of this volume.

The chapters by Stephen G. Brooks and William C. Wohlforth, Christopher Layne, Robert Kagan, and James F. Hoge Jr. each examine the balance of international power from a realist perspective. Brooks and Wohlforth argue that U.S. dominance will prove lasting well into the future, while Layne contends that U.S. power will provoke balancing efforts by a unifying Europe. Kagan views the gap in power between the United States and Europe as the key source of differences between the two over the roles of international institutions and military force in world politics. Hoge argues that U.S. power will be challenged in the coming decades by the rise of China and India. The realist assumptions shared among these authors do not preclude differing assessments of the current and future distribution of international power.

Both the selections by Robert F. Ellsworth and Dimitri K. Simes and by Jeffrey Record offer realist critiques of the Bush administration's policies toward terrorism and Iraq. Each reflects realist skepticism about the moralistic aspects of Bush's approach to dealing with international threats and the promotion of democracy abroad.

By contrast, democratic nationalists Max Boot, Niall Ferguson, and Michael Ignatieff each endorse a "liberal imperial" role for the United States as a positive force for the spread of freedom and democracy. In the cases of Ferguson and Ignatieff, however, their enthusiasm for more assertive U.S. leadership is qualified by doubts about the ability of the United States to stay the course in the long run and to pay the costs necessary to ensure the triumph of a stable liberal order. Also in keeping with the democratic nationalist perspective, Charles Krauthammer rejects both isolationism and liberal institutionalism while endorsing a viewpoint that infuses realism with a sense of moral purpose and a commitment to spreading democratic values.

These democratic nationalist themes are well articulated in the Bush administration's 2002 National Security Strategy report to the Congress. This official overview of U.S. strategy includes a defense of the unilateralist option in U.S. foreign policy, a focus on rogue and failed states as the principal sources of threat to U.S. security, a preference for preemptive military action and regime change over deterrence, and faith in the U.S.-sponsored spread of democratic institutions and values as the key to a more stable world order.

A number of contributors strike liberal internationalist themes. Rejecting realism's exclusive focus on military resources, Joseph S. Nye Jr. argues for the growing salience of "soft power" and the importance to the United States of maintaining an international reputation for benign leadership. Michael Mandelbaum, John B. Judis, and Ralph G. Carter all stress the critical role that international institutions can play in the promotion of liberal ideas and practices such as democracy and free markets. Carter's contribution emphasizes the costs of unilateralism, while G. John Ikenberry provides a theoretical and historical defense of liberal institutionalism. Francis Fukuyama calls for a new era of institution building in U.S. foreign policy focused upon the long-term and noncoercive promotion of democracy.

Some of the contributions that follow do not easily fit within a realist, democratic nationalist, and liberal institutionalist classification scheme. Andrew J. Bacevich warns of the dangers associated with the growing strength of militarism in American institutions and culture. Christopher Hitchens offers a liberal rationale for supporting the Iraq war based upon the dire humanitarian consequences of Saddam Hussein's rule. Paul W. Schroeder's commentary on the contemporary debate over U.S. imperialism represents an effort to distinguish between empire and hegemony. Minxin Pei examines the roots of American nationalism and the ways in which American political culture affects U.S. policies toward the world. Selections by Todd S. Sechser and the Pew Global Attitudes Project analyze the findings of public opinion polling in the United States and abroad on America's role in the world and related issues. Stephen M. Walt examines the varied ways that other states have sought to tame or resist the unilateral exercise of American power. Philip H. Gordon asks whether the foreign policy adjustments

that international and domestic pressures have forced upon the Bush administration signal that the Bush revolution in foreign policy is already at
an end. Together, these contributions provide important perspective and
background information for evaluating the broader debate over U.S. foreign
policy in a changing world.

CONCLUSION

The end of the cold war launched a new era in U.S. foreign policy. The
United States entered a period of unprecedented global power; this era, however, was also characterized by new conflicts, challenges, and paradoxes.
The terrorist attacks of 9/11 and the subsequent U.S. military operations in
Afghanistan and Iraq have cast a spotlight on continuing debates over how
the United States should best use its considerable international power to secure safety for Americans and stability in the world.

These debates center on two crucial questions: Should U.S. foreign policy focus on securing vital interests narrowly defined or should the United
States seek as well to spread American institutions and values to other societies? Should the United States seek maximum independence in the exercise of American power abroad or work principally through multilateral institutions?

Realists and democratic nationalists share a preference for unilateralism
but differ over the relative emphasis to be placed upon interests versus values. Democratic nationalists and liberal institutionalists each view the
spread of liberalism, democracy, and markets as critical to global stability
but differ over whether such goals are best pursued through unilateral or
multilateral means. These varying conceptual and normative assumptions
produce markedly diverging policy preferences, as illustrated by the range
of opinions and perspectives represented in the readings that follow.

I

U.S. Dominance and Its Limits

OVERVIEW

Few analysts dispute the fact that America's current military, technological, and economic resources dwarf those of any other country in the world today. Surveying the vast concentration of global power in American hands, Stephen G. Brooks and William C. Wohlforth comment that "if today's American primacy does not constitute unipolarity, then nothing ever will."

Yet disagreement remains over several important questions surrounding the issue of American dominance: Which sources of power—military, economic, or cultural—will prove most salient in coming decades? What are the limits of American power, or, in other words, what kinds of problems are beyond the ability of even the United States to resolve? Will other countries find American power so threatening that they form balancing coalitions designed to check the United States? How long before one or more rising powers manage to narrow the gap with the United States?

The readings contained in this section offer a range of views on these questions and others. Brooks and Wohlforth are the most bullish on the staying power of American dominance. The comprehensive nature of American power and the size of the gap between the United States and its nearest competitors ensure that the United States will enjoy a long period of primacy. Brooks and Wohlforth dismiss the idea that other states might combine in a balancing coalition against the United States. The geographic isolation of the United States from other major powers makes American military primacy seem relatively unthreatening. Indeed, most states worry more about proximate rivals than about the United States, and some rely upon U.S. security guarantees for their protection. This further reduces the likelihood that other states will combine in an effort to contain U.S. power. Despite much international criticism of U.S. foreign policy in recent years, only China, among the major powers, seems engaged in a serious effort to upgrade its military resources, and even the Chinese buildup offers little threat to U.S. primacy. The unusual degree and stability of U.S. dominance provide U.S. policymakers, according to Brooks and Wohlforth, unprecedented freedom of choice in how to use that power.

Nevertheless, Joseph S. Nye Jr. urges caution about embracing a triumphalist perspective on American power. Despite its great military might, the United States has suffered a decline in what Nye refers to as "soft power": the ability to influence the behavior of others through the attraction of America's culture, values, and institutions. What many around the world view as arrogant and unilateralist U.S. behavior abroad has diminished the global appeal of the American example. U.S. efforts to counter such perceptions through public diplomacy have been halfhearted and ineffective. Nye advocates greater efforts to communicate the American message abroad, more openness to educational and cultural exchanges, greater cultural sensitivity in U.S. diplomacy, and a willingness to listen and take into account the views of other states. These measures, he argues, will enhance the ability of the United States to influence international outcomes through the employment of soft power.

Michael Mandelbaum also stresses the limits of American power. U.S. interests will be most secure in a world favorable to the spread of peace, democracy, and free markets. Yet despite its vast resources, the ability of the United States to ensure the persistence of a world order built upon these foundations is uncertain. Peace, democracy, and free markets are international public goods that depend upon the support of strong international institutions. These international institutions are costly to create and sustain, in terms of both financial resources and lost policy autonomy. States have a rational incentive to "free ride"—relying upon others to provide the necessary support for international public goods while avoiding such costs themselves.

During the cold war, the dominance of the United States, combined with the presence of a serious and sustained common threat—the power of the Soviet Union—gave American policymakers sufficient incentive to pay the lion's share of the costs of supporting strong international institutions. With the end of the cold war, however, the United States has proven less willing to cover such costs. Indeed, the United States itself has sought to "free ride" on the efforts of others while pursuing an increasingly unilateralist foreign policy. In the absence of international leadership, the institutions necessary to the survival of a world order built upon peace, democracy, and free markets seem likely to weaken.

A second challenge Mandelbaum identifies arises from the difficulties of establishing peace and implanting democracy and free markets in societies where these institutions remain tenuous or absent. While the United States can offer a powerful example to others, democracy and free markets can only arise within a society through internal processes of change. The enormous resources available to American policymakers are insufficient to impose the Western model on societies whose people and culture are resistant. If the United States is unwilling to support strong international institutions necessary to the spread of peace, democracy, and free markets and unable to impose these conditions on societies where they do not yet exist, then the ability of the United States to guarantee international stability will remain limited in spite of American dominance.

The coming decades could also bring growing regional challenges to U.S. power in Europe and Asia. Christopher Layne argues that the growing diplomatic rupture between the United States and Europe is a predictable consequence of the end of the cold war. Although Europe chafed under U.S. domination during the cold war, European dependence upon U.S. power in order to counter the greater threat posed by the Soviet Union generally dictated deference to U.S. leadership. With the collapse of the Soviet Union, many Europeans now aspire to greater independence from U.S. control. The push to unify Europe and pool its collective resources is in part driven by this desire to balance U.S. hegemony. The potential inclusion of Russia, and perhaps even China, in a European-led balancing coalition could undermine the basis for U.S. global dominance in the coming decades.

James F. Hoge Jr. points to the economic rise of China and India as harbingers of potentially broader political and military realignments in the Asian theater. The United States has traditionally relied upon its naval strength in the region and bilateral defense treaties with Japan, South Korea, and other countries as tools for promoting stability and discouraging local security dilemmas. China's growing economic and military power, and to a lesser extent that of India, poses new challenges to this strategy. Several regional flash points—North Korea, Taiwan, and Kashmir—hold the potential for escalating conflict while Japan and other nearby states remain uneasy about China's ultimate ambitions. The U.S. role must be to manage China and India's rise while dampening regional insecurities.

In short, agreement among most observers about the dominant international position that the United States presently enjoys leaves plenty of room for disagreement about the relative salience of different forms of power, the relevance of American power for ensuring a favorable international order, and the likelihood that other powers will close the gap with the United States over time. Most important, the authors represented here each raise, in somewhat different ways, the following question: How will the choices made by American policymakers over how to wield U.S. power affect the future position of the United States and the prospects for international peace and stability? This important question lies at the heart of the debates featured in subsequent parts of this book.

DISCUSSION QUESTIONS

1. What measures are most important in measuring the distribution of power among the world's leading states? How can we assess the relative significance of military, economic, and cultural sources of international influence?

2. How do other countries view American dominance? Is U.S. power viewed as relatively benign or as potentially threatening?

3. Why have other powers been slow to form military balancing coalitions in order to counter U.S. dominance? What other options do states possess for resisting U.S. power?

4. What is "soft power" and why does Joseph Nye believe that its significance is rising? How do the foreign policy choices that U.S. leaders make affect the ability of the United States to successfully exercise soft power?

5. Is it possible to foresee a day when one or more countries will close the power gap with the United States? Which country or countries are most likely to challenge U.S. dominance? How should the United States respond to the rising power of other states?

SUGGESTED READINGS

Ikenberry, G. John, ed. *America Unrivaled: The Future of the Balance of Power.* Ithaca, N.Y.: Cornell University Press, 2002.

Kapstein, Ethan B., and Michael Mastanduno, eds. *Unipolar Politics: Realism and State Strategies after the Cold War.* New York: Columbia University Press, 1999.

Kupchan, Charles. *The End of the American Era: U.S. Foreign Policy and the Geopolitics of the Twenty-first Century.* New York: Knopf, 2002.

Mearsheimer, John J. *The Tragedy of Great Power Politics.* New York: Norton, 2001.

Nye, Joseph S., Jr. *The Paradox of American Power: Why the World's Only Superpower Can't Go It Alone.* New York: Oxford University Press, 2002.

1

American Primacy in Perspective

*Stephen G. Brooks and
William C. Wohlforth*

FROM STRENGTH TO STRENGTH

More than a decade ago, political columnist Charles Krauthammer pro-claimed . . . the arrival of what he called a "unipolar moment," a period in which one superpower, the United States, stood clearly above the rest of the international community. In the following years the Soviet Union collapsed, Russia's economic and military decline accelerated, and Japan stagnated, while the United States experienced the longest and one of the most vigor-ous economic expansions in its history. Yet toward the close of the century readers could find political scientist Samuel Huntington arguing . . . that unipolarity had already given way to a "uni-multipolar" structure, which in turn would soon become unambiguously multipolar. And despite the boast-ing rhetoric of American officials, Huntington was not alone in his views. Polls showed that more than 40 percent of Americans had come to agree that the United States was now merely one of several leading powers—a number that had risen steadily for several years.

Why did the unipolarity argument seem less persuasive to many even as U.S. power appeared to grow? Largely because the goal posts were moved. Krauthammer's definition of unipolarity, as a system with only one pole, made sense in the immediate wake of a Cold War that had been so clearly shaped by the existence of two poles. People sensed intuitively that a world with no great power capable of sustaining a focused rivalry with the United States would be very different in important ways.

But a decade later what increasingly seemed salient was less the absence of a peer rival than the persistence of a number of problems in the world that Washington could not dispose of by itself. This was the context for Huntington's new definition of unipolarity, as a system with "one super-power, no significant major powers, and many minor powers." The dominant power in such a system, he argued, would be able to "effectively re-solve important international issues alone, and no combination of other states would have the power to prevent it from doing so." The United States had no such ability and thus did not qualify.

The terrorist attacks last fall appeared to some to reinforce this point, re-vealing not only a remarkable degree of American vulnerability but also a deep vein of global anti-American resentment. Suddenly the world seemed a more threatening place, with dangers lurking at every corner and eternal vigilance the price of liberty. Yet as the success of the military campaign in Afghanistan demonstrated, vulnerability to terror has few effects on U.S. strength in more traditional interstate affairs. If anything, America's re-sponse to the attacks—which showed its ability to project power in several places around the globe simultaneously, and essentially unilaterally, while effortlessly increasing defense spending by nearly $50 billion—only rein-forced its unique position.

If today's American primacy does not constitute unipolarity, then noth-ing ever will. The only things left for dispute are how long it will last and what the implications are for American foreign policy.

PICK A MEASURE, ANY MEASURE

To understand just how dominant the United States is today, one needs to look at each of the standard components of national power in succession. In the military arena, the United States is poised to spend more on defense in 2003 than the next 15–20 biggest spenders combined. The United States has overwhelming nuclear superiority, the world's dominant air force, the only truly blue-water navy, and a unique capability to project power around the globe. And its military advantage is even more apparent in qual-ity than in quantity. The United States leads the world in exploiting the mil-itary applications of advanced communications and information technology and it has demonstrated an unrivaled ability to coordinate and process in-formation about the battlefield and destroy targets from afar with extraor-dinary precision. Washington is not making it easy for others to catch up, moreover, given the massive gap in spending on military research and de-velopment (R&D), on which the United States spends three times more than the next six powers combined. Looked at another way, the United

States currently spends more on military R&D than Germany or the United Kingdom spends on defense in total.

No state in the modern history of international politics has come close to the military predominance these numbers suggest. And the United States purchases this preeminence with only 3.5 percent of its GDP. As historian Paul Kennedy notes, "being Number One at great cost is one thing; being the world's single superpower on the cheap is astonishing."

America's economic dominance, meanwhile—relative to either the next several richest powers or the rest of the world combined—surpasses that of any great power in modern history, with the sole exception of its own position after 1945 (when World War II had temporarily laid waste every other major economy). The U.S. economy is currently twice as large as its closest rival, Japan. California's economy alone has risen to become the fifth largest in the world (using market exchange-rate estimates), ahead of France and just behind the United Kingdom.

It is true that the long expansion of the 1990s has ebbed, but it would take an experience like Japan's in that decade—that is, an extraordinarily deep and prolonged domestic recession juxtaposed with robust growth elsewhere—for the United States just to fall back to the economic position it occupied in 1991. The odds against such relative decline are long, however, in part because the United States is the country in the best position to take advantage of globalization. Its status as the preferred destination for scientifically trained foreign workers solidified during the 1990s, and it is the most popular destination for foreign firms. In 1999 it attracted more than one-third of world inflows of foreign direct investment.

U.S. military and economic dominance, finally, is rooted in the country's position as the world's leading technological power. Although measuring national R&D spending is increasingly difficult in an era in which so many economic activities cross borders, efforts to do so indicate America's continuing lead. Figures from the late 1990s showed that U.S. expenditures on R&D nearly equaled those of the next seven richest countries combined.

Measuring the degree of American dominance in each category begins to place things in perspective. But what truly distinguishes the current international system is American dominance in all of them simultaneously. Previous leading states in the modern era were either great commercial and naval powers or great military powers on land, never both. The British Empire in its heyday and the United States during the Cold War, for example, each shared the world with other powers that matched or exceeded them in some areas. . . .

Today, in contrast, the United States has no rival in any critical dimension of power. There has never been a system of sovereign states that contained one state with this degree of dominance. The recent tendency to equate unipolarity with the ability to achieve desired outcomes single-handedly on all issues only reinforces this point; in no previous international system would it ever have occurred to anyone to apply such a yardstick.

CAN IT LAST?

Many who acknowledge the extent of American power, however, regard it as necessarily self-negating. Other states traditionally band together to restrain potential hegemons, they say, and this time will be no different. As German political commentator Josef Joffe has put it, "the history books say that Mr. Big always invites his own demise. Nos. 2, 3, 4 will gang up on him, form countervailing alliances and plot his downfall. That happened to Napoleon, as it happened to Louis XIV and the mighty Hapsburgs, to Hitler and to Stalin. Power begets superior counterpower; it's the oldest rule of world politics."

What such arguments fail to recognize are the features of America's post–Cold War position that make it likely to buck the historical trend. Bounded by oceans to the east and west and weak, friendly powers to the north and south, the United States is both less vulnerable than previous aspiring hegemons and also less threatening to others. The main potential challengers to its unipolarity, meanwhile—China, Russia, Japan, and Germany— are in the opposite position. They cannot augment their military capabilities so as to balance the United States without simultaneously becoming an immediate threat to their neighbors. Politics, even international politics, is local. Although American power attracts a lot of attention globally, states are usually more concerned with their own neighborhoods than with the global equilibrium. Were any of the potential challengers to make a serious run at the United States, regional balancing efforts would almost certainly help contain them, as would the massive latent power capabilities of the United States, which could be mobilized as necessary to head off an emerging threat.

When analysts refer to a historical pattern of balancing against potentially preponderant powers, they rarely note that the cases in question—the Hapsburg ascendancy, Napoleonic France, the Soviet Union in the Cold War, and so forth—featured would-be hegemons that were vulnerable, threatening, centrally located, and dominant in only one or two components of power. Moreover, the would-be hegemons all specialized in precisely the form of power—the ability to seize territory—most likely to scare other states into an antihegemonic coalition. American capabilities, by contrast, are relatively greater and more comprehensive than those of past hegemonic aspirants, they are located safely offshore, and the prospective balancers are close regional neighbors of one another. U.S. power is also at the command of one government, whereas the putative balancers would face major challenges in acting collectively to assemble and coordinate their military capabilities.

Previous historical experiences of balancing, moreover, involved groups of status quo powers seeking to contain a rising revisionist one. The balancers had much to fear if the aspiring hegemon got its way. Today, however, U.S. dominance is the status quo. Several of the major powers in the system have been closely allied with the United States for decades and derive substantial benefits from their position. Not only would they have to forego those benefits if they tried to balance, but they would have to find some way of putting together a durable, coherent alliance while America was watching. This is a profoundly important point, because although there may be several precedents for a coalition of balancers preventing a hegemon from emerging, there is none for a group of subordinate powers joining to topple a hegemon once it has already emerged, which is what would have to happen today.

The comprehensive nature of U.S. power, finally, also skews the odds against any major attempt at balancing, let alone a successful one. The United States is both big and rich, whereas the potential challengers are all either one or the other. It will take at least a generation for today's other big countries (such as China and India) to become rich, and given declining birth rates the other rich powers are not about to get big, at least in relative terms. During the 1990s, the U.S. population increased by 32.7 million—a figure equal to more than half the current population of France or the United Kingdom.

Some might argue that the European Union is an exception to the big-or-rich rule. It is true that if Brussels were to develop impressive military capabilities and wield its latent collective power like a state, the EU would clearly constitute another pole. But the creation of an autonomous and unified defense and defense-industrial capacity that could compete with that of the United States would be a gargantuan task. The EU is struggling to put together a 60,000-strong rapid reaction force that is designed for smaller operations such as humanitarian relief, peacekeeping, and crisis management, but it still lacks military essentials such as capabilities in intelligence gathering, airlift, air-defense suppression, air-to-air refueling, sea transport, medical care, and combat search and rescue—and even when it has those capacities, perhaps by the end of this decade, it will still rely on NATO command and control and other assets.

Whatever capability the EU eventually assembles, moreover, will matter only to the extent that it is under the control of a statelike decision-making body with the authority to act quickly and decisively in Europe's name. Such authority, which does not yet exist even for international financial matters, could be purchased only at the price of a direct frontal assault on European nations' core sovereignty. And all of this would have to occur as the EU expands to add ten or more new member states, a process that will complicate further deepening. Given these obstacles, Europe is unlikely to emerge as a dominant actor in the military realm for a very long time, if ever.

Most analysts looking for a future peer competitor to the United States, therefore, focus on China, since it is the only power with the potential to match the size of the U.S. economy over the next several decades. Yet even if China were eventually to catch up to the United States in terms of aggregate GDP, the gaps in the two states' other power capabilities—technological, military, and geographic—would remain.

Since the mid-1990s, Chinese strategists themselves have become markedly less bullish about their country's ability to close the gap in what they call "comprehensive national power" any time soon. The latest estimates by China's intelligence agency project that in 2020 the country will possess between slightly more than a third and slightly more than half of U.S. capabilities. Fifty percent of China's labor force is employed in agriculture, and relatively little of its economy is geared toward high technology. In the 1990s, U.S. spending on technological development was more than 20 times China's. Most of China's weapons are decades old. And nothing China can do will allow it to escape its geography, which leaves it surrounded by countries that have the motivation and ability to engage in balancing of their own should China start to build up an expansive military force.

These are not just facts about the current system; they are recognized as such by the major players involved. As a result, no global challenge to the United States is likely to emerge for the foreseeable future. No country, or group of countries, wants to maneuver itself into a situation in which it will have to contend with the focused enmity of the United States.

Two of the prime causes of past great-power conflicts—hegemonic rivalry and misperception—are thus not currently operative in world politics. At the dawn of the twentieth century, a militarily powerful Germany challenged the United Kingdom's claim to leadership. The result was World War I. In the middle of the twentieth century, American leadership seemed under challenge by a militarily and ideologically strong Soviet Union. The result was the Cold War. U.S. dominance today militates against a comparable challenge, however, and hence against a comparable global conflict. Because the United States is too powerful to balance, moreover, there is far less danger of war emerging from the misperceptions, miscalculations, arms races, and so forth that have traditionally plagued balancing attempts. Pundits often lament the absence of a post–Cold War Bismarck. Luckily, as long as unipolarity lasts, there is no need for one.

UNIPOLAR POLITICS AS USUAL

The conclusion that balancing is not in the cards may strike many as questionable in light of the parade of ostensibly anti-U.S. diplomatic combinations in recent years: the "European troika" of France, Germany, and Russia; the "special relationship" between Germany and Russia; the "strategic triangle" of Russia, China, and India; the "strategic partnership" between China and Russia; and so on. Yet a close look at any of these arrangements reveals their rhetorical as opposed to substantive character. Real balancing involves real economic and political costs, which neither Russia, nor China, nor indeed any other major power has shown any willingness to bear.

The most reliable way to balance power is to increase defense outlays. Since 1995, however, military spending by most major powers has been declining relative to GDP, and in the majority of cases in absolute terms as well. At most, these opposing coalitions can occasionally succeed in frustrating U.S. policy initiatives when the expected costs of doing so remain conveniently low. At the same time, Beijing, Moscow, and others have demonstrated a willingness to cooperate with the United States periodically on strategic matters and especially in the economic realm. This general tendency toward bandwagoning was the norm before September 11 and has only become more pronounced since then.

Consider the Sino-Russian "strategic partnership," the most prominent instance of apparent balancing to date. The easy retort to overheated rhetoric about a Moscow-Beijing "axis" would involve pointing out how it failed to slow, much less stop, President Vladimir Putin's geopolitical sprint toward Washington in the aftermath of the September 11 attacks. More telling, however, is just how tenuous the shift was even before it was thrown off track. At no point did the partnership entail any costly commitment or policy coordination against Washington that might have risked a genuine confrontation. The keystone of the partnership—Russia's arms sales to China—reflects a symmetry of weaknesses, rather than the potential of combined strengths. The sales partially offset China's backward military technology while helping to slow the decline of Russia's defense industries. Most of the arms in question are legacies of the R&D efforts of the Soviet military-industrial complex, and given Moscow's paltry R&D budget today, few of these systems will long remain competitive with their U.S. or NATO analogues.

Even as the two neighbors signed cooperative agreements, moreover, deep suspicions continued to plague their relationship, economic ties between them remained anemic and unlikely to grow dramatically, and both were highly dependent on inflows of capital and technology that could come only from the West. Russian and Chinese leaders highlighted their desire for a world of reduced U.S. influence not because this was a goal toward which they had actually started moving, but because it was one general principle on which they could agree.

Balancing rhetoric is obviously partly the reflection of genuine sentiment. The world finds it unfair, undemocratic, annoying, and sometimes downright frightening to have so much power concentrated in the hands of one state, especially when the United States aggressively goes its own way. But given the weight and prominence of U.S. power on the world stage, some unease among other countries is inevitable no matter what

Washington does. Foreign governments frequently rail against what they regard as excessive U.S. involvement in their affairs. Yet inflated expectations
about what the United States can do to solve global problems (such as the
Israeli-Palestinian conflict) can lead to frustration with supposed U.S. un-
derengagement as well. Nothing the United States could do short of abdi-
cating its power would solve the problem completely. . . .

SO WHAT?

The first and most important practical consequence of unipolarity for the
United States is notable for its absence: the lack of hegemonic rivalry. During the Cold War the United States confronted a military superpower with
the potential to conquer all the industrial power centers of Europe and
Asia. To forestall that catastrophic outcome, for decades the United States
committed between 5 and 14 percent of its GDP to defense spending and
maintained an extended nuclear deterrent that put a premium on the credibility of its commitments. Largely to maintain a reputation for resolve,
85,000 Americans lost their lives in two Asian wars while U.S. presidents repeatedly engaged in brinkmanship that ran the risk of escalation to global
thermonuclear destruction.

Today the costs and dangers of the Cold War have faded into history,
but they need to be kept in mind in order to assess unipolarity accurately.
For decades to come, no state is likely to combine the resources, geography, and growth rates necessary to mount a hegemonic challenge on such
a scale—an astonishing development. Crowns may generally lie uneasy,
but America's does not.

Some might question the worth of being at the top of a unipolar system
if that means serving as a lightning rod for the world's malcontents. When
there was a Soviet Union, after all, it bore the brunt of Osama bin Laden's
anger, and only after its collapse did he shift his focus to the United States.
. . . But terrorism has been a perennial problem in history, and multipolarity did not save the leaders of several great powers from assassination by
anarchists around the turn of the twentieth century. In fact, a slide back toward multipolarity would actually be the worst of all worlds for the United
States. In such a scenario it would continue to lead the pack and serve as
a focal point for resentment and hatred by both state and nonstate actors,
but it would have fewer carrots and sticks to use in dealing with the situation. The threats would remain, but the possibility of effective and coordinated action against them would be reduced.

The second major practical consequence of unipolarity is the unique
freedom it offers American policymakers. Many decisionmakers labor
under feelings of constraint, and all participants in policy debates defend
their preferred courses of action by pointing to the dire consequences that

will follow if their advice is not accepted. But the sources of American strength are so varied and so durable that U.S. foreign policy today operates in the realm of choice rather than necessity to a greater degree than any other power in modern history. Whether the participants realize it or not, this new freedom to choose has transformed the debate over what the U.S. role in the world should be.

Historically, the major forces pushing powerful states toward restraint and magnanimity have been the limits of their strength and the fear of overextension and balancing. Great powers typically checked their ambitions and deferred to others not because they wanted to but because they had to in order to win the cooperation they needed to survive and prosper. It is thus no surprise that today's champions of American moderation and international benevolence stress the constraints on American power rather than the lack of them. Political scientist Joseph Nye, for example, insists that "[the term] unipolarity is misleading because it exaggerates the degree to which the United States is able to get the results it wants in some dimensions of world politics. . . . American power is less effective than it might first appear." And he cautions that if the United States "handles its hard power in an overbearing, unilateral manner," then others might be provoked into forming a balancing coalition.

Such arguments are unpersuasive, however, because they fail to acknowledge the true nature of the current international system. The United States cannot be scared into meekness by warnings of inefficacy or potential balancing. Isolationists and aggressive unilateralists see this situation clearly, and their domestic opponents need to as well. Now and for the foreseeable future, the United States will have immense power resources it can bring to bear to force or entice others to do its bidding on a case-by-case basis.

But just because the United States is strong enough to act heedlessly does not mean that it should do so. Why not? Because it can afford to reap the greater gains that will eventually come from magnanimity. Aside from a few cases in a few issue areas, ignoring others' concerns avoids hassles today at the cost of more serious trouble tomorrow. Unilateralism may produce results in the short term, but it is apt to reduce the pool of voluntary help from other countries that the United States can draw on down the road, and thus in the end to make life more difficult rather than less. Unipolarity makes it possible to be the global bully—but it also offers the United States the luxury of being able to look beyond its immediate needs to its own, and the world's, long-term interests.

RESISTING TEMPTATION

Consider the question that preoccupied many observers before September 11: whether to engage or contain potential great-power challengers such as

China. Supporters of engagement argued that the best way to moderate Chinese behavior (both internal and external) was to tie the country into the international political and economic system as thoroughly as possible. Supporters of containment, meanwhile, argued that this course was far too risky, because it might hasten the emergence of a strong but still tyrannical power. To the extent that the above analysis of unipolarity is correct, however, the risks that accompany engagement are minor, because the margin of U.S. superiority is so great that China is unlikely to pose a significant challenge to U.S. dominance for decades, no matter what policy is followed. Although engagement may not succeed, therefore, the chance that it might makes it worth a try, and there will be plenty of time to reverse course if it fails. . . .

Washington also needs to be concerned about the level of resentment that an aggressive unilateral course would engender among its major allies. After all, it is influence, not power, that is ultimately most valuable. The further one looks beyond the immediate short term, the clearer become the many issues—the environment, disease, migration, and the stability of the global economy, to name a few—that the United States cannot solve on its own. Such issues entail repeated dealings with many partners over many years. Straining relationships now will lead only to a more challenging policy environment later on. . . .

Magnanimity and restraint in the face of temptation are tenets of successful statecraft that have proved their worth from classical Greece onward. Standing taller than leading states of the past, the United States has unprecedented freedom to do as it pleases. It can play the game for itself alone or for the system as a whole; it can focus on small returns today or larger ones tomorrow. If the administration truly wants to be loved as well as feared, the policy answers are not hard to find.

2

The Decline of America's Soft Power

Joseph S. Nye Jr.

Anti-Americanism has increased in recent years, and the United States' soft power—its ability to attract others by the legitimacy of U.S. policies and the values that underlie them—is in decline as a result. According to Gallup International polls, pluralities in 29 countries say that Washington's policies have had a negative effect on their view of the United States. A Eurobarometer poll found that a majority of Europeans believes that Washington has hindered efforts to fight global poverty, protect the environment, and maintain peace. Such attitudes undercut soft power, reducing the ability of the United States to achieve its goals without resorting to coercion or payment.

Skeptics of soft power . . . claim that popularity is ephemeral and should not guide foreign policy. The United States, they assert, is strong enough to do as it wishes with or without the world's approval and should simply accept that others will envy and resent it. The world's only superpower does not need permanent allies; the issues should determine the coalitions, not vice-versa, according to [Secretary of Defense Donald] Rumsfeld.

But the recent decline in U.S. attractiveness should not be so lightly dismissed. It is true that the United States has recovered from unpopular policies in the past (such as those regarding the Vietnam War), but that was often during the Cold War, when other countries still feared the Soviet Union as the greater evil. It is also true that the United States' sheer size and association with disruptive modernity make some resentment unavoidable today. But wise policies can reduce the antagonisms that these realities engender. Indeed, that is what Washington achieved after World War II: it used soft-power resources to draw others into a system of alliances and institutions that has lasted for 60 years. The Cold War was won with a strategy of containment that used soft power along with hard power.

The United States cannot confront the new threat of terrorism without the cooperation of other countries. Of course, other governments will often cooperate out of self-interest. But the extent of their cooperation often depends on the attractiveness of the United States.

Soft power, therefore, is not just a matter of ephemeral popularity; it is a means of obtaining outcomes the United States wants. When Washington discounts the importance of its attractiveness abroad, it pays a steep price. When the United States becomes so unpopular that being pro-American is a kiss of death in other countries' domestic politics, foreign political leaders are unlikely to make helpful concessions . . . . And when U.S. policies lose their legitimacy in the eyes of others, distrust grows, reducing U.S. leverage in international affairs.

Some hard-line skeptics might counter that, whatever its merits, soft power has little importance in the current war against terrorism; after all, Osama bin Laden and his followers are repelled, not attracted, by American culture and values. But this claim ignores the real metric of success in the current war, articulated in Rumsfeld's now-famous memo that was leaked in February 2003: "Are we capturing, killing or deterring and dissuading more terrorists every day than the madrassas and the radical clerics are recruiting, training and deploying against us?"

The current struggle against Islamist terrorism is not a clash of civilizations; it is a contest closely tied to the civil war raging within Islamic civilization between moderates and extremists. The United States and its allies will win only if they adopt policies that appeal to those moderates and use public diplomacy effectively to communicate that appeal. Yet the world's only superpower, and the leader in the information revolution, spends as little on public diplomacy as does France or the United Kingdom—and is all too often outgunned in the propaganda war by fundamentalists hiding in caves.

LOST SAVINGS

With the end of the Cold War, soft power seemed expendable, and Americans became more interested in saving money than in investing in soft power. Between 1989 and 1999, the budget of the United States Information Agency (USIA) decreased ten percent; resources for its mission in Indonesia, the world's largest Muslim nation, were cut in half. By the time it was taken over by the State Department at the end of the decade, USIA had only 6,715 employees (compared to 12,000 at its peak in the mid-1960s).

During the Cold War, radio broadcasts funded by Washington reached half the Soviet population and 70 to 80 percent of the population in Eastern Europe every week; on the eve of the September 11 attacks, a mere two percent of Arabs listened to the Voice of America (VOA). The annual number of academic and cultural exchanges, meanwhile, dropped from 45,000 in 1995 to 29,000 in 2001. Soft power had become so identified with fighting the Cold War that few Americans noticed that, with the advent of the information revolution, soft power was becoming more important, not less.

It took the September 11 attacks to remind the United States of this fact. But although Washington has rediscovered the need for public diplomacy, it has failed to master the complexities of wielding soft power in an information age. Some people in government now concede that the abolition of USIA was a mistake, but there is no consensus on whether to re-create it or to reorganize its functions, which were dispersed within the State Department after the Clinton administration gave in to the demands of Senator Jesse Helms (R-N.C.). The board that oversees the VOA, along with a number of specialized radio stations, has taken some useful steps—such as the establishment of Radio Sawa to broadcast in Arabic, Radio Farda to broadcast in Farsi, and the Arabic-language TV station Al Hurra. The White House has created its own Office of Global Communications. But much more is needed, especially in the Middle East.

Autocratic regimes in the Middle East have eradicated their liberal opposition, and radical Islamists are in most cases the only dissenters left. They feed on anger toward corrupt regimes, opposition to U.S. policies, and popular fears of modernization. Liberal democracy, as they portray it, is full of corruption, sex, and violence—an impression reinforced by American movies and television and often exacerbated by the extreme statements of some especially virulent Christian preachers in the United States.

Nonetheless, the situation is not hopeless. Although modernization and American values can be disruptive, they also bring education, jobs, better health care, and a range of new opportunities. Indeed, polls show that much of the Middle East craves the benefits of trade, globalization, and improved communications. American technology is widely admired, and American culture is often more attractive than U.S. policies. Given such widespread (albeit ambivalent) moderate views, there is still a chance of isolating the extremists.

Democracy, however, cannot be imposed by force. The outcome in Iraq will be of crucial importance, but success will also depend on policies that open regional economies, reduce bureaucratic controls, speed economic growth, improve educational systems, and encourage the types of gradual political changes currently taking place in small countries such as Bahrain, Oman, Kuwait, and Morocco. The development of intellectuals, social groups, and, eventually, countries that show that liberal democracy is not inconsistent with Muslim culture will have a beneficial effect like that of

Japan and South Korea, which showed that democracy could coexist with indigenous Asian values. But this demonstration effect will take time—and the skillful deployment of soft-power resources by the United States in concert with other democracies, nongovernmental organizations, and the United Nations.

FIRST RESPONDERS

In the wake of September 11, Americans were transfixed by the question "Why do they hate us?" But many in the Middle East do not hate the United States. As polls consistently show, many fear, misunderstand, and oppose U.S. policies, but they nonetheless admire certain American values and aspects of American culture. The world's leader in communications, however, has been inept at recognizing and exploiting such opportunities.

In 2003, a bipartisan advisory group on public diplomacy for the Arab and Muslim world found that the United States was spending only $150 million on public diplomacy in majority-Muslim countries, including $25 million on outreach programs. In the advisory group's words, "to say that financial resources are inadequate to the task is a gross understatement." They recommended appointing a new White House director of public diplomacy, building libraries and information centers, translating more Western books into Arabic, increasing the number of scholarships and visiting fellowships, and training more Arabic speakers and public relations specialists.

The development of effective public diplomacy must include strategies for the short, medium, and long terms. In the short term, the United States will have to become more agile in responding to and explaining current events. New broadcasting units such as Radio Sawa, which intersperses news with popular music, is a step in the right direction, but Americans must also learn to work more effectively with Arab media outlets such as Al Jazeera.

In the medium term, U.S. policymakers will have to develop a few key strategic themes in order to better explain U.S. policies and "brand" the United States as a democratic nation. The charge that U.S. policies are indifferent to the destruction of Muslim lives, for example, can be countered by pointing to U.S. interventions in Bosnia and Kosovo that saved Muslim lives, and to assistance to Muslim countries for fostering development and combating AIDS. As Assistant Secretary of State for Near Eastern Affairs William Burns has pointed out, democratic change must be embedded in "a wider positive agenda for the region, alongside rebuilding Iraq, achieving the president's two-state vision for Israelis and Palestinians, and modernizing Arab economies."

Most important will be a long-term strategy, built around cultural and educational exchanges, to develop a richer, more open civil society in Middle

Eastern countries. To this end, the most effective spokespeople are not Americans but indigenous surrogates who understand American virtues and faults. Corporations, foundations, universities, and other nongovernmental organizations—as well as governments—can all help promote the development of open civil society. Corporations can offer technology to modernize educational systems. Universities can establish more exchange programs for students and faculty. Foundations can support institutions of American studies and programs to enhance the professionalism of journalists. Governments can support the teaching of English and finance student exchanges.

In short, there are many strands to an effective long-term strategy for creating soft-power resources and the conditions for democracy. Of course, even the best advertising cannot sell an unpopular product: a communications strategy will not work if it cuts against the grain of policy. Public diplomacy will not be effective unless the style and substance of U.S. policies are consistent with a broader democratic message.

ANTE UP

The United States' most striking failure is the low priority and paucity of resources it has devoted to producing soft power. The combined cost of the State Department's public diplomacy programs and U.S. international broadcasting is just over a billion dollars, about four percent of the nation's international affairs budget. That total is about three percent of what the United States spends on intelligence and a quarter of one percent of its military budget. If Washington devoted just one percent of its military spending to public diplomacy—in the words of Newton Minow, former head of the Federal Communications Commission, "one dollar to launch ideas for every 100 dollars we invest to launch bombs"—it would mean almost quadrupling the current budget.

It is also important to establish more policy coherence among the various dimensions of public diplomacy, and to relate them to other issues. The Association of International Educators reports that, despite a declining share of the market for international students, "the U.S. government seems to lack overall strategic sense of why exchange is important. . . . In this strategic vacuum, it is difficult to counter the day-to-day obstacles that students encounter in trying to come here." There is, for example, little coordination of exchange policies and visa policies. As the educator Victor Johnson noted, "while greater vigilance is certainly needed, this broad net is catching all kinds of people who are no danger whatsoever." By needlessly discouraging people from coming to the United States, such policies undercut American soft power.

Public diplomacy needs greater support from the White House. A recent Council on Foreign Relations task force recommended the creation of a

"White House Public Diplomacy Coordinating Structure," led by a presidential designee, and a nonprofit "Corporation for Public Diplomacy" to help mobilize the private sector. And ultimately, a successful strategy must focus not only on broadcasting American messages, but also on two-way communication that engages all sectors of society, not just the government.

IT GOES BOTH WAYS

Above all, Americans will have to become more aware of cultural differences; an effective approach requires less parochialism and more sensitivity to perceptions abroad.

The first step, then, is changing attitudes at home. Americans need a better understanding of how U.S. policies appear to others. Coverage of the rest of the world by the U.S. media has declined dramatically since the end of the Cold War. Training in foreign languages has lagged. Fewer scholars are taking up Fulbright visiting lectureships. Historian Richard Pells notes "how distant we are from a time when American historians—driven by a curiosity about the world beyond both the academy and the United States—were able to communicate with the public about the issues, national and international, that continue to affect us all."

Wielding soft power is far less unilateral than employing hard power—a fact that the United States has yet to recognize. To communicate effectively, Americans must first learn to listen.

3

The Inadequacy of American Power

Michael Mandelbaum

ALONE AT THE TOP

It is a truth universally acknowledged that the central feature of the world at the outset of the twenty-first century is the enormous power of the United States. This country possesses the most formidable military forces and the largest and most vibrant national economy on the planet. From within its borders emanate the social and cultural trends that exercise the greatest influence on other societies. In the league standings of global power, the United States occupies first place—and by a margin so large that it recalls the preponderance of the Roman Empire of antiquity. So vast is American superiority that the distinction bestowed upon it and its great rival, the Soviet Union, during the Cold War no longer applies. The United States is no longer a mere superpower; it has ascended to the status of "hyperpower."

The fact of American supremacy tends to polarize opinion. For those who deem such supremacy desirable, the great question of twenty-first century international politics is how to perpetuate it. On the other hand, those who regard U.S. power as unwelcome seek to discover how it can be curtailed. The undoubted fact of American supremacy, however, raises a prior question: For what purpose is all this power to be used? The proper answer to that question puts American power in a different light, and that answer derives from the singular and unprecedented character of the world in which we now live.

The contemporary world is dominated by three major ideas' peace as the preferred basis for relations among countries, democracy as the optimal way to organize political life within them, and the free market as the indispensable vehicle for producing wealth. Peace, democracy, and free markets are the ideas that conquered the world. They are not, of course, universally practiced, and not all sovereign states accept each of them. But for the first time since they were introduced—at the outset of the period that began with the French and Industrial Revolutions and is known as the modern era—they have no serious, fully articulated rivals as principles for organizing the world's military relations, politics, and economics. They have become the world's orthodoxy. The traditional ideas with which they contended in the nineteenth century and the illiberal ideas, embodied by the fascist and communist powers, with which they did battle in the twentieth have all been vanquished.

From these new circumstances follow the central purpose of the United States in the twenty-first century and the principal use for American power: to defend, maintain, and expand peace, democracy, and free markets. Achieving this goal, however, involves two separate tasks, and for these American power, great though it is, is not necessarily sufficient.

The first task is to sustain the international institutions and practices, concerning both security and economics, within which these three ideas can flourish. The second is to strengthen peaceful foreign policies, democratic politics, and free markets where they are not securely rooted above all, in Russia and China and install them where they do not exist at all, notably in the Arab world. For the first of these two tasks American power may prove in practice to be inadequate, and for the second that enormous power is hardly relevant. . . .

INTERNATIONAL PUBLIC GOODS

A public good is something the benefits of which no potential consumer can be prevented from enjoying. Such goods are difficult to obtain because, for that very reason, no consumer has an incentive to pay for them. National defense and clean air and water are three examples. The mechanism that makes it possible to obtain them is government—the state—which, with its monopoly on the legitimate use of force, can compel people to pay for them. If there is no conductor to collect fares on a bus, everyone will ride free. But in that case there will be no funds to pay for bus service and ultimately no one will be able to ride at all. Economists have termed this inherent difficulty in providing public goods the "free rider" problem, a problem to which government is the solution.

Peace in Europe and East Asia, nuclear nonproliferation, and access to Persian Gulf oil are all public goods, but of a different sort: they are international public goods. Their "consumers" are not individuals but sovereign states, over which there is no supreme authority. Because no world government exists, international public goods are therefore difficult—but not impossible—to provide.

Public goods tend to be provided even without government when power and wealth are unevenly distributed within the relevant group optimally, when one member far surpasses all the others in both. In such cases, the powerful and the wealthy are more likely to pay the costs themselves. This is particularly likely when providing the public good in question is believed to be a matter of urgency.

Both conditions were fulfilled during the Cold War. The United States towered over all others in wealth and military might and had an urgent reason to pay the costs of international public goods: the Cold War itself. Americans considered sustaining military alliances in Europe and East Asia to be necessary for their own security, even if that meant assuming a disproportionate share of the costs of doing so.

Now, however, the Cold War is over. In its wake American political leaders have frequently invoked the need for the United States to continue to exercise global leadership. The essence of such leadership is paying a disproportionate share of the costs of international public goods. But leading the world is not only no longer as urgent as it once was, it has also ceased to seem a heroic enterprise. Leadership involves not so much marching gloriously at the head of the parade as paying quietly for the parade permit and the cleanup afterward. Leading the world means acting not as its commander in chief but as its concierge. Thus, where maintaining the framework of security within which peace and democracy—and free markets as well—can flourish is concerned, the question that American power raises is whether the United States will mobilize enough of it to continue, in different circumstances, the role it played during the Cold War.

Favoring continuity is the fact that the price of that role has decreased. It is no longer necessary to gird for a global conflict against a powerful adversary. The terrorist attacks on New York City and Washington of September 11, 2001, do not alter this calculus. Moreover, those attacks have partially re-created the Cold War basis for American military operations abroad. Also favoring continuity are habits ingrained over the second half of the twentieth century. Americans have become accustomed to the duties and burdens as well as the prerogatives of international leadership. Or rather, some Americans are accustomed to them, for the habits are concentrated in one sector of American society.

In the United States, as in other countries, foreign policy is the preoccupation of only a small part of the population. But carrying out any American foreign policy requires the support of the wider public. Whereas for the foreign policy elite, the need for American leadership in the world is a matter of settled conviction, in the general public the commitment to global leadership is weaker. This is not surprising. That commitment depends on a view of its effects on the rest of the world and the likely consequences of its absence. These are views for which most Americans, like most people in most countries, lack the relevant information because they are not ordinarily interested enough to gather it.

The politics of American foreign policy thus resembles a firm in which the management—the foreign policy elite—has to persuade the shareholders—the public—to authorize expenditures. This was true as well during the Cold War. But in its wake, the willingness of the public to authorize such spending requests has diminished, even though the expenditures required are smaller than in the past. And if there are reasons to expect the public to be forthcoming with the support needed for American global leadership, there are also post–Cold War currents pushing in the other direction.

The chief obstacle to an expansive American international role stems from what the country has in common with others. The United States has the same incentive to be a free rider as all other countries. The circumstances that suppressed this incentive during the second half of the twentieth century were exceptional. To the extent that Americans are reluctant to pay for international public goods, they are no different from any other people. A disinclination to pay also arises from Americans' fundamental political principles, which place a higher value on individual wishes than on collective aspirations, and greater emphasis on domestic goals than on international objectives. The Declaration of Independence, the founding document of the American republic, asserts the right to "life, liberty, and the pursuit of happiness," presumably individual happiness—not the right to earn military glory or provide foreign tutelage or international stability.

International leadership imposes a kind of tax on the people of the United States, and the normal attitude toward taxation is expressed in a ditty attributed to the former chairman of the Senate Finance Committee, Russell Long (D–La.)

Don't tax you
Don't tax me
Tax that man behind the tree.

Although the terrorist attacks on New York and Washington gave the American people new and potent reasons for involving themselves heavily with the rest of the world, it is nonetheless conceivable that they will tire of being the man behind the tree, especially if the threat of terrorism fades. And the war against terrorism, whatever its scope and duration, provides little incentive to sustain the other frameworks crucial for peace, democracy, and free markets around the world: those involving the international economy. . . .

THE USELESSNESS OF POWER

There is reason for optimism that, in the course of the twenty-first century, peace, democracy, and free markets will become more widely distributed and firmly rooted around the world. Virtually every country pays at least rhetorical tribute to all three, and many are actually trying to adopt them, particularly free markets. In fact, these efforts dominate the global agenda today. But the direct use of American power contributes little, if anything, to the process.

The struggle to achieve peace, democracy, and free markets involves the creation of a particular kind of state, which is the key to putting those ideas into practice. It is a state strong enough to protect property and liberty but not powerful, ambitious, or intrusive enough to suppress them. It is a state able and willing to enforce the law but not disposed to violate it. Such a state is likely to conduct peaceful foreign policies.

The construction of such a state, however, is a task for the countries themselves: others can do little to help. This was not always so. Historically, state institutions were implanted by an occupier. Thus did Roman practices spread throughout Europe in ancient times, and British institutions around the world in the modern age. But the pattern is highly unlikely to be repeated in the post–Cold War era, and will certainly not be repeated where the creation of this kind of state is most important: in Russia and China.

To be sure, the example set by the United States and the countries of western Europe and Japan carries unprecedented weight. Like individuals, collectives change by observing and learning, and as political and economic models for the rest of the world the liberal democracies have no competition. But to this process of state-building, American foreign policy has no direct contribution to make, for its tools—guns, money, and words promising or suggesting the use of either or both—are not effective. . . . In inducing the wish to establish peace, democracy, and free markets and the kind of state that makes them possible, the American and Western example exercises a powerful effect. But in bringing these ends about, American foreign policy is of little use. . . .

Even when aspirant societies wish to equip themselves with the appropriate kind of state, success is not assured. The capacity to develop and operate one depends heavily on whether a society's dominant values equip it for the task. In many cases they do not. So an important step in building a market economy and in making a commitment to peace and democracy is the acquisition of the appropriate cultural underpinnings.

Acquiring such a culture cannot happen overnight. The pertinent unit of time is the generation, for a shift in a society's prevailing values requires that people whose formative experiences have equipped them with one set of norms be replaced by others who have embraced, at later times and in other circumstances, different values. So although cultures do change and have always changed, and although they have changed more rapidly and broadly in the modern period than ever before, they cannot readily be changed by acts of official policy, not even by the foreign policy of the most powerful country on earth.

Thus for the diffusion of peace, democracy, and free markets—the supreme American international goal in the twenty-first century—the United States finds itself today in a position similar to that of Nathan Rothschild more than 150 years ago. The richest man in the world in the early decades of the nineteenth century, Rothschild died in 1837 of an infection of which the poorest Englishman could easily have been cured in the next century by readily available antibiotics. All of Rothschild's wealth could not give him what had not yet been invented, and all of the vast military and economic might of the United States cannot secure what lies beyond the power of guns to compel and money to buy.

4

America as a European Hegemon

Christopher Layne

As the wisest of all American philosophers, Yogi Berra, has insightfully observed, making predictions is hard, especially about the future. And he might have added—pointing to the predictions of an impending Euro-American rupture that have been a staple of debates about U.S.-European relations at least since the 1956 Suez crisis—prognosticating accurately about the future of Transatlantic relations is extra hard. Through all the ups and downs in U.S.-European relations over the years, those many Chicken Littles who have gone out on a limb to forecast an impending drifting apart of Europe and the United States never have had their predictions validated by events.

Until now, perhaps?

The Iraq War has produced a very different kind of rift. The damage inflicted on Washington's ties to Europe by the Bush Administration's policy is likely to prove real, lasting and, at the end of the day, irreparable. . . .

To understand why this crisis is different, we must understand its causes. The rupture between the United States and Europe is not, as some have asserted, mainly about an alleged Transatlantic rift in the realm of culture, values and ideology. It is not about the relative merits of unilateralism versus multilateralism. It is not even about the issues that framed the debate about Iraq during the run-up to war. . . . For sure, Iraq was a catalyst for Transatlantic dispute, but this crisis has been about American power—specifically about American hegemony.

39

OF BALANCE AND HEGEMONY

When future historians write about how American hegemony ended, they may well point to January 22, 2003 as a watershed. On that day, commemorating the 40th anniversary of the Franco-German Treaty negotiated by Charles de Gaulle and Konrad Adenauer as a bulwark against American hegemony, French President Jacques Chirac and German Chancellor Gerhard Schröder jointly declared that Paris and Berlin would work together to oppose the Bush Administration's evident intent to resolve the Iraqi question by force of arms. Later that day, in a Pentagon briefing, Secretary of Defense Donald Rumsfeld responded to the Franco-German declaration by contemptuously dismissing those partners as representing the "Old Europe," thereby triggering a Transatlantic earthquake, the geopolitical aftershocks of which will be felt for a long time. And well they should, for these contratemps reflect what is already a very old issue.

The problem of hegemony has been a major issue in U.S.-European relations since the United States emerged as a great power at the end of the 19th century. The United States fought two big wars in Europe out of fear that if a single power (in those cases, Germany) attained hegemony in Europe, it would be able to mobilize the continent's resources and threaten America in its own backyard, the Western Hemisphere. The conventional wisdom holds that America's post–World War II initiatives—the Marshall Plan, the North Atlantic Treaty—were driven by similar fears of possible Soviet hegemony in Europe. Indeed, many American strategic thinkers define America's traditional European strategy as a text-book example of "offshore balancing."

As an offshore balancer, the United States supposedly remains on the sidelines with respect to European security affairs unless a single great power threatens to dominate the continent. America's European grand strategy, therefore, is said to be counter-hegemonic: the United States intervenes in Europe only when the continental balance of power appears unable to thwart the rise of a would-be hegemon without U.S. assistance. The most notable proponent of this view of America's European grand strategy toward Europe is University of Chicago political scientist John J. Mearsheimer. He argues that the United States is not a global hegemon. Rather, because of what he describes as the "stopping power of water," the United States is a hegemon only in its own region (the Western Hemisphere), and acts as an offshore balancer toward Europe. He predicts that the United States soon will end its "continental commitment" because there is no European hegemon looming on the geopolitical horizon. As an offshore balancer, Mearsheimer says, the United States will not remain in Europe merely to play the role of regional stabilizer or pacifier.

There is just one thing wrong with this view: it does not fit the facts.

If American strategy toward Europe is indeed one of counter-hegemonic offshore balancing, it should have been over, over there, for the United States when the Soviet Union collapsed. By a different but not far-fetched reckoning, it should have been over in the early 1960s, when the Europeans were capable of deterring a Soviet military advance westward without the United States. With no hegemonic threat to contain, American military power should have been retracted from Europe after 1991, and NATO should have contracted into non-existence rather than undergoing two rounds of expansion. Of course, it may be that America will ultimately be ejected from the continent by the Europeans, but there are no signs that the United States will voluntarily pack up and go home any time soon.

It is not a "time lag," or mere inertia, that has kept American military power on the European continent more than a decade after the Soviet Union ceased to exist. There is a better explanation for why U.S. troops are still in Europe and NATO is still in business. It is because the Soviet Union's containment was never the driving force behind America's post–World War II commitment to Europe. There is a well-known quip that NATO was created to "keep the Russians out, the Germans down, and the Americans in." It would be more accurate to say that the Atlantic Alliance's primary raison d'être, from Washington's standpoint, was to keep America in—and on top—so that Germans could be kept down, Europe could be kept quiet militarily, and the Europeans would lack any pressing incentive to unite politically. The attainment of America's postwar grand strategic objectives on the continent required that the United States establish its own hegemony over Western Europe, something it would probably have done even in the absence of the Cold War. In other words, NATO is still in business to advance long-standing American objectives that existed independently of the Cold War and hence survived the Soviet Union's collapse.

AMERICAN AIMS

We usually look to history to help us understand the present and predict the future. But the reverse can be true, as well: sometimes recent events serve to shed light on what happened in the past, and why it happened. Many may react skeptically to the claim that America's postwar European grand strategy was driven at least as much—probably more—by non–Cold War factors as by the Soviet threat. But Washington's post–Cold War behavior provides a good deal of support for this thesis.

For starters, when the Berlin Wall fell and the Soviet Union began to unravel, the first Bush Administration did not feel in the least bit compelled to reconsider the relevance of, or need for, either the U.S. military commitment to Europe or NATO. As Philip Zelikow and Condoleezza Rice, both of whom served that administration as senior foreign policy officials, have observed:

> [The] administration believed strongly that, even if the immediate military threat from the Soviet Union diminished, the United States should maintain a significant military presence in Europe for the foreseeable future . . . . The American troop presence thus also served as the ante to ensure a central place for the United States as a player in European politics. The Bush administration placed a high value on retaining such influence, underscored by Bush's flat statement that the United States was and would remain "a European power.". . . The Bush administration was determined to maintain crucial features of the NATO system for European security even if the Cold War ended.

The Clinton Administration took a similar view. As one former State Department official avers, NATO had to be revitalized after the Cold War because American interests in Europe "transcended" the Soviet threat. . . .

The fact that American policymakers did not miss a beat when the Cold War ended with respect to reaffirming NATO's continuing importance reveals a great deal about the real nature of the interests that shaped America's European grand strategy after World War II, and that continue to do so today. The truth is that, from its inception, America's postwar European grand strategy reflected a complex set of interlocking "Open Door" interests. These interests are at once economic, strategic and broadly political in nature.

The first of these is that U.S. postwar officials believed that America had crucial economic interests in Europe. Even if there was no communist threat to Western Europe, State Department Policy Planning Staff Director George F. Kennan argued in 1947, the United States had a vital interest in facilitating Western Europe's economic recovery: "The United States people have a very real economic interest in Europe. This stems from Europe's role in the past as a market and as a major source of supply for a variety of products and services." These interests required that Europe's antiquated economic structure of small, national markets be fused into a large, integrated market that would facilitate efficiencies and economies of scale. . . .

To prevent far Left parties (especially the communists) from coming to power on the Continent's western half after World War II, U.S. aims also required political and social stability there. Washington was not really so concerned that such governments would drift into Moscow's political orbit, but it was very concerned that they would embrace the kinds of nationalist, or autarkic, economic policies that were anathema to America's goal of an open international economy. . . .

Second, American strategists perceived that U.S. economic interests would be jeopardized if postwar Europe relapsed into its bad habits of nationalism, great power rivalries and realpolitik. To ensure stability in Europe after World War II, the United States sought to create a militarily de-nationalized and economically integrated—but not politically unified—Europe. Washington would assume primary responsibility for European security, thereby precluding the re-emergence of the security dilemmas (especially that between France and Germany) that had sparked the two world wars. In turn, Western Europe's economic integration and interdependence—under the umbrella of America's military protectorate—would contribute to building a peaceful and stable Western Europe. In this respect, U.S. economic and security objectives meshed nicely.

Postwar U.S. policymakers viewed Europe's traditional balance of power security architecture as a "fire trap" and, as Undersecretary of State Robert Lovett said following World War II, Washington wanted to make certain that this fire trap was not rebuilt. Starting with those who were "present at the creation," successive generations of U.S. policymakers feared the continent's reversion to its (as Americans see it) dark past—a past defined by war, militarism, nationalism and an unstable multipolar balance of power. For American officials, Europe indeed has been a dark continent whose wars spilled over across the Atlantic, threatened American interests and invariably drew in the United States. . . .

After World War II, Rumsfeld's cabinet predecessors sought to maintain U.S. interests by breaking the Old Europe of its bad old geopolitical habits. As Secretary of State John Foster Dulles put it in 1953,

> Surely there is an urgent, positive duty on all of us to seek to end that danger which comes from within. It has been the cause of two world wars and it will be disastrous if it persists.

. . . The U.S. goal of embedding a militarily de-nationalized, but economically integrated Western Europe within the structure of an American-dominated "Atlantic Community" dovetailed neatly with another of Washington's key post-1945 grand strategic objectives: preventing the emergence of new poles of power in the international system—in the form either of a resurgent Germany or a united Europe—that could challenge America's geopolitical pre-eminence. Since the 1940s, Washington has had to perform a delicate balancing act with respect to Europe. To be sure, for economic reasons, the United States encouraged Western Europe's integration into a single common market, but the United States sought to prevent that from leading to its political unification.

To prevent the emergence of a politically unified Western Europe, successive U.S. administrations sought to "denationalize" the region by establishing a military protectorate that integrated Western Europe's military forces under, and subordinated them to, American command. The goal was to neuter Western Europe geopolitically and thereby circumscribe its ability to act independently of the United States in the high political realms of foreign and security policy. Embedding West European integration in the American-dominated Atlantic community would prevent the Europeans from veering off in the wrong direction. . . .

Europe's military absorption into the Atlantic Community went hand in hand with its economic integration. By persuading the West Europeans to "pool" their military and economic sovereignty, Washington aimed to strip them of the capacity to take unilateral national action. . . .

For the United States, therefore, institutions such as NATO, the aborted European Defense Community, the European Coal and Steel Community (ECSC) and the Common Market were the instruments it employed to contain the West Europeans. As the State Department said, the United States hoped that "cautious initial steps toward military, political, and economic cooperation will be followed by more radical departures from traditional concepts of sovereignty." The American aim was to create "institutional machinery to ensure that separate national interests are subordinated to the best interests of the community," and achieving this subordination was deemed essential if the United States was to accomplish its grand strategic purposes in Europe.

THE CONTINENTAL RESPONSE

Just as fear of a European hegemon led the United States to intervene in Europe's two great wars of the 20th century, the West Europeans after World War II understood that America had established its own hegemony over them. As realist international relations theory suggests, Western Europe tried to do something about it.

To be sure, West European balancing against the United States was constrained. On the one hand, although the West Europeans feared American power, they feared the Soviet Union even more during the Cold War. In a more positive sense, too, following World War II, Washington was able to use the carrot of economic assistance—notably, the Marshall Plan—to keep Western Europe aligned . . . with the United States. Nevertheless, throughout the post–World War II era, West European inclinations to balance against American power were never far from the surface.

In the five years or so after the end of World War II, it was Britain that hoped to emerge as a "Third Force" in world politics to balance both the United States and the Soviet Union. . . . The accelerating decline of Britain's relative power, of course, put paid to London's Third Force aspirations, but continental Europe's Third Force aspirations remained. In the late 1940s and 1950s, one of the hopes of the founding fathers of today's European Union was that the European Coal and Steel Community, and then the Common Market, would prove to be the embryo of a united Europe that could act as a geopolitical and economic counterweight to the United States. . . .

. . . Jean Monnet, author of the Schuman Plan that led to the ECSC and the "father" of European integration, first toyed with the idea of an Anglo-

French federation in the late 1940s because he saw this as the basis of a European bloc that could stand apart from both the United States and the Soviet Union. . . .

By the early 1960s, French President Charles de Gaulle believed that Western Europe had recovered sufficiently from World War II's dislocations and was poised to re-emerge as an independent pole of power in the international system. De Gaulle, clearly one of the 20th century's towering figures, was well versed in the realities of international politics. Following Washington's successful facing-down of the Soviet Union in the 1962 Cuban missile crisis, he concluded then that the world had become "unipolar"—dominated by a hegemonic America. To balance U.S. hegemony, de Gaulle pushed for France to acquire independent nuclear capabilities, and he sought to build a West European pole of power based on a Franco-German axis. That is what the 1963 treaty—the one Chirac and Schröder were commemorating on January 22—was all about, a fact that Washington apprehended clearly. U.S. policymakers were deeply concerned that Paris would lure West Germany out of the "Atlantic" (that is, U.S.) orbit, because such a Euro-centric strategic axis, as a 1966 State Department cable explicitly said, "would fragment Europe and divide the Atlantic world." In plainer English, the foundations of America's European hegemony would be undermined.

Washington recognized the Gaullist challenge for what it was—a direct assault on U.S. preponderance in Western Europe—and reacted by reasserting its own hegemonic prerogatives on the Continent. President Kennedy gave eloquent expression to the fear that Western Europe's emergence as an independent pole of power in the international system would be inimical to U.S. interests. . . . Kennedy voiced concern that U.S. leverage over Europe might be waning because the West Europeans, having staged a vigorous postwar recovery, were no longer dependent on the United States economically. Noting that "the European states are less subject to our influence," Kennedy expressed the fear that "if the French and other European powers acquire a nuclear capability they would be in a position to be entirely independent and we might be on the outside looking in." By pushing for a Multilateral Nuclear Force for Western Europe (in reality, one that kept Washington's finger firmly on the trigger), the United States sought—unsuccessfully—to derail France's nuclear ambitions.

With considerably more success, however, the United States did manage to take the teeth out of the Franco-German Treaty. In so doing, Washington played the hardest kind of hegemonic hardball. Threatening to rescind the security guarantee that protected West Germany from the Soviets, the U.S. government insisted that the Bundestag insert a preamble to the treaty reaffirming that Bonn's Atlantic connection to the United States and NATO took supremacy over its ties with Paris. . . .

WHAT'S NEW?

Now, forty years later, the United States and Europe are still playing the same game. America still asserts its hegemony, and France and Germany still seek (so far without much success) to create a European counterweight. As has been the case in the past, too, Washington is employing a number of strategies to keep Europe apart.

First, the United States is still actively discouraging Europe from either collective, or national, efforts to acquire the full spectrum of advanced military capabilities. Specifically, the United States has opposed the EU's Rapid Reaction Force (the nucleus of a future EU army), insisting that any European efforts must not duplicate NATO capabilities and must be part of an effort to strengthen the Alliance's "European pillar." The United States is also encouraging European NATO members to concentrate individually on carving out "niche" capabilities that will complement U.S. power rather than potentially challenge it.

Second, Washington is engaged in a game of divide and rule in a bid to thwart the EU's political unification process. The United States is pushing hard for the enlargement of the EU—and especially the admission of Turkey—in the expectation that a bigger EU will prove unmanageable and hence unable to emerge as a politically unified actor in international politics. The United States also has encouraged NATO expansion in a similar vein, in the hope that the "New Europe" (Poland, Hungary, the Czech Republic and Romania)—which, with the exception of Romania, will join the EU in 2004—will side with Washington against France and Germany on most issues of significance. For the United States, a Europe that speaks with many voices is optimal, which is why the United States is trying to ensure that the EU's "state-building" process fails, thereby heading off the emergence of a united Europe that could become an independent pole of power in the international system. . . .

Washington's aim of keeping Europe apart paid apparent dividends when, at the end of January, the leaders of Britain, Spain, Italy, Portugal, Denmark, Poland, Hungary and the Czech Republic signed a letter urging Europe and the international community to unite behind Washington's Iraq policy. This letter was notable especially because it illustrated that the United States is having some success in using the "New Europe" to balance against the "Old" Franco-German core. Clearly, Washington hopes that states such as Poland, Hungary, the Czech Republic and Romania will not only line up behind the United States within NATO, but will also represent Atlanticist interests over European ones within the EU itself.

In short, U.S. policy seeks to encourage an intra-European counterweight that will block French and German aspirations to create a united Europe counterweight to American hegemony. Indeed, in the wake of the Iraq War,

Transatlantic relations are characterized by a kind of "double containment" in Europe: the hard core of Old Europe (centered around France and Germany, and possibly supported by Russia) seeks to brake America's aspirations for global hegemony, while the United States and its "New European" allies in central and eastern Europe seek to contain Franco-German power on the Continent. It is an old game, in a new form.

THE WIDENING ATLANTIC

In the decade between the Soviet Union's collapse and 9/11, American hegemony . . . was the central issue in American grand strategy debates. It still is. Although American policymakers have developed a number of (too) clever rationales to convince themselves that the United States will escape the fate that invariably befalls hegemons, the fallout of the Iraq crisis on the Transatlantic relationship illustrates that concern with America's hegemonic power—and the way it is exercised—is not confined to the Middle East and Persian Gulf.

Why do France, Germany and much of the rest of the world, including other major powers such as Russia and China, worry about American hegemony? The simple answer is that international politics remains fundamentally what it has always been: a competitive arena in which states struggle to survive. States are always worried about their security. Thus when one state becomes overwhelmingly powerful—that is, hegemonic—others fear for their safety.

Doubtless the Bush Administration's fervent hegemonists will scoff at the idea that the United States will become the object of counter-hegemonic balancing. They clearly believe that the United States can do as it pleases because it is so far ahead in terms of hard power that no other state (or coalition of states) can possibly hope to balance against it. They also know, and know that Europeans know, that the United States does not and will never literally threaten Europe with its military power. This confidence is misplaced, however, because it overlooks the effects of what can be called "the hegemon's temptation."

A hegemonic power like the United States today has overwhelming hard power—especially military power—and indeed there is no state or coalition with commensurate power capable of restraining the United States from exercising that power. For hegemons, the formula of overwhelming power and lack of opposition creates powerful incentives to expand the scope of its geopolitical interests. But over time, the cumulative effects of expansion for the United States—wars and subsequent occupations in the Balkans, the Persian Gulf, Afghanistan and the War on Terrorism; possible future wars against North Korea, Iran, Syria, or China over Taiwan—will have an enervating impact on U.S. power.

At the end of the day, hegemonic decline results from the interplay of overextension abroad and domestic economic weakness. Over time, the costs of America's hegemonic vocation will interact with its economic vulnerabilities—endless budget deficits fueled in part by burgeoning military spending, and the persistent balance of payments deficit—to erode America's relative power advantage over the rest of the world. As the relative power gap between the United States and potential new great powers begins to shrink, the costs and risks of challenging the United States will decrease, and the pay-off for doing so will increase. As the British found out toward the end of the 19th century, a seemingly unassailable international power position can melt away with unexpected rapidity.

There are already today other potential poles of power in the international system waiting in the wings that could quickly emerge as counterweights to the United States. And with the Iraq crisis revealing the stark nature of American hegemony, these new power centers have increasingly greater incentive to do so. Here, by facilitating "soft" balancing against the United States, the Iraq crisis may have paved the way for "hard" balancing as well. Since the end of World War II, policymakers and analysts on both sides of the Atlantic have realized that Europe is a potential pole of power in the international system. Will France and Germany provide the motor to unite Europe in opposition to the United States? Time, of course, will tell.

But for sure, this is not 1963. The Cold War is over, and France and Germany are freer to challenge American hegemony. The EU is in the midst of an important constitutional convention that is laying the foundation for a politically unified Europe. And even as the Iraq War proceeded, there were straws in the wind pointing in the direction of hard balancing against the United States. Most notable are indications that France, Germany, Belgium and Luxemburg may act together to create Europe's own version of a coalition of the willing—by forming a "hard core" of enhanced defense cooperation among themselves.

In the short term, however, Paris and Berlin—supported by Russia—have led the way in soft balancing to counter American hegemony. By using international organizations like the United Nations to marshal opposition to the United States, France and Germany—and similarly inclined powers such as Russia and China—are beginning to develop new habits of diplomatic cooperation to oppose Washington. . . .

At the end of the day, the most telling piece of evidence that the Iraq War marks a turning point in Transatlantic relations, and with respect to American hegemony, is this: Despite widespread predictions that they would fold diplomatically and acquiesce in a second UN resolution authorizing the United States and Great Britain to forcibly disarm Iraq, Paris and Berlin (and Moscow) held firm. Rather than being shocked and awed by America's power and strong-arm diplomacy, they stuck to their guns . . . and refused to fall into line behind Washington. What this shows, at the very least, is that it is easier to be Number One when there is a Number Two that threatens Numbers Three, Four, Five and so on. It also suggests that a hegemon so clearly defied is a hegemon on a downward arc.

Many throughout the world now have the impression that the United States is acting as an aggressive hegemon engaged in the naked aggrandizement of its own power. The notion that the United States is a "benevolent" hegemon has been shredded. America is inviting the same fate as that which has overtaken previous contenders for hegemony. In the sweep of history, the Bush Administration will not be remembered for conquering Baghdad, but for a policy that galvanized both soft and hard balancing against American hegemony. At the end of the day, what the administration trumpets as "victory" in the Persian Gulf may prove, in reality, to have pushed NATO into terminal decline, given the decisive boost to the political unification of Europe (at least the most important parts of it), and marked the beginning of the end of America's era of global preponderance.

5

A Global Power Shift in the Making

James F. Hoge Jr.

IS THE UNITED STATES READY?

The transfer of power from West to East is gathering pace and soon will dramatically change the context for dealing with international challenges—as well as the challenges themselves. Many in the West are already aware of Asia's growing strength. This awareness, however, has not yet been translated into preparedness. And therein lies a danger: that Western countries will repeat their past mistakes.

Major shifts of power between states, not to mention regions, occur infrequently and are rarely peaceful. In the early twentieth century, the imperial order and the aspiring states of Germany and Japan failed to adjust to each other. The conflict that resulted devastated large parts of the globe. Today, the transformation of the international system will be even bigger and will require the assimilation of markedly different political and cultural traditions. This time, the populous states of Asia are the aspirants seeking to play a greater role. Like Japan and Germany back then, these rising powers are nationalistic, seek redress of past grievances, and want to claim their place in the sun. Asia's growing economic power is translating into greater political and military power, thus increasing the potential damage of conflicts. Within the region, the flash points for hostilities—Taiwan, the Korean Peninsula, and divided Kashmir—have defied peaceful resolution. Any of them could explode into large-scale warfare that would make the current

Middle East confrontations seem like police operations. In short, the stakes in Asia are huge and will challenge the West's adaptability.

Today, China is the most obvious power on the rise. But it is not alone: India and other Asian states now boast growth rates that could outstrip those of major Western countries for decades to come. China's economy is growing at more than nine percent annually, India's at eight percent, and the Southeast Asian "tigers" have recovered from the 1997 financial crisis and resumed their march forward. China's economy is expected to be double the size of Germany's by 2010 and to overtake Japan's, currently the world's second largest, by 2020. If India sustains a six percent growth rate for 50 years, as some financial analysts think possible, it will equal or overtake China in that time.

Nevertheless, China's own extraordinary economic rise is likely to continue for several decades—if, that is, it can manage the tremendous disruptions caused by rapid growth, such as internal migration from rural to urban areas, high levels of unemployment, massive bank debt, and pervasive corruption. At the moment, China is facing a crucial test in its transition to a market economy. It is experiencing increased inflation, real-estate bubbles, and growing shortages of key resources such as oil, water, electricity, and steel. Beijing is tightening the money supply and big bank lending, while continuing efforts to clean up the fragile banking sector. It is also considering raising the value of its dollar-pegged currency, to lower the cost of imports. If such attempts to cool China's economy—which is much larger and more decentralized than it was ten years ago, when it last overheated—do not work, it could crash.

Even if temporary, such a massive bust would have dire consequences. China is now such a large player in the global economy that its health is inextricably linked to that of the system at large. China has become the engine driving the recovery of other Asian economies from the setbacks of the 1990s. Japan, for example, has become the largest beneficiary of China's economic growth, and its leading economic indicators, including consumer spending, have improved as a result. The latest official figures indicate that Japan's real GDP rose at the annual rate of 6.4 percent in the last quarter of 2003, the highest growth of any quarter since 1990. Thanks to China, Japan may finally be emerging from a decade of economic malaise. But that trend might not continue if China crashes.

India also looms large on the radar screen. Despite the halting progress of its economic reforms, India has embarked on a sharp upward trajectory; propelled by its thriving software and business-service industries, which support corporations in the United States and other advanced economies. Regulation remains inefficient, but a quarter-century of partial reforms has allowed a dynamic private sector to emerge. Economic success is also starting to change basic attitudes: after 50 years, many Indians are finally discarding their colonial-era sense of victimization.

Other Southeast Asian states are steadily integrating their economies into a large web through trade and investment treaties. Unlike in the past, however, China—not Japan or the United States—is at the hub. . . .

THE STRAINS OF SUCCESS

Asia's rise is just beginning, and if the big regional powers can remain stable while improving their policies, rapid growth could continue for decades. Robust success, however, is inevitably accompanied by various stresses.

The first and foremost of these will be relations among the region's major players. For example, China and Japan have never been powerful at the same time: for centuries, China was strong while Japan was impoverished, whereas for most of the last 200 years, Japan has been powerful and China weak. Having both powerful in the same era will be an unprecedented challenge. Meanwhile, India and China have not resolved their 42-year-old border dispute and still distrust each other. Can these three powers now coexist, or will they butt heads over control of the region, access to energy sources, security of sea-lanes, and sovereignty over islands in the South China Sea? . . .

Taiwan is the most dangerous example of this risk. It has now been more than 30 years since the United States coupled recognition of one China with a call for a peaceful resolution of the Taiwan question. Although economic and social ties between the island and the mainland have since grown, political relations have soured. Taiwan, under its current president, seems to be creeping toward outright independence, whereas mainland China continues to seek its isolation and to threaten it by positioning some 500 missiles across the Taiwan Strait. The United States, acting on its commitment to Taiwan's security, has provided the island with ever more sophisticated military equipment. Despite U.S. warnings to both sides, if Taiwan oversteps the line between provisional autonomy and independence or if China grows impatient, the region could explode.

Kashmir remains divided between nuclear-armed India and Pakistan. Since 1989, the conflict there has taken 40,000 lives, many in clashes along the Line of Control that separates the two belligerents. India and Pakistan have recently softened their hawkish rhetoric toward each other, but neither side appears ready for a mutually acceptable settlement. Economic or political instabilities within Pakistan could easily ignite the conflict once more.

North Korea is another potential flash point. Several recent rounds of six-party talks held under Chinese auspices have so far failed to persuade Kim Jong Il to scrap his nuclear weapons program in exchange for security guarantees and aid to North Korea's decrepit economy. Instead, the talks have brought recriminations: toward the United States, for offering too little; toward North Korea, for remaining intransigent; and toward China, for applying insufficient pressure on its dependent neighbor. Now recently disclosed evidence suggests that North Korea's nuclear efforts are even more advanced than was previously believed. As Vice President Dick Cheney warned China's leaders during an April trip, time may be running out for a negotiated resolution to the crisis.

SHIFTING PRIORITIES

For more than half a century, the United States has provided stability in the Pacific through its military presence there, its alliances with Japan and South Korea, and its commitment to fostering economic progress. Indeed, in its early days, the Bush administration stressed its intention to strengthen those traditional ties and to treat China more as a strategic competitor than as a prospective partner. Recent events, however—including the attacks of September 11, 2001—have changed the emphasis of U.S. policy. Today, far less is expected of South Korea than in the past, thanks in part to Seoul's new leaders, who represent a younger generation of Koreans enamored of China, disaffected with the United States, and unafraid of the North.

Japan, meanwhile, faced with a rising China, a nuclear-armed North Korea, and increasing tension over Taiwan, is feeling insecure. It has thus signed on to develop a missile defense system with U.S. aid and is considering easing constitutional limits on the development and deployment of its military forces.

Such moves have been unsettling to Japan's neighbors, which would become even more uncomfortable if Japan lost faith in its U.S. security guarantee and opted to build its own nuclear deterrent instead. Even worse, from the American perspective, would be if China and Japan were to seek a strategic alliance between themselves rather than parallel relations with the United States. To forestall this, Washington must avoid, in all its maneuverings with China and the two Koreas, sowing any doubt in Japan about its commitment to the region.

Yet Japan, given its ongoing economic and demographic problems, cannot be the center of any new power arrangement in Asia. Instead, that role will be played by China and, eventually, India. Relations with these two growing giants are thus essential to the future, and engagement must be the order of the day, even though some Bush officials remain convinced that the United States and China will ultimately end up rivals. For them, the strategic reality is one of incompatible vital interests.

Militarily, the United States is hedging its bets with the most extensive realignment of U.S. power in half a century. Part of this realignment is the opening of a second front in Asia. No longer is the United States poised with several large, toehold bases on the Pacific rim of the Asian continent; today, it has made significant moves into the heart of Asia itself, building a network of smaller, jumping-off bases in Central Asia. The ostensible rationale for these bases is the war on terrorism. But Chinese analysts suspect that the unannounced intention behind these new U.S. positions, particularly when coupled with Washington's newly intensified military cooperation with India, is the soft containment of China.

For its part, China is modernizing its military forces, both to improve its ability to win a conflict over Taiwan and to deter U.S. aggression. Chinese military doctrine now focuses on countering U.S. high-tech capabilities—information networks, stealth aircraft, cruise missiles, and precision guided bombs.

Suspicious Americans have interpreted larger Chinese military budgets as signs of Beijing's intention to roll back America's presence in East Asia. Washington is thus eager to use India, which appears set to grow in economic and military strength, as a counterbalance to China as well as a strong proponent of democracy in its own right. To step into these roles, India needs to quicken the pace of its economic reforms and avoid the Hindu nationalism espoused by the Bharatiya Janata Party (BJP). . . .

. . . To date, the aberrant religious ideology that opposes all secular government has developed only moderate traction among the large Muslim populations of India and the surrounding states of Central and Southeast Asia. For example, fundamentalist Islamic political parties fared poorly in winter and spring parliamentary elections in Malaysia and Indonesia. In other ways, however, radical Islamists are becoming a serious threat to the region. Weak governments and pervasive corruption there provide fertile ground for back shop operations: training, recruitment, and equipping of terrorists. Evidence points to a loose network of disparate Southeast Asian terrorist groups that help each other with funds and operations.

Recent public-opinion polls show that sympathy is growing for the anti-American posturing of the radical Islamists, in large part due to U.S. activities in Iraq and U.S. support of the Sharon government in Israel. The full impact of outrage over the mistreatment of Iraqi prisoners is still to be determined. But deep anger is already in place among Muslim communities worldwide over the perceived slighting of Palestinian interests by the Bush administration. A settlement of the Israeli-Palestinian conflict would not end terrorism, and Muslims themselves must lead the ideological battle within Islam. Yet the United States could strengthen the hand of moderates in the Muslim world with a combination of policy changes and effective public diplomacy. The United States must do more than set up radio and television stations to broadcast alternative views of U.S. intentions in the Middle East. It must replenish its diminished public diplomacy resources to recruit more language experts, reopen foreign libraries and cultural centers, and sponsor exchange programs. Given the large number of traditionally tolerant Muslims in Asia, the United States must vigorously assist the creation of attractive alternatives to radical Islamism.

NEEDED CHANGES

To accommodate the great power shift now rapidly occurring in Asia, the United States needs vigorous preparation by its executive branch and Congress. The Bush administration's embrace of engagement with China is an improvement over its initial posture, and the change has been reflected in Washington's efforts to work with Beijing in the battle against terrorism and negotiations with North Korea. The change has also been reflected in the reluctance to settle trade and currency differences by imposing duties. In other ways, however, Washington has yet to shift its approach. On the ground, the United States appears undermanned. Despite a huge increase in the workload, the work force at the U.S. embassy in China numbers approximately 1,000, which is half the employees envisioned for the new embassy in Iraq. Training in Asian languages for U.S. government officials has been increased only marginally. As for the next generation, only several thousand American students are now studying in China, compared to the more than 50,000 Chinese who are now studying in U.S. schools.

Going forward, the United States must provide the leadership to forge regional security arrangements, along the lines of the pending U.S.-Singapore accord to expand cooperation in the fight against terrorism and the proliferation of weapons of mass destruction. It must also champion open economies or risk being left out of future trade arrangements. The United States must also avoid creating a self-fulfilling prophecy of strategic rivalry with China. Such a rivalry may in fact come to pass, and the United States should be prepared for such a turn of events. But it is not inevitable; cooperation could still produce historic advancements.

At the international level, Asia's rising powers must be given more representation in key institutions, starting with the UN Security Council. This important body should reflect the emerging configuration of global power, not just the victors of World War II. The same can be said of other key international bodies. . . .

The credibility and effectiveness of international bodies depend on such changes; only then will they be able to contribute significantly to peace among nations. Although hardly foolproof, restructuring institutions to reflect the distribution of power holds out more hope than letting them fade into irrelevance and returning to unrestrained and unpredictable balance-of-power politics and free-for-all economic competition.

II

An American Empire?

OVERVIEW

Among the surprising turns in political and intellectual debate since 9/11 has been the discussion of whether the United States is an imperialist power. The accusation itself is not unexpected, given recent American moves to topple regimes in Afghanistan and Iraq by military force. During periods of intensified U.S. military intervention abroad, opponents of such policies have often employed the language of anti-imperialism in sharpening their critiques. Such appeals, designed to awaken anticolonial reflexes rooted in America's own founding, have resurfaced in recent years.

Uniquely in the present case, however, a group of writers generally placed on the conservative side of the political spectrum have embraced the label of American empire in an approving fashion. Some call upon the United States to emulate the British imperial example of the nineteenth century, which is recast in a positive light. While no author calls for a revival of colonialism in its prior forms, many argue that the United States should self-confidently impose order and bring democracy to regions plagued by instability or despotism—even if this involves the employment of military force and infringements on the principles of sovereignty.

The course of the twentieth century witnessed the dismantlement of European empires around the world in the face of growing resistance by subject peoples. The imperial ideal—the norms and ideals that surrounded such projects—was seemingly forever discredited in favor of the principle of self-determination. Against this backdrop, it is striking—and surprising— to encounter defenses of U.S. military action abroad framed in terms of the merits of empire.

This debate is reflected in the selections that make up this section. To better understand the issues at stake, we can frame the discussion with three questions: Is the United States an imperial power? Would an American empire be good for Americans or for the world? Is the United States suited to an imperial role?

The United States: An Imperial Power?

Most Americans would balk at the idea that the United States is an imperial power. After all, their country won its independence by overthrowing British colonialism. Moreover, the United States never assembled the vast overseas possessions acquired by some European countries during the nineteenth century. Nevertheless, the early European settlers of North America were colonizers as well as colonists. The westward expansion of European settlement, both before and after independence, depended upon the violent displacement of native peoples, the conquest of Mexican territories in the southwest, and the purchase of other lands from various European powers.

Also, the United States was not entirely absent from the game of overseas colonial expansion. Victory in the Spanish-American War of 1898 left the United States in possession of colonies in Cuba and the Philippines. During the first decades of the twentieth century, the United States established informal control over much of the Caribbean and Central America, intervening with military force on numerous occasions and at times for lengthy periods in order to reverse unwelcome political developments and install friendly governments.

Yet the imperial project never represented the central thrust of U.S. foreign policy. Anti-imperialist sentiment runs deep in America's collective consciousness. At the turn of the twentieth century, the United States opposed the European dismemberment of China through its Open Door policy. In the wake of World War I, Woodrow Wilson championed the cause of self-determination and called for the breakup of Europe's colonial empires. World War II was fought to counter the expansionist ambitions of Germany and Japan. The United States voluntarily granted independence to its major colonial possessions in Cuba and the Philippines and eschewed territorial demands after each of the two world wars. As John B. Judis points out in his chapter, America's early-twentieth-century flirtation with imperialist policies proved unsatisfying and short-lived.

But what of the present era, a time when the United States possesses economic and military resources that dwarf those of competing states? Historian Paul W. Schroeder argues that the United States is not a true empire. Defining imperialism as "the possession of final authority by one entity over the vital political decisions of another," Schroeder concludes that the United States lacks the desire for territorial expansion or political control over other societies that has characterized imperial powers of the past.

Schroeder prefers the label *hegemon* to describe the dominant position that the United States currently enjoys. A hegemon exercises influence not through coercion and control but through leadership based at least in part on the consent of other states. Schroeder emphasizes the point that supreme power alone does not qualify a state or its foreign policies as imperialist. The term *imperialism* implies something more about how and for what purposes power is employed.

Yet even under Schroeder's criteria, the frequency of U.S. interventions to topple and replace out-of-favor governments in countries such as Panama, Haiti, Liberia, Somalia, Bosnia, Kosovo, Afghanistan, and Iraq might be viewed as the behavior of an imperial power, whatever the merits of intervention in any particular case. And Schroeder himself concedes that the current Bush administration may have imperial ambitions.

Other authors argue that U.S. power serves imperial functions, even if today's American empire differs in structure and appearance from those of the past. Andrew J. Bacevich suggests that today's U.S. military establishment far exceeds any reasonable defensive need and serves instead as a tool for projecting American power abroad. The ever-more-frequent resort to military force undercuts the potential for peaceful diplomatic solutions to international conflict and erodes the health of American democracy at home.

Beyond America's military presence, U.S. power extends into other societies through its economic muscle and predominance over key global economic institutions, such as the International Monetary Fund, the World Bank, and the World Trade Organization. U.S. influence also flows through American leadership in information technologies—especially the Internet and the global appeal of American popular culture and media. Considering America's global role, Michael Ignatieff asks, "what word but 'empire' describes the awesome thing that America is becoming?"

The Cases for and against American Imperialism

Advocates of modern-day imperialism are careful to qualify their application of the term *empire* to the United States. Ignatieff refers to "empire lite" and Max Boot to America's "liberal and humanitarian imperialism." These terms are meant to distinguish American imperialism from the exploitative legacies of past imperialisms. The purposes of U.S. imperialism are instead defensive and humanitarian, according to these authors. The United States must intervene, with force if necessary, to reconstruct both failed states and rogue states into pluralistic democracies with market economies. The application of U.S. power for these purposes serves both to bring a better life to the inhabitants of such societies and to protect the United States and its friends from the dangers created when terrorists find safe haven in failed states or when aggressive dictators seek weapons of mass destruction.

This mixture of self-interested and idealist rationales for imperialism has many precedents. British imperialists claimed that their enlightened form of colonial rule brought progress and the rule of law to subject peoples, along with profits from mining, plantations, and commerce for the British themselves. The French justified colonial rule as a means of bringing "civilization," or at least the French version of it, to backward societies. America's own efforts at what is today called "nation building" rest upon the presumed universal applicability of democracy, human rights, and market capitalism. Nevertheless, critics of a new American imperialism argue that the moral rationales advanced in support of U.S. intervention abroad are little more than cloaks for more self-serving motivations, such as control over oil resources abroad or the protection of American business interests.

The Practicality of American Imperialism

Apart from the rightness or wrongness of a new American imperialism are questions about its practicality. Schroeder and Judis both argue that democracy cannot be successfully advanced in other societies through imperial imposition because imperialism inevitably produces nationalist resistance. Michael Ignatieff, who is ambivalent about American empire, warns that imperial societies are given to hubris and run the danger of overreaching and overextension.

Niall Ferguson is convinced that a world given order by a benevolent imperial power such as the United States is preferable to the chaos that would result from the retraction of American influence. Yet he frets that American society is too parochial, too impatient, and too self-conscious about its imperial role to build and sustain an effective empire. Implanting the seeds of democracy and capitalism abroad requires considerable time and a firm, self-confident hand. Yet when the United States does overthrow a tyrant abroad or intervene for humanitarian purposes, Americans immediately begin looking for an "exit strategy."

Conclusion

The varied perspectives reflected in the readings contained in this part suggest the difficulties that Americans (and non-Americans) currently experience in coming to grips with the character, purposes, and responsibilities of America's enormous international power. Disagreements over what terminology to use in referring to America's world role—superpower? hegemon? empire?—reflect the complex and politically charged nature of the problem.

Given the combination of American's vast power and equally wide-ranging commitments abroad, disagreements over the uses and abuses of this country's global influence are likely to animate American political discourse for years to come.

DISCUSSION QUESTIONS

1. What criteria might be applied in determining whether a country is engaged in "imperialist" behavior abroad? What indicators would allow us to distinguish imperialist policies from nonimperialist policies? ·

2. Is it possible for a state to pursue a "liberal and humanitarian imperialism?" Or does this phrase contain a contradiction in terms?

3. Is the exercise of American influence abroad driven mainly by idealism or self-interest?

4. Can democracy be imposed through external force? Or is democracy only viable if it arises through internal processes?

5. How does Great Britain's imperial role during the nineteenth century differ from that of the United States today? Why does Niall Ferguson believe that the United States is poorly suited to the task of empire building?

6. How, according to Andrew Bacevich, have perceptions about the proper role of the military in U.S. society changed since the early post–Vietnam War era?

SUGGESTED READINGS

Bacevich, Andrew J. *American Empire: The Realities and Consequences of U.S. Diplomacy.* Cambridge, Mass.: Harvard University Press, 2002.

Brawley, Mark R. *Afterglow or Adjustment? Domestic Institutions and Responses to Overstretch.* New York: Columbia University Press, 1999.

Chomsky, Noam. *Hegemony or Survival: America's Quest for Global Dominance.* New York: Metropolitan Books, 2003.

Doyle, Michael W. *Empires.* Ithaca, N.Y.: Cornell University Press, 1986.

Ferguson, Niall. *Colossus: The Price of America's Empire.* New York: Penguin Books, 2004.

Hardt, Michael, and Antonio Negri. *Empire.* Cambridge, Mass.: Harvard University Press, 2001.

Johnson, Chalmers. *The Sorrows of Empire: Militarism, Secrecy, and the End of the Republic.* New York: Metropolitan, 2004.

Khalidi, Rashid. *Resurrecting Empire: Western Footprints and America's Perilous Path in the Middle East*. Boston: Beacon Press, 2004.

Kinzer, Stephen. *Overthrow: America's Century of Regime Change from Hawaii to Iraq*. New York: Times Books, 2006.

Lal, Deepak. *In Praise of Empires: Globalization and Order*. New York: Palgrave Macmillan, 2004.

6

History Lesson

What Woodrow Wilson
Can Teach Today's Imperialists

John B. Judis

History is not physics. Studying the past does not yield objective laws that can unerringly predict the course of events. But peoples do draw lessons from history and change their behavior accordingly. Western European countries, for instance, took the experience of two world wars as reason to change radically their relations with one another. . . .

Historical lessons can also be unlearned or forgotten. The New Left of the 1960s, for instance, forgot the lessons of an earlier "God that failed" and projected the same hopes for a communist utopia onto Castro's Cuba or Ho Chi Minh's Vietnam that earlier generations had projected onto the Soviet Union. And, today, the right is going through its own bout of historical amnesia. Conservatives, forgetting the lessons of the early twentieth century, are attempting to rehabilitate the long-discredited strategy of imperialism.

The revival is centered in East Coast journals and think tanks, from *National Review* and *The Wall Street Journal* editorial page in New York to the American Enterprise Institute, *The Weekly Standard, Policy Review,* and the Project for the New American Century in Washington. In an October 2001 *Weekly Standard* cover story, Max Boot called on the United States "unambiguously to embrace its imperial role." In *Foreign Affairs* last July, Thomas Donnelly, a former Lockheed official who is a senior fellow at the Project for the New American Century, wrote that "American imperialism can bring with it new hopes of liberty, security, and prosperity." In *Policy Review* last April, Stanley Kurtz called for a new "democratic imperialism."

Although the Bush administration's foreign policy is a mix of different ideologies, it has clearly been influenced by this new imperialism. Evidence can be found in the cultlike popularity of Theodore Roosevelt, the president many conservatives take as their guide to a neo-imperial strategy. . . . More important, it is evident in the administration's attitude toward international institutions, its arguments for invading and occupying Iraq, its case for preventive war, and even its international economic strategy.

This new imperialism differs in some respects from the older U.S. imperialism of Roosevelt and Senator Henry Cabot Lodge—the new imperialists don't assume, for instance, the superiority of the Anglo-Saxon race or seek the spread of Christian civilization—but it is sufficiently similar to raise the question of whether these new imperialists are reviving a strategy that failed the United States 80 years ago. That failure was understood most clearly by Woodrow Wilson, who offered not only the most compelling critique of U.S. imperialism but also the most thoughtful alternative—a liberal internationalism that served the United States well in the second half of the twentieth century and could guide Americans again today.

There have been empires since the Greeks and Romans, but modern imperialism, and the term "imperialism" itself, appeared in the late nineteenth century. From 1870 to 1914, when World War I began, the great European powers and Japan carved up Asia and Africa into colonies, protectorates, and client regimes. The United States, still recovering from the Civil War and having not yet completed its continental expansion, initially forswore any imperial ambitions. But, by the 1890s, a powerful lobby led by Roosevelt (who would become assistant secretary of the Navy in the McKinley administration) and Lodge was calling for an "expansionist" foreign policy.

Like their European counterparts, the American imperialists were worried about ensuring national prosperity. They contended, particularly after the depression of the mid-1890s, that, if the United States failed to gain a foothold in Asia and Africa, it would be denied access to raw materials and important markets for the surplus of goods that its factories could now produce. But Roosevelt and Lodge also saw imperialism through the prism of geopolitics, social Darwinism, and evangelical Protestantism. Roosevelt regarded it as integral to a struggle for the "domination of the world" that the United States must either win or lose. If the United States failed to seize the Hawaiian Islands, Roosevelt warned in 1898, they could be "transformed into the most dangerous possible base of operations against our Pacific cities." Imperialism also offered a way to provide moral uplift to Americans—by fostering a spirit of what Roosevelt called "national greatness"—and to extend the benefits of American, and more broadly Anglo-Saxon and Christian, civilization to the "barbarous" peoples of Asia and Africa. Wrote Roosevelt in 1901, "It is our duty toward the people living in barbarism to see that they are freed from their chains."

The American imperialists first got their chance in 1898. Accusing the Spanish of blowing up the battleship *Maine* in the Havana harbor (the explosion later turned out to be from a defective boiler), the United States declared war on Spain and seized its possessions in the Caribbean and the Pacific, including Cuba and the Philippines. The United States, it seemed, had enthusiastically entered the imperial fray.

Yet, in less than a decade, the United States would abandon its imperial mission and, five years after that, explicitly repudiate it. The abandonment of imperialism began, ironically, with Roosevelt. While publicly continuing to support an imperialist foreign policy, Roosevelt actually allowed U.S. possessions to shrink during his two terms as president (1901–1908) and resisted pleas to establish new U.S. bases in China and the Caribbean. In 1902, he wrote to prominent New York lawyer Frederick Coudert, "Barring the possible necessity of fortifying the Isthmian canal or getting a naval station, I hope it will not become our duty to take a foot of soil south of us."

Like Roosevelt, Wilson was an early advocate of imperialism—for example, arguing in 1902 that the "impulse to expansion is the natural and wholesome impulse, which comes from a consciousness of matured strength"— but refrained from endorsing it once he ascended to the presidency. In 1913, his first year in office, Wilson withdrew America's support for a bank consortium in China that the United States, along with Britain and other occupying powers, had established to parcel out China's economy. "I will not help any man buy a power which he ought not to exercise over fellow beings," he commented. He also pressured Congress to grant early independence to the Philippines and citizenship to Puerto Ricans.

Most important, Wilson made self-determination and an end to colonialism the hallmarks of his plan for ending World War I and preventing future wars. During the Senate debate in 1920 over the League of Nations, Wilson argued that Americans had "a choice between . . . the ideal of democracy, which represents the rights of free peoples everywhere to govern themselves, and . . . the ideal of imperialism, which seeks to dominate by force and unjust power." Imperialism, to Wilson, was not an instrument of democracy but an obstacle to it.

What initially turned Roosevelt privately and Wilson publicly against imperialism were the nationalist backlashes that America's imperialist policies provoked. Roosevelt and other American imperialists had believed they could impose U.S. civilization upon conquered peoples as readily as they had transformed the continental frontier. But, in the first decades of the twentieth century, they were to discover that imperial intervention inspired anti-imperial nationalist movements that frustrated U.S. objectives. Roosevelt had promised to "civilize" the Filipinos, but, soon after the United States took power in 1898, it faced a succession of violent national rebellions. By 1902, at least 4,000 Americans and 200,000 Filipinos had been killed. When World War I began, Roosevelt finally urged U.S. withdrawal from the Philippines.

Wilson experienced similar frustration in Mexico. The Mexican Revolution had begun in 1910, and the next year liberal constitutionalist Francisco Madero overthrew dictator Porfirio Díaz. In 1913, Madero was murdered and replaced by General Victoriano Huerta. With Mexico on the verge of civil war, Wilson landed troops in Veracruz to depose the unpopular Huerta. "I am going to teach the South American republics to elect good men," Wilson declared. But Huerta used Wilson's intervention to rally support against Yankee imperialism. And Huerta's successor, the revolutionary Venustiano Carranza, fearful of being identified with the Yankee invaders, rebuffed Wilson's diplomatic overtures. Wilson, biographer Kendrick A. Clements writes, was "stunned by the fury with which the invasion was greeted by Mexicans of all political persuasions." Although Roosevelt and others urged him to impose a pliant regime on Mexico by force, Wilson instead withdrew the troops and recognized Carranza. . . .

Wilson's opposition to imperialism was hardened by World War I. Proponents of empire had previously argued that imperial expansion would reduce the chances of global war by eliminating unstable regimes in Africa and Asia. "Peace cannot be had until the civilized nations have expanded in some shape over the barbarous nations," wrote Roosevelt in 1894. But, by making the struggle for imperial domination integral to a nation's power and prosperity, imperialism instead led to a succession of conflicts culminating in world war: the Russo-Japanese war in 1904–1905 over Manchuria and Korea; the clashes between Germany and France over French North Africa in 1906 and in 1911; the Anglo-German naval arms race for control of the seas and the world's commerce; the growing tensions in the Middle East, where oil had been discovered; and, finally, the outbreak of war in 1914 between Austria and Russia over Turkey's former possessions in the Balkans, a conflict that quickly pulled in all of Europe's great powers. When the United States entered the war in 1917, Wilson would publicly blame it on German militarism. But, when it came to making proposals to prevent future wars, Wilson showed that he believed imperial rivalry lay at the root of the conflagration. "For my own part," he told the Senate in 1920, "I am as intolerant of imperialistic designs on the part of other nations as I was of such designs on the part of Germany."

Wilson saw imperialism not simply as a strategy or policy but as a system of international relations that had to be thoroughly uprooted. It was characterized by a hierarchy of power in which the larger, more powerful nations competed violently with each other to dominate the smaller, less powerful ones. To the extent it didn't immediately lead to war, it was because of a coincidental and transient balance of power among the larger powers. The system itself, he believed, was inherently unstable as well as unjust.

Wilson didn't believe he could eliminate hierarchies of power, but he contrived to create a mediating system of international law and organizations that would protect the sovereignty and independence of smaller, weaker nations. Within this realm, all nations would become equal, just as all citizens were legally equal, regardless of their strength or wealth, within a democracy. In his Fourteen Points, which he announced to Congress in January 1918, and in the draft charter of a new League of Nations that he wrote and introduced the next year, Wilson called for phasing out colonialism, eliminating protectionist trade barriers, and establishing a worldwide system of free trade. "There must be, not a balance of power, but a community of power," he explained, "not organized rivalries, but an organized common peace."

Like Roosevelt, Wilson believed that Americans were chosen to transform the backward nations of the world. He thought of the United States "as the light of the world as created to lead the world in the assertion of the rights of peoples and the rights of free nations." Citing this commitment to global democracy, some of today's neoconservatives . . . have argued that they are the true heirs of Wilsonianism. But, unlike the turn-of-the-century imperialists or today's neoconservatives, Wilson did not believe the world's great powers, acting individually, should impose their political beliefs or economic systems on former colonies or protectorates. Instead, Wilson believed the great nations had to act together within an organization such as the League of Nations. He proposed a "mandate system" by which the transition to self-government in Africa or Asia would be overseen by smaller, non-imperial nations, such as Sweden. Wilson believed in spreading democracy and Christian civilization, but he believed the United States had to do it through international organizations and outside the framework of imperial power.

At Versailles, America's allies rejected Wilson's proposals for free trade and an end to imperialism. They insisted that German aggression was the sole cause of World War I and sought to curb it through reparations and a divvying up of German colonies. Back home, Lodge and conservative Republicans rejected even the weakened League of Nations because they feared it put America's foreign policy at the mercy of an international organization.

Wilson's internationalism was shelved for two decades, but the outbreak of World War II, precipitated by Germany, Italy, and Japan's efforts to conquer Europe, Africa, and Asia, confirmed Wilson's warnings that the system of imperialism, if not uprooted, would again lead to war. And so the Franklin Roosevelt and Truman administrations adopted the outlines of Wilson's approach. They made ending imperialism and dismantling trade and currency blocs one of their principal war aims; and, rejecting Wilson's reliance on a single organization, they built many international organizations—including the United Nations, NATO, the International Monetary Fund (IMF), and the

World Bank—that attempted to create a "community of power" without ignoring existing disparities of power.

The events of the last 50 years have confirmed the correctness of this neo-Wilsonian strategy. The second half of the twentieth century, when compared with the first, was prosperous and pacific. The international institutions the United States built helped to win the cold war against the Soviet Union, which under Stalin became heir to czarist Russia's imperial ambitions. The British, French, Germans, Italians, and Dutch abandoned their empires and subordinated their national ambitions to a new, supranational organization, the European Union. Under the IMF, GATT, and now the World Trade Organization, the world has tempered the older cycle of boom and extreme bust.

In addition, the World Bank—along with the United Nations, the European Union, and NATO—has, to a considerable extent, taken over the civilizing and stabilizing functions that the imperial nations once claimed for themselves. Some of these efforts have been less than successful, but, in Africa and Asia, these organizations have helped guide former colonies toward self-government. As a last resort, the United Nations and NATO have sanctioned the use of force to protect or expand the community of power—in 1991, the United Nations backed the coalition that drove Saddam Hussein out of Kuwait, defending the sovereignty of a smaller, weaker nation, and, in 1995 and 1999, NATO took action against Slobodan Milosevic in the former Yugoslavia.

Republican conservatives embraced this Wilsonian approach grudgingly during the cold war, backing NATO, if not the United Nations, as a means to defeat communism. But, after the fall of the Berlin Wall in 1989, conservatives divided into two camps. Some, led by former Reagan official Pat Buchanan and House Republicans, reverted to the isolationism and protectionism of 1920s Republicans. Others, led by neoconservatives such as Paul Wolfowitz, William Kristol, Richard Perle, and Robert Kagan, continued to advocate the transformation of the world in America's image, but they repudiated Wilson's internationalist methods in favor of Roosevelt's imperial strategy. As Kristol explained in *Commentary* in January 2000, "There is a fundamental difference between us and the true Wilsonians—between, that is, the muscular patriotism of Teddy Roosevelt and Ronald Reagan and the utopian multilateralism of Woodrow Wilson and Bill Clinton."

Like Roosevelt and the late-nineteenth-century expansionists, the new imperialists want to transform the politics and allegiances of countries and regions, and they are willing to use force unilaterally to do so. Like the old imperialists, the new ones see overseas intervention in evangelical, although secular, terms. They believe in what the Hoover Institution's Dinesh d'Souza has called "America's evident moral superiority" and see the United States as having a special responsibility to transform the world in its image. "Imperialism as the midwife of democratic self-rule is an undeniable good,"

Stanley Kurtz writes. And, like Roosevelt, they see the politics of this new imperialism as an expression of patriotism and of support for "national greatness."

The new imperialists are even less equivocal than the old in rejecting multilateral institutions. Now that the United States has become the premier world power, they argue, it has no need for international organizations except on an ad hoc basis. Unlike Wilson, or contemporary Wilsonians such as Bill Clinton, they actually prefer for the United States to act alone or in ad hoc coalitions that the United States dominates. And they despise the United Nations, which Perle has described as the "chatterbox on the Hudson" and columnist Charles Krauthammer has opined should "sink . . . into irrelevance."

Wilson wanted a world in which the community of power would eventually overshadow the balance of power. The new imperialists regard that as a dangerous illusion. They think the United States will always have to depend on superior military power for its security; employing it, if necessary, to eliminate or intimidate potential competitors and adversaries. Wilson wanted a mediating realm of equal, independent nations governed by Kantian moral universality, in which what is justifiable for one country must be justifiable for all. The new imperialists invoke America's global mission to limit the prerogatives of other nations but not the United States. They support sustained violations of other nations' sovereignty, for instance, in the name of nonproliferation and human rights, but reject virtually any infringements on U.S. sovereignty at all. As Stephen Peter Rosen wrote in *The National Interest,* "The organizing principle of empire rests . . . on the existence of an overarching power that creates and enforces the principle of hierarchy, but is not itself bound by such rules."

During Bush's presidency, the primary goal of the new imperialists has been winning support for an invasion of Iraq that would overthrow Saddam's regime and transform the entire region. By democratizing Iraq and pulling its oil industry out of the Saudi-dominated OPEC, they believed they could bring the region into America's orbit in much the way the older imperialists had imagined turning the western Pacific into an American sphere of influence. . . .

Americans generally interpret this growing Islamic radicalism as a new phenomenon. And to some extent it is. But it is also a particularly ugly manifestation of a Third World nationalism that has frustrated imperialist efforts since China's Boxer Rebellion of 1900. In neighboring Iran, for instance, the Islamic radicals of the late '70s saw themselves as the successors to nationalist Prime Minister Mohammed Mossadeq, whom the United States had helped overthrow in 1953. Olivier Roy, an authority on and critic of radical Islam, wrote in *The New York Times* this month, "The United States cannot stand alone when dealing with the driving force in the Middle East. This is neither Islamism nor the appetite for democracy, but simply nationalism—

whether it comes in the guise of democracy, secular totalitarianism or Islamic fervor." . . .

The Bush administration's rejection of international institutions, its readiness to wage aggressive, preventive wars to dominate a vital region, and its protectionist trade strategy have already aroused considerable popular opposition—not just in surrounding Arab nations, but in Europe and Asia as well. . . . This popular opposition is already sparking a challenge to U.S. hegemony. Initially, such a challenge is taking the form of terrorism by Islamic radicals—asymmetric military challenges, in the current jargon—and of what political scientists call "soft balancing." These latter tactics focus on economic policy and on diplomacy in the United Nations, NATO, and other international organizations. . . .

There is also growing discussion in Europe of expanding the European Union to meet the challenge of U.S. hegemony. In a recent report on Europe's economic future, France's leading think tank, the Institut Français des Relations Internationales, warned that, if Europe doesn't want to be dominated by the United States, it must create an economic bloc that would stretch to Russia in the east and to Arab North Africa in the south. Such a bloc would enjoy natural resources and a pool of well-educated professionals and low-wage service workers.

Eventually, attempts to balance America's imperial efforts may even take "hard," military forms. The U.S. war in Iraq pushed the EU countries closer to developing an independent military, with Germany, France, Belgium, and Luxembourg meeting in April to plan a new, multinational force. The war also brought France, Germany, and Russia closer together. A military, as well as economic, alliance between Western Europe and nuclear-armed Russia could one day pose a real threat to U.S. dominance. Together with the inevitable growth of China as an economic and military power, it could lead to a world divided into hostile U.S., Euro-Russian, and Chinese power blocs. That's highly speculative, of course, but this disaggregation of a "unipolar" world dominated by a single imperial power into hostile alliances has happened once before—during the last era of British-dominated great-power imperialism.

The new American imperialists, who view the world as a hierarchy governed by military power, would argue that the development of such blocs is inevitable—unless the United States actively discourages its allies as well as rogue states from competing against it. But Wilsonians see the world and the future differently. They would argue that, by encouraging supranational institutions and agreements, and by exercising its authority benignly, the United States stands a far better chance of preventing the older imperial rivalries from reemerging. . . .

The best way for the United States to retain its superiority, in other words, is to repudiate the very strategy that the new imperialists have devised to perpetuate it. An imperial strategy is inherently self-defeating. Wilson understood that paradox in 1919, and it was borne out by America's experience in the last half of the twentieth century. But it is a historical lesson being ignored by the conservatives who now shape foreign policy in Washington. They believe the United States has entered a new world in which the lessons of the old no longer apply. That is almost certainly wrong. History is not physics. But we ignore its lessons at our peril.

7

Is the U.S. an Empire?

Paul W. Schroeder

American Empire is the current rage—whether hailed or denounced, accepted as inevitable or greeted as an historic opportunity. Common to the discourse is an assumption, shared also by friends and foes abroad, that America already enjoys a world-imperial position and is launched on an imperial course.

But that assumption involves another: that America is already an empire simply by being the world's only superpower, by virtue of its military supremacy, economic power, global influence, technological and scientific prowess, and world-wide alliances. The term "empire," in short, describes America's current condition and world status, and is equivalent to phrases like "unipolar moment" or "unchallenged hegemony."

This is a misleading, unhistorical understanding of empire, ignoring crucial distinctions between empire and other relationships in international affairs and obscuring vital truths about the fate of empires and bids for empire within the modern international system. A better understanding of empire can point us to historical generalizations we ignore at our peril.

First a definition: empire means political control exercised by one organized political unit over another unit separate from and alien to it. Many factors enter into empire—economics, technology, ideology, religion, above all military strategy and weaponry—but the essential core is political: the possession of final authority by one entity over the vital political decisions of another. This need not mean direct rule exercised by formal occupation and administration; most empires involve informal, indirect rule. But real empire requires that effective final authority, and states can enjoy various forms of superiority or even domination over others without being empires.

This points to a critical distinction between two terms frequently employed as synonyms: hegemony and empire. These are two essentially different relationships. Hegemony means clear, acknowledged leadership and dominant influence by one unit within a community of units not under a single authority. A hegemon is first among equals; an imperial power rules over subordinates. A hegemonic power is the one without whom no final decision can be reached within a given system; its responsibility is essentially managerial, to see that a decision is reached. An imperial power rules the system, imposes its decision when it wishes.

Powerful implications flow from this definition and distinction. First, hegemony in principle is compatible with the international system we now have, composed of autonomous, coordinate units enjoying juridical equality (status, sovereignty, rights, and international obligations) regardless of differences in power. Empire is not.

Second, those who speak of an American empire bringing freedom and democracy to the world are talking of dry rain and snowy blackness. In principle and by definition, empire is the negation of political freedom, liberation, and self-determination.

This empire/hegemony dialectic yields some profound historical lessons, offered here without proof, though historical evidence is abundant:

1) There are circumstances (the absence or breakdown of inter-state or inter-community order) under which empires have historically provided a certain order and stability, though almost always accompanied by overt and latent violence, disorder, and war. Where, however, a relatively stable international system of autonomous units already exists, attempts to make that system work and endure through empire have not only regularly failed, but overwhelmingly produced massive instability, disorder, and war.

2) Recurrently throughout modern history leading powers have at critical junctures chosen empire over hegemony, and thereby triggered large-scale disorder and war. In some instances, the choice was conscious and demonstrable, in many others less clear-cut and more debatable. Nonetheless, the historian can point to repeated instances over the last five centuries where leaders and powers, having the option between empire and hegemony, chose the path of empire, and thereby ruined themselves and the system.

3) The converse also holds. Where real advances in international order, stability, and peace have been achieved (and they have been), they have been connected with choices leading powers have made for durable, tolerable hegemony rather than empire.

4) Recent developments reshaping the international system (e.g., globalization, the rise of new states, the growth of non-governmental actors and

international institutions, developments in weaponry, etc.) reinforce this longstanding trend, making empire increasingly unworkable and counterproductive as a principle of order, and hegemony more possible, more needed, and more potentially stable and beneficial.

These are not academic propositions. They illuminate the choice for America today. It is not an empire—not yet. But it is at this moment a wannabe empire, poised on the brink. The Bush Doctrine proclaims unquestionably imperialist ambitions and goals, and its armed forces are poised for war for empire—formal empire in Iraq through conquest, occupation, and indefinite political control, and informal empire over the whole Middle East through exclusive paramountcy. The administration pursues this path even in the face of a far graver challenge by North Korea to both its imperial pretensions and its own and the world's security.

History here warrants a prediction, based not on analogies or examples from the past but on sober analysis of what can and cannot succeed in this international world. If America goes down the path of empire, it will ultimately fail. How, when, and with what consequences, no one can tell—but fail it will, and harm itself and the world in the process. Not the least harm will come from thereby wrecking an American hegemony now clearly possible, needed, and potentially durable and beneficial.

In July 1878, at the end of the Berlin Congress that patched up peace in the Balkans after a Russo-Turkish war, Prince Bismarck told an Ottoman delegate, "This is your last chance—and if I know you, you will not take it." Bismarck's words, slightly altered, apply today. This is our best chance—and knowing us, we will not take it. But there is hope. Circumstances, the frictions of war, the pressures and pleas of allies, the maneuvers and resistances of opponents, new foreign dangers, challenges, and distractions, and domestic problems and politics could yet deter this country from a potentially tragic choice of empire and compel it to settle for hegemony. In other words, that special Providence Bismarck once said was reserved for fools, drunkards, and the United States of America may again come to our rescue.

8

The New American Militarism

Andrew J. Bacevich

. . . At the end of the Cold War, Americans said yes to military power. The skepticism about arms and armies that pervaded the American experiment from its founding, vanished. Political leaders, liberals and conservatives alike, became enamored with military might.

The ensuing affair had and continues to have a heedless, Gatsby-like aspect, a passion pursued in utter disregard of any consequences that might ensue. Few in power have openly considered whether valuing military power for its own sake or cultivating permanent global military superiority might be at odds with American principles. Indeed, one striking aspect of America's drift toward militarism has been the absence of dissent offered by any political figure of genuine stature. . . .

For example, when Senator John Kerry, Democrat of Massachusetts, ran for the presidency in 2004, he framed his differences with George W. Bush's national security policies in terms of tactics rather than first principles. Kerry did not question the wisdom of styling the U.S. response to the events of 9/11 as a generations-long "global war on terror." It was not the prospect of open-ended war that drew Kerry's ire. It was rather the fact that the war had been "extraordinarily mismanaged and ineptly prosecuted." Kerry faulted Bush because, in his view, U.S. troops in Iraq lacked "the preparation and hardware they needed to fight as effectively as they could." Bush was expecting too few soldiers to do too much with too little. Declaring that "keeping our military strong and keeping our troops as safe as they can be should be our highest priority," Kerry promised if elected to fix these deficiencies. Americans could count on a President Kerry to expand the armed forces and to improve their ability to fight.

Yet on this score Kerry's circumspection was entirely predictable. It was the candidate's way of signaling that he was sound on defense and had no intention of departing from the prevailing national security consensus.

Under the terms of that consensus, mainstream politicians today take as a given that American military supremacy is an unqualified good, evidence of a larger American superiority. They see this armed might as the key to creating an international order that accommodates American values. One result of that consensus over the past quarter century has been to militarize U.S. policy and to encourage tendencies suggesting that American society itself is increasingly enamored with its self-image as the military power nonpareil.

This new American militarism manifests itself in several different ways. It does so, first of all, in the scope, cost, and configuration of America's present-day military establishment.

Through the first two centuries of U.S. history, political leaders in Washington gauged the size and capabilities of America's armed services according to the security tasks immediately at hand. A grave and proximate threat to the nation's well-being might require a large and powerful military establishment. In the absence of such a threat, policymakers scaled down that establishment accordingly. With the passing of crisis, the army raised up for the crisis went immediately out of existence. This had been the case in 1865, in 1918, and in 1945. . . .

Since the end of the Cold War, having come to value military power for its own sake, the United States has abandoned this principle and is committed as a matter of policy to maintaining military capabilities far in excess of those of any would-be adversary or combination of adversaries. This commitment finds both a qualitative and quantitative expression, with the U.S. military establishment dwarfing that of even America's closest ally. Thus, whereas the U.S. Navy maintains and operates a total of twelve large attack aircraft carriers, the once-vaunted [British] Royal Navy has none—indeed, in all the battle fleets of the world there is no ship even remotely comparable to a Nimitz-class carrier, weighing in at some ninety-seven thousand tons fully loaded, longer than three football fields, cruising at a speed above thirty knots, and powered by nuclear reactors that give it an essentially infinite radius of action. Today, the U.S. Marine Corps possesses more attack aircraft than does the entire Royal Air Force—and the United States has two other even larger "air forces," one an integral part of the Navy and the other officially designated as the U.S. Air Force. Indeed, in terms of numbers of men and women in uniform, the U.S. Marine Corps is half again as large as the entire British Army—and the Pentagon has a second, even larger "army" actually called the U.S. Army—which in turn also operates its own "air force" of some five thousand aircraft.

All of these massive and redundant capabilities cost money. Notably, the present-day Pentagon budget, adjusted for inflation, is 12 percent larger than the average defense budget of the Cold War era. In 2002, American defense spending exceeded by a factor of twenty-five the *combined* defense budgets of the seven "rogue states" then comprising the roster of U.S. enemies. Indeed, by some calculations, the United States spends more on defense than all other nations in the world together. This is a circumstance without historical precedent.

Furthermore, in all likelihood, the gap in military spending between the United States and all other nations will expand further still in the years to come. Projected increases in the defense budget will boost Pentagon spending in real terms to a level higher than it was during the Reagan era. According to the Pentagon's announced long-range plans, by 2009 its budget will exceed the Cold War average by 23 percent—despite the absence of anything remotely resembling a so-called peer competitor. However astonishing this fact might seem, it elicits little comment, either from political leaders or the press. It is simply taken for granted. The truth is that there no longer exists any meaningful context within which Americans might consider the question "How much is enough?"

On a day-to-day basis, what do these expensive forces exist to do? Simply put, for the Department of Defense and all of its constituent parts, defense per se figures as little more than an afterthought. The primary mission of America's far-flung military establishment is global power projection, a reality tacitly understood in all quarters of American society. To suggest that the U.S. military has become the world's police force may slightly overstate the case, but only slightly.

That well over a decade after the collapse of the Soviet Union the United States continues to maintain bases and military forces in several dozens of countries—by some counts well over a hundred in all—rouses minimal controversy, despite the fact that many of these countries are perfectly capable of providing for their own security needs. That even apart from fighting wars and pursuing terrorists, U.S. forces are constantly prowling around the globe—training, exercising, planning, and posturing—elicits no more notice (and in some cases less) from the average American than the presence of a cop on a city street corner. Even before the Pentagon officially assigned itself the mission of "shaping" the international environment, members of the political elite, liberals and conservatives alike, had reached a common understanding that scattering U.S. troops around the globe to restrain, inspire, influence, persuade, or cajole paid dividends. Whether any correlation exists between this vast panoply of forward-deployed forces on the one hand and antipathy to the United States abroad on the other has remained for the most part a taboo subject.

The indisputable fact of global U.S. military preeminence also affects the collective mindset of the officer corps. For the armed services, dominance constitutes a baseline or a point of departure from which to scale the heights of ever greater military capabilities. Indeed, the services have come to view outright supremacy as merely adequate and any hesitation in efforts to increase the margin of supremacy as evidence of falling behind.

Thus, according to one typical study of the U.S. Navy's future, "sea supremacy beginning at our shore lines and extending outward to distant theaters is a necessary condition for the defense of the U.S." Of course, the U.S. Navy already possesses unquestioned global preeminence; the real point of the study is to argue for the urgency of radical enhancements to that preeminence. The officer-authors of this study express confidence that given sufficient money the Navy can achieve ever greater supremacy, enabling the Navy of the future to enjoy "overwhelming precision firepower," "pervasive surveillance," and "dominant control of a maneuvering area, whether sea, undersea, land, air, space or cyberspace." In this study and in virtually all others, political and strategic questions implicit in the proposition that supremacy in distant theaters forms a prerequisite of "defense" are left begging—indeed, are probably unrecognized. At times, this quest for military dominion takes on galactic proportions. Acknowledging that the United States enjoys "superiority in many aspects of space capability," a senior defense official nonetheless complains that "we don't have space dominance and we don't have space supremacy." Since outer space is "the ultimate high ground," which the United States must control, he urges immediate action to correct this deficiency. When it comes to military power, mere superiority will not suffice.

The new American militarism also manifests itself through an increased propensity to use force, leading, in effect, to the normalization of war. There was a time in recent memory, most notably while the so-called Vietnam Syndrome infected the American body politic, when Republican and Democratic administrations alike viewed with real trepidation the prospect of sending U.S. troops into action abroad. Since the advent of the new Wilsonianism, however, self-restraint regarding the use of force has all but disappeared. During the entire Cold War era, from 1945 through 1988, large-scale U.S. military actions abroad totaled a scant six. Since the fall of the Berlin Wall, however, they have become almost annual events. The brief period extending from 1989's Operation Just Cause (the overthrow of Manuel Noriega) to 2003's Operation Iraqi Freedom (the overthrow of Saddam Hussein) featured nine major military interventions. And that count does not include innumerable lesser actions such as Bill Clinton's signature cruise missile attacks against obscure targets in obscure places, the almost daily bombing of Iraq throughout the late 1990s, or the quasi-combat missions that have seen GIs dispatched to Rwanda, Colombia, East Timor, and the Philippines. Altogether, the tempo of U.S. military interventionism has become nothing short of frenetic.

As this roster of incidents lengthened, Americans grew accustomed to—perhaps even comfortable with—reading in their morning newspapers the latest reports of U.S. soldiers responding to some crisis somewhere on the other side of the globe. As crisis became a seemingly permanent condition so too did war. The Bush administration has tacitly acknowledged as much in describing the global campaign against terror as a conflict likely to last decades and in promulgating—and in Iraq implementing—a doctrine of preventive war.

In former times American policymakers treated (or at least pretended to treat) the use of force as evidence that diplomacy had failed. In our own time they have concluded (in the words of Vice President Dick Cheney) that force "makes your diplomacy more effective going forward, dealing with other problems." Policymakers have increasingly come to see coercion as a sort of all-purpose tool. Among American war planners, the assumption has now taken root that whenever and wherever U.S. forces next engage in hostilities, it will be the result of the United States consciously choosing to launch a war. As President Bush has remarked, the big lesson of 9/11 was that "this country must go on the offense and stay on the offense." The American public's ready acceptance of the prospect of war without foreseeable end and of a policy that abandons even the pretense of the United States fighting defensively or viewing war as a last resort shows clearly how far the process of militarization has advanced.

Reinforcing this heightened predilection for arms has been the appearance in recent years of a new aesthetic of war. This is the third indication of advancing militarism.

The old twentieth-century aesthetic of armed conflict as barbarism, brutality, ugliness, and sheer waste grew out of World War I, as depicted by writers such as Ernest Hemingway, Erich Maria Remarque, and Robert Graves. World War II, Korea, and Vietnam reaffirmed that aesthetic, in the latter case with films like *Apocalypse Now*, *Platoon*, and *Full Metal Jacket*.

The intersection of art and war gave birth to two large truths. The first was that the modern battlefield was a slaughterhouse, and modern war an orgy of destruction that devoured guilty and innocent alike. The second, stemming from the first, was that military service was an inherently degrading experience and military institutions by their very nature repressive and inhumane. After 1914, only fascists dared to challenge these truths. Only fascists celebrated war and depicted armies as forward-looking—expressions of national unity and collective purpose that paved the way for utopia. To be a genuine progressive, liberal in instinct, enlightened in sensibility, was to reject such notions as preposterous.

But by the turn of the twenty-first century, a new image of war had emerged, if not fully displacing the old one at least serving as a counterweight. To many observers, events of the 1990s suggested that war's very nature was undergoing a profound change. The era of mass armies, going back to the time of Napoleon, and of mechanized warfare, an offshoot of industrialization, was coming to an end. A new era of high-tech warfare, waged by highly skilled professionals equipped with "smart" weapons, had commenced. Describing the result inspired the creation of a new lexicon of military terms: war was becoming surgical, frictionless, postmodern, even abstract or virtual. It was "coercive diplomacy"—the object of the exercise no longer to kill but to persuade. By the end of the twentieth century, Michael Ignatieff of Harvard University concluded, war had become "a spectacle." It had transformed itself into a kind of "spectator sport," one offering "the added thrill that it is real for someone, but not, happily, for the spectator." Even for the participants, fighting no longer implied the prospect of dying for some abstract cause, since the very notion of "sacrifice in battle had become implausible or ironic." . . .

Combat in the information age promised to overturn all of "the hoary dictums about the fog and friction" that had traditionally made warfare such a chancy proposition. American commanders, affirmed General Tommy Franks, could expect to enjoy "the kind of Olympian perspective that Homer had given his gods."

In short, by the dawn of the twenty-first century the reigning postulates of technology-as-panacea had knocked away much of the accumulated blood-rust sullying war's reputation. Thus reimagined—and amidst widespread assurances that the United States could be expected to retain a monopoly on this new way of war—armed conflict regained an aesthetic respectability, even palatability, that the literary and artistic interpreters of twentieth-century military cataclysms were thought to have demolished once and for all. In the right circumstances, for the right cause, it now turned out, war could actually offer an attractive option—cost-effective, humane, even thrilling. Indeed, as the Anglo-American race to Baghdad conclusively demonstrated in the spring of 2003, in the eyes of many, war has once again become a grand pageant, performance art, or a perhaps temporary diversion from the ennui and boring routine of everyday life. As one observer noted with approval, "public enthusiasm for the whiz-bang technology of the U.S. military" had become "almost boyish." . . .

This new aesthetic has contributed, in turn, to an appreciable boost in the status of military institutions and soldiers themselves, a fourth manifestation of the new American militarism.

Since the end of the Cold War, opinion polls surveying public attitudes toward national institutions have regularly ranked the armed services first. While confidence in the executive branch, the Congress, the media, and even organized religion is diminishing, confidence in the military continues to climb. Otherwise acutely wary of having their pockets picked, Americans count on men and women in uniform to do the right thing in the right way for the right reasons. Americans fearful that the rest of society may be teetering on the brink of moral collapse console themselves with the thought that the armed services remain a repository of traditional values and old fashioned virtue. . . .

Confidence in the military has found further expression in a tendency to elevate the soldier to the status of national icon, the apotheosis of all that is great and good about contemporary America. The men and women of the armed services, gushed *Newsweek* in the aftermath of Operation Desert Storm, "looked like a Norman Rockwell painting come to life. They were young, confident, and hardworking, and they went about their business with poise and élan." A writer for *Rolling Stone* reported after a more recent and extended immersion in military life that "the Army was not the awful thing that my [anti-military] father had imagined"; it was instead "the sort of America he always pictured when he explained . . . his best hopes for the country." According to the old post-Vietnam-era political correctness, the armed services had been a refuge for louts and mediocrities who probably couldn't make it in the real world. By the turn of the twenty-first century a different view had taken hold. Now the United States military was "a place where everyone tried their hardest. A place where everybody . . . looked out for each other. A place where people—intelligent, talented people—said honestly that money wasn't what drove them. A place where people spoke openly about their feelings." Soldiers, it turned out, were not only more virtuous than the rest of us, but also more sensitive and even happier. Contemplating the GIs advancing on Baghdad in March 2003, the classicist and military historian Victor Davis Hanson saw something more than soldiers in battle. He ascertained "transcendence at work." According to Hanson, the armed services had "somehow distilled from the rest of us an elite cohort" in which virtues cherished by earlier generations of Americans continued to flourish.

Soldiers have tended to concur with this evaluation of their own moral superiority. In a 2003 survey of military personnel, "two-thirds [of those polled] said they think military members have higher moral standards than the nation they serve . . . Once in the military, many said, members are wrapped in a culture that values honor and morality." Such attitudes leave even some senior officers more than a little uncomfortable. Noting with regret that "the armed forces are no longer representative of the people they serve," retired admiral Stanley Arthur has expressed concern that "more and more, enlisted as well as officers are beginning to feel that they are special, better than the society they serve." Such tendencies, concluded Arthur, are "not healthy in an armed force serving a democracy."

In public life today, paying homage to those in uniform has become obligatory and the one unforgivable sin is to be found guilty of failing to "support the troops." In the realm of partisan politics, the political Right has shown considerable skill in exploiting this dynamic, shamelessly pandering to the military itself and by extension to those members of the public laboring under the misconception, a residue from Vietnam, that the armed services are under siege from a rabidly anti-military Left.

In fact, the Democratic mainstream—if only to save itself from extinction—has long since purged itself of any dovish inclinations. "What's the point of having this superb military that you're always talking about," Madeleine Albright demanded of General Colin Powell, "if we can't use it?" As Albright's question famously attests, when it comes to advocating the use of force, Democrats can be positively gung ho. Moreover, in comparison to their Republican counterparts, they are at least as deferential to military leaders and probably more reluctant to question claims of military expertise.

Even among Left-liberal activists, the reflexive anti-militarism of the 1960s has given way to a more nuanced view. Although hard-pressed to match self-aggrandizing conservative claims of being one with the troops, progressives have come to appreciate the potential for using the armed services to advance their own agenda. Do-gooders want to harness military power to their efforts to do good. Thus, the most persistent calls for U.S. intervention abroad to relieve the plight of the abused and persecuted come from the militant Left. In the present moment, writes Michael Ignatieff, "empire has become a precondition for democracy." Ignatieff, a prominent human rights advocate, summons the United States to "use imperial power to strengthen respect for self-determination [and] to give states back to abused, oppressed people who deserve to rule them for themselves." . . .

Occasionally, albeit infrequently, the prospect of an upcoming military adventure still elicits opposition, even from a public grown accustomed to war. For example, during the run-up to the U.S. invasion of Iraq in the spring of 2003, large-scale demonstrations against President Bush's planned intervention filled the streets of many American cities. The prospect of the United States launching a preventive war without the sanction of the U.N. Security Council produced the largest outpouring of public protest that the country had seen since the Vietnam War. Yet the response of the political classes to this phenomenon was essentially to ignore it. No politician of national stature offered himself or herself as the movement's champion. No would-be statesman nursing even the slightest prospects of winning high national office was willing to risk being tagged with not supporting those whom President Bush was ordering into harm's way. When the Congress took up the matter, Democrats who denounced George W. Bush's policies in every other respect dutifully authorized him to invade Iraq. For up-and-coming politicians, opposition to war had become something of a third rail: only the very brave or the very foolhardy dared to venture anywhere near it. . . .

More recently still, this has culminated in George W. Bush styling himself as the nation's first full-fledged warrior-president. The staging of Bush's victory lap shortly after the conquest of Baghdad in the spring of 2003—the dramatic landing on the carrier *USS Abraham Lincoln*, with the president decked out in the full regalia of a naval aviator emerging from the cockpit to bask in the adulation of the crew—was lifted directly from the triumphant final scenes of the movie *Top Gun*, with the boyish George Bush standing in for the boyish Tom Cruise. For this nationally televised moment, Bush was not simply mingling with the troops; he had merged his identity with their own and made himself one of them—the president as warlord. In short order, the marketplace ratified this effort; a toy manufacturer offered for $39.99 a Bush look-alike military action figure advertised as "Elite Force Aviator: George W. Bush—U.S. President and Naval Aviator." . . .

Thus has the condition that worried C. Wright Mills in 1956 come to pass in our own day. "For the first time in the nation's history," Mills wrote, "men in authority are talking about an 'emergency' without a foreseeable end." While in earlier times Americans had viewed history as "a peaceful continuum interrupted by war," today planning, preparing, and waging war has become "the normal state and seemingly permanent condition of the United States." And "the only accepted 'plan' for peace is the loaded pistol."

9

The American Empire

The Burden

Michael Ignatieff

In a speech to graduating cadets at West Point in June, President Bush declared, "America has no empire to extend or utopia to establish." When he spoke to veterans assembled at the White House in November, he said: America has "no territorial ambitions. We don't seek an empire. Our nation is committed to freedom for ourselves and for others."

Ever since George Washington warned his countrymen against foreign entanglements, empire abroad has been seen as the republic's permanent temptation and its potential nemesis. Yet what word but "empire" describes the awesome thing that America is becoming?

It is the only nation that polices the world through five global military commands; maintains more than a million men and women at arms on four continents; deploys carrier battle groups on watch in every ocean; guarantees the survival of countries from Israel to South Korea; drives the wheels of global trade and commerce; and fills the hearts and minds of an entire planet with its dreams and desires.

If Americans have an empire, they have acquired it in a state of deep denial. But Sept. 11 was an awakening, a moment of reckoning with the extent of American power and the avenging hatreds it arouses. Americans may not have thought of the World Trade Center or the Pentagon as the symbolic headquarters of a world empire, but the men with the box cutters certainly did, and so do numberless millions who cheered their terrifying exercise in the propaganda of the deed.

America's empire is not like empires of times past, built on colonies, conquest and the white man's burden. The 21st century imperium is a new invention in the annals of political science, an empire lite, a global hegemony whose grace notes are free markets, human rights and democracy, enforced by the most awesome military power the world has ever known.

It is the imperialism of a people who remember that their country secured its independence by revolt against an empire, and who like to think of themselves as the friend of freedom everywhere. It is an empire without consciousness of itself as such, constantly shocked that its good intentions arouse resentment abroad. But that does not make it any less of an empire, with a conviction that it alone, in Herman Melville's words, bears "the ark of the liberties of the world."

In this vein, the President's National Security Strategy, announced in September, commits America to lead other nations toward "the single sustainable model for national success," by which he meant free markets and liberal democracy. This is strange rhetoric for a Texas politician who ran for office opposing nation-building abroad and calling for a more humble America overseas.

But Sept. 11 changed everyone, including a laconic and anti-rhetorical President. His messianic note may be new to him, but it is not new to his office. It has been present in the American vocabulary at least since Woodrow Wilson went to Versailles in 1919 and told the world that he wanted to make it safe for democracy.

At the beginning of the first volume of "The Decline and Fall of the Roman Empire," published in 1776, Edward Gibbon remarked that empires endure only so long as their rulers take care not to overextend their borders.

The characteristic delusion of imperial power is to confuse global power with global domination. The Americans may have the former, but they do not have the latter. They cannot rebuild each failed state or appease each anti-American hatred, and the more they try, the more they expose themselves to the overreach that eventually undermined the classical empires of old.

The Secretary of Defense may be right when he warns the North Koreans that America is capable of fighting on two fronts—in Korea and Iraq—simultaneously, but Americans at home cannot be overjoyed at such a prospect, and if two fronts are possible at once, a much larger number of fronts is not.

If conflict in Iraq, North Korea or both becomes a possibility, al-Qaeda can be counted on to seek to strike a busy and overextended empire in the back. What this suggests is not just that overwhelming power never confers the security it promises but also that even the overwhelmingly powerful need friends and allies.

Empires survive when they understand that diplomacy, backed by force, is always to be preferred to force alone. Looking into the more distant future, say a generation ahead, resurgent Russia and China will demand recognition both as world powers and as regional hegemons.

America needs to share the policing of nonproliferation and other threats with these powers, and if it tries, as the current National Security Strategy suggests, to prevent the emergence of any competitor to American global dominance, it risks everything that Gibbon predicted: overextension followed by defeat.

America will also remain vulnerable, despite its overwhelming military power, because its primary enemy, Iraq and North Korea notwithstanding, is not a state, susceptible to deterrence, influence and coercion, but a shadowy cell of fanatics who have proved that they cannot be deterred and coerced and who have hijacked a global ideology—Islam—that gives them a bottomless supply of recruits and allies.

After 1991 and the collapse of the Soviet empire, American presidents thought they could have imperial domination on the cheap, ruling the world without putting in place any new imperial architecture—new military alliances, new legal institutions, new international development organisms—for a postcolonial, post-Soviet world.

The Greeks taught the Romans to call this failure hubris. It was also, in the 1990s, a general failure of the historical imagination, an inability of the post-Cold-War West to grasp that the emerging crisis of state order in so many overlapping zones of the world—from Egypt to Afghanistan—would eventually become a security threat at home.

Radical Islam would never have succeeded in winning adherents if the Muslim countries that won independence from the European empires had been able to convert dreams of self-determination into the reality of competent, rule-abiding states. America has inherited this crisis of self-determination from the empires of the past.

Its solution—to create democracy in Iraq, then hopefully roll out the same happy experiment throughout the Middle East—is both noble and dangerous: noble because, if successful, it will finally give these peoples the self-determination they vainly fought for against the empires of the past; dangerous because, if it fails, there will be nobody left to blame but the Americans.

The dual nemeses of empire in the 20th century were nationalism, the desire of peoples to rule themselves free of alien domination, and narcissism, the incurable delusion of imperial rulers that the "lesser breeds" aspired only to be versions of themselves. Both nationalism and narcissism have threatened the American reassertion of global power since Sept. 11.

The core beliefs of our time are the creations of the anticolonial revolt against empire: the idea that all human beings are equal and that each human group has a right to rule itself free of foreign interference. It is at least ironic that American believers in these ideas have ended up supporting the creation of a new form of temporary colonial tutelage for Bosnians, Kosovars and Afghans—and could for Iraqis.

The age of empire ought to have been succeeded by an age of independent, equal and self-governing nation-states. But that has not come to pass. America has inherited a world scarred not just by the failures of empires past but also by the failure of nationalist movements to create and secure free states—and now, suddenly, by the desire of Islamists to build theocratic tyrannies on the ruins of failed nationalist dreams.

Those who want America to remain a republic rather than become an empire imagine rightly, but they have not factored in what tyranny or chaos can do to vital American interests. The case for empire is that it has become, in a place like Iraq, the last hope for democracy and stability alike.

Even so, empires survive only by understanding their limits. Sept. 11 pitched the Islamic world into the beginning of a long and bloody struggle to determine how it will be ruled and by whom: the authoritarians, the Islamists or perhaps the democrats.

America can help repress and contain the struggle, but even though its own security depends on the outcome, it cannot ultimately control it. Only a very deluded imperialist would believe otherwise.

10

The Case for American Empire

Max Boot

Many have suggested that the September 11 attack on America was payback for U.S. imperialism. . . . The solution is obvious: The United States must become a kinder, gentler nation, must eschew quixotic missions abroad, must become, in Pat Buchanan's phrase, "a republic, not an empire." In fact this analysis is exactly backward: The September 11 attack was a result of insufficient American involvement and ambition; the solution is to be more expansive in our goals and more assertive in their implementation.

It has been said, with the benefit of faulty hindsight, that America erred in providing the mujahedeen with weapons and training that some of them now turn against us. But this was amply justified by the exigencies of the Cold War. The real problem is that we pulled out of Afghanistan after 1989. In so doing, the George H. W. Bush administration was following a classic realpolitik policy. We had gotten involved in this distant nation to wage a proxy war against the Soviet Union. Once that larger war was over, we could safely pull out and let the Afghans resolve their own affairs. And if the consequence was the rise of the Taliban—homicidal mullahs driven by a hatred of modernity itself—so what? . . . So said the wise elder statesmen. The "so what" question has now been answered definitively; the answer lies in the rubble of the World Trade Center and Pentagon.

We had better sense when it came to the Balkans, which could without much difficulty have turned into another Afghanistan. When Muslim Bosnians rose up against Serb oppression in the early 1990s, they received support from many of the same Islamic extremists who also backed the Mujahedeen in Afghanistan. The Muslims of Bosnia are not particularly fundamentalist—after years of Communist rule, most are not all that religious—but they might have been seduced by the siren song of the mullahs if no one else had come to champion their cause. Luckily, someone else did. NATO and the United States intervened to stop the fighting in Bosnia, and later in Kosovo. Employing its leverage, the U.S. government pressured the Bosnian government into expelling the Mujahedeen. . . . U.S. imperialism—a liberal and humanitarian imperialism, to be sure, but imperialism all the same—appears to have paid off in the Balkans.

The problem is that, while the Clinton administration eventually did something right in the Balkans, elsewhere it was scandalously irresolute in the assertion of U.S. power. By cutting and running from Somalia after the deaths of 18 U.S. soldiers, Bill Clinton fostered a widespread impression that we could be chased out of a country by anyone who managed to kill a few Americans. . . . After the attacks on the U.S. embassies in Kenya and Tanzania in 1998, Clinton sent cruise missiles—not soldiers—to strike a symbolic blow against bin Laden's training camps in Afghanistan and a pharmaceutical factory in Sudan. Those attacks were indeed symbolic, though not in the way Clinton intended. They symbolized not U.S. determination but rather passivity in the face of terrorism. And this impression was reinforced by the failure of either Bill Clinton or George W. Bush to retaliate for the attack on the USS *Cole* in October 2000, most likely carried out by Osama bin Laden's al Qaeda network. All these displays of weakness emboldened our enemies to commit greater and more outrageous acts of aggression, much as the failure of the West to contest Japan's occupation of Manchuria in the 1930s, or Mussolini's incursion into Abyssinia, encouraged the Axis powers toward more spectacular depravities.

The problem, in short, has not been excessive American assertiveness but rather insufficient assertiveness. The question is whether, having now been attacked, we will act as a great power should. . . .

It is striking—and no coincidence—that America now faces the prospect of military action in many of the same lands where generations of British colonial soldiers went on campaigns. . . . In Afghanistan, the British suffered a serious setback in 1842 when their forces had to retreat from Kabul and were massacred—all but Dr. William Brydon, who staggered into Jalalabad to tell the terrible tale. This British failure has been much mentioned in recent weeks to support the proposition that the Afghans are invincible fighters. Less remembered is the sequel. An army under Major General George Pollock forced the Khyber Pass, recaptured Kabul, burned down the Great Bazaar to leave "some lasting mark of the just retribution of an outraged nation," and then marched back to India.

Thirty-six years later, in 1878, the British returned to Afghanistan. The highlight of the Second Afghan War was Lieutenant General Frederick Roberts's once-famous march from Kabul to Kandahar. Although the British were always badly outnumbered, they repeatedly bested larger Afghan armies. The British did not try to impose a colonial administration in Kabul, but Afghanistan became in effect a British protectorate with its foreign policy controlled by the Raj. This arrangement lasted until the Third Afghan War in 1919, when Britain, bled dry by World War I, finally left the Afghans to their own devices.

Afghanistan and other troubled lands today cry out for the sort of enlightened foreign administration once provided by self-confident Englishmen in jodhpurs and pith helmets. Is imperialism a dusty relic of a long-gone era? Perhaps. But it's interesting to note that in the 1990s East Timor, Cambodia, Kosovo, and Bosnia all became wards of the international community (Cambodia only temporarily). This precedent could easily be extended . . . into a formal system of United Nations mandates modeled on the mandatory territories sanctioned by the League of Nations in the 1920s. Following the defeat of the German and Ottoman empires, their colonial possessions were handed out to the Allied powers, in theory to prepare their inhabitants for eventual self-rule. . . . This was supposed to be "for the good of the natives," a phrase that once made progressives snort in derision, but may be taken more seriously after the left's conversion (or, rather, reversion) in the 1990s to the cause of "humanitarian" interventions.

The mealy-mouthed modern euphemism is "nation-building," but "state building" is a better description. Building a national consciousness, while hardly impossible . . . is a long-term task. Building a working state administration is a more practical short-term objective that has been achieved by countless colonial regimes, including the United States in Haiti (1915–1933), the Dominican Republic (1916–1924), Cuba (1899–1902, 1906–1909), and the Philippines (1899–1935), to say nothing of the achievements of generals Lucius Clay in Germany and Douglas MacArthur in Japan.

Unilateral U.S. rule may no longer be an option today. But the United States can certainly lead an international occupation force under U.N. auspices, with the cooperation of some Muslim nations. This would be a huge improvement in any number of lands that support or shelter terrorists. . . .

Long before British and American armies had returned to the continent of Europe—even before America had entered the struggle against Germany and Japan—Winston Churchill and Franklin Roosevelt met on a battleship in the North Atlantic to plan the shape of the postwar world. The Atlantic Charter of August 14, 1941, pledged Britain and America to creating a liberal world order based on peace and national self-determination. The leaders of America, and of the West, should be making similar plans today.

Once they do, they will see that ambitious goals—such as "regime change"—are also the most realistic. Occupying Iraq and Afghanistan will hardly end the "war on terrorism," but it beats the alternatives. Killing bin Laden is important and necessary; but it is not enough. New bin Ladens could rise up to take his place. We must not only wipe out the vipers but also destroy their nest and do our best to prevent new nests from being built there again.

11

The Empire Slinks Back

Niall Ferguson

. . . Let me come clean. I am a fully paid-up member of the neoimperialist gang. Long before it was fashionable to say so, I was already arguing that it would be "desirable for the United States to depose" tyrants like Saddam Hussein. "Capitalism and democracy," I wrote, "are not naturally occurring, but require strong institutional foundations of law and order. The proper role of an imperial America is to establish these institutions where they are lacking, if necessary . . . by military force." Today this argument is in danger of becoming commonplace. . . . [W]riters as diverse as Max Boot, Andrew Bacevich and Thomas Donnelly have drawn explicit (and in Boot's case, approving) comparisons between the pax Britannica of Queen Victoria's reign and the pax Americana they envisage in the reign of George II. Boot has gone so far as to say that the United States should provide places like Afghanistan and other troubled countries with "the sort of enlightened foreign administration once provided by self-confident Englishmen in jodhpurs and pith helmets."

I agree. The British Empire has had a pretty lousy press from a generation of "postcolonial" historians anachronistically affronted by its racism. But the reality is that the British were significantly more successful at establishing market economies, the rule of law and the transition to representative government than the majority of postcolonial governments have been. The policy "mix" favored by Victorian imperialists reads like something just published by the International Monetary Fund, if not the World Bank: free trade, balanced budgets, sound money, the common law, incorrupt administration and investment in infrastructure financed by international loans. These are precisely the things Iraq needs right now. If the scary-sounding "American empire" can deliver them, then I am all for it. The catch is whether or not America has the one crucial character trait without which the whole imperial project is doomed: stamina. The more time I spend here in the United States, the more doubtful I become about this.

The United States unquestionably has the raw economic power to build an empire—more, indeed, than the United Kingdom ever had at its disposal. In 1913, for example, Britain's share of total world output was 8 percent, while the equivalent figure for the United States in 1998 was 22 percent. There's "soft" power too—the endlessly innovative consumer culture that Joseph Nye argues is an essential component of American power—but at its core, as we have seen in Afghanistan and now in Iraq, American power is far from soft. It can be very, very hard. The trouble is that it is ephemeral. It is not so much Power Lite as Flash Power—here today, with a spectacular bang, but gone tomorrow.

Besides the presidential time frame—which is limited by the four-year election cycle—the most obvious symptom of its short-windedness is the difficulty the American empire finds in recruiting the right sort of people to run it. America's educational institutions excel at producing young men and women who are both academically and professionally very well trained. It's just that the young elites have no desire whatsoever to spend their lives running a screwed-up, sun-scorched sandpit like Iraq. America's brightest and best aspire not to govern Mesopotamia, but to manage MTV; not to rule Hejaz, but to run a hedge fund; not to be a C.B.E., or Commander of the British Empire, but to be a C.E.O. And that, of course, is one reason so many of the Americans currently in Iraq are first-generation immigrants to the United States. . . .

America's British allies have been here before. Having defeated the previous Ottoman rulers in the First World War, Britain ran Iraq as a "mandate" between 1920 and 1932. For the sake of form, the British installed one of their Arab clients, the Hashemite prince Faisal, as king. But there was no doubt who was really running the place. Nor did the British make any bones about why they were there. When two Standard Oil geologists entered Iraq on a prospecting mission, the British civil commissioner handed them over to the chief of police of Baghdad; in 1927 the British takeover paid a handsome dividend when oil was struck at Baba Gurgur, in the northern part of Iraq. Although they formally relinquished power to the ruling dynasty in 1932, the British remained informally in control of Iraq throughout the 1930's. Indeed, they only really lost their grip on Baghdad with the assassination of their clients Faisal II and his prime minister, Nuri es-Said, in the revolution of 1958.

The crucial point is this: when the British went into Iraq, they stuck around. To be precise, there were British government representatives, military and civilian, in Baghdad uninterruptedly for almost exactly 40 years. And that brings up a simple question: Who in today's United States would like to be based in Baghdad as long as the British were—which would be from now until 2043?

"Don't even go there!" is one of those catch phrases you hear every day in New York. Somehow it sums up exactly what is flawed about the whole post-9/11 crypto-imperial project. Despite their vast wealth and devastating weaponry, Americans have no interest in the one crucial activity without which a true empire cannot enduringly be established. They won't actually go there. . . .

The British regarded long-term occupation as an inherent part of their self-appointed "civilizing mission." This did not mean forever. The assumption was that British rule would end once a country had been sufficiently "civilized"—read: anglicized—to ensure the continued rule of law and operation of free markets (not to mention the playing of cricket). But that clearly meant decades, not days; when the British intervened in a country like Iraq, they simply didn't have an exit strategy. The only issue was whether to rule directly—installing a British governor—or indirectly, with a British "secretary" offering "advice" to a local puppet like Faisal.

In other words, the British did go there. Between 1900 and 1914, 2.6 million Britons left the United Kingdom for imperial destinations (by 1957 the total had reached nearly 6 million). Admittedly, most of them preferred to migrate to the temperate regions of a select few colonies—Canada, Australia, New Zealand and South Africa—that soon became semiautonomous "dominions." Nevertheless, a significant number went to the much less hospitable climes of Asia and Africa. At the end of the 1930's, for example, the official Colonial Service in Africa was staffed by more than 7,500 expat Brits. The substantial expatriate communities they established were crucial to the operation of the British Empire. They provided the indispensable "men on the spot" who learned the local languages, perhaps adopted some local customs—though not usually to the fatal extent of "going native"—and acted as the intermediaries between a remote imperial authority and the indigenous elites upon whose willing collaboration the empire depended.

Expat life was not all tiffin and gin. As Rudyard Kipling saw it, governing India was a hard slog: "Year by year England sends out fresh drafts for the first fighting-line, which is officially called the Indian Civil Service. These die, or kill themselves by overwork, or are worried to death or broken in health and hope." Yet this was a service that could confidently expect to attract the very brightest and best products of the elite British universities. Of 927 recruits to the Colonial Service between 1927 and 1929, nearly half had been to Oxford or Cambridge. The proportion in the Indian Civil Service was even higher.

Why were so many products of Britain's top universities willing to spend their entire working lives so far from the land of their birth, running infernally hot, disease-ridden countries? Why, to pick a typical example, did one Evan Machonochie, an Oxford graduate who passed the grueling Indian Civil Service exam, set off for Bengal in 1887 and spend the next 40 years in India? One clue lies in his Celtic surname. The Scots were heavily over-represented not just in the colonies of white settlement, but also in the commercial and professional elites of cities like Calcutta and Hong Kong and Cape Town. The Irish too played a disproportionate role in enforcing British rule, supplying a huge proportion of the officers and men of the British army. Not for nothing is Kipling's representative Indian Army N.C.O. named Mulvaney. For young men growing up on the rainy, barren and poorer fringes of the United Kingdom, the empire offered opportunities.

Yet economics alone cannot explain what motivated Machonochie. . . . The imperial impulse arose from a complex of emotions: racial superiority, yes, but also evangelical zeal; profit, perhaps, but also a sincere belief that spreading "commerce, Christianity and civilization" was not just in Britain's interest but in the interests of her colonial subjects too.

The contrast with today's "wannabe" imperialists in the United States—call them "nation-builders" if you prefer euphemism—could scarcely be more stark. Five points stand out.

First, not only do the overwhelming majority of Americans have no de-sire to leave the United States; millions of non-Americans are also eager to join them here. Unlike the United Kingdom a century ago, the United States is an importer of people, with a net immigration rate of 3.5 per 1,000 and a total foreign-born population of 32.5 million (more than 1 in 10 residents of the United States).

Second, when Americans do opt to reside abroad, they tend to stick to the developed world. As of 1999, there were an estimated 3.8 million Amer-icans living abroad. That sounds like a lot. But it is a little more than a tenth the number of the foreign-born population in the United States. And of these expat Americans, almost three-quarters were living in the two other NAFTA countries (more than one million in Mexico, 687,700 in Canada) or in Europe (just over a million). Of the 294,000 living in the Middle East, nearly two-thirds were in Israel. A mere 37,500 were in Africa.

Third, whereas British imperial forces were mostly based abroad, most of the American military is normally stationed at home. Even the B-2 Stealth bombers that pounded Serbia into quitting Kosovo in 1999 were flying out of Knob Noster, Mo. And it's worth remembering that 40 percent of Amer-ican overseas military personnel are located in Western Europe, no fewer than 71,000 of them in Germany. Thus, whereas the British delighted in building barracks in hostile territories precisely in order to subjugate them, Americans today locate a quarter of their overseas troops in what is ar-guably the world's most pacifist country.

Fourth, when Americans do live abroad they generally don't stay long and don't integrate much, preferring to inhabit Mini Me versions of

America, ranging from military bases to five-star "international" (read: American) hotels. . . .

The fifth and final contrast with the British experience is perhaps the most telling. It is the fact that the products of America's elite educational institutions are the people least likely to head overseas, other than on flying visits and holidays. The Americans who serve the longest tours of duty are the volunteer soldiers, a substantial proportion of whom are African-Americans (12.9 percent of the population, 25.4 percent of the Army Reserve). It's just possible that African-Americans will turn out to be the Celts of the American empire, driven overseas by the comparatively poor opportunities at home. Indeed, if the occupation of Iraq is to be run by the military, then it can hardly fail to create career opportunities for the growing number of African-American officers in the Army. . . .

The British, however, were always wary about giving the military too much power in their imperial administration. Their parliamentarians had read enough Roman history to want to keep generals subordinate to civilian governors. The "brass hats" were there to inflict the Victorian equivalent of "shock and awe" whenever the "natives" grew restive. Otherwise, colonial government was a matter for Oxbridge-educated, frock-coated mandarins.

Now, ask yourself in light of this: how many members of Harvard's or Yale's class of 2003 are seriously considering a career in the postwar administration of Iraq? The number is unlikely to be very high. In 1998/99 there were 47,689 undergraduate course registrations at Yale, of which just 335 (less than 1 percent) were for courses in Near Eastern languages and civilizations. There was just one, lone undergraduate senior majoring in the subject (compared with 17 doing film studies). If Samuel Huntington is right and we are witnessing a "clash of civilizations," America's brightest students show remarkably little interest in the civilization of the other side.

After graduation, too, the members of America's academic elite generally subscribe to the "Wizard of Oz" principle: "There's no place like home." According to a 1998 survey, there were 134,798 registered Yale alumni. Of these, little more than 5 percent lived outside the United States. A mere handful—roughly 70—lived in Arab countries.

Sure, the bolder products of the Kennedy School may be eager for "tours of duty" in postwar Baghdad. And a few of the star Harvard economists may want to do for Iraq what a couple of their professors did for post-Soviet Russia back in the early 90's. But what that means is flying back and forth, writing a bunch of papers on "transition economics," pocketing some fat consultancy fees and then heading for home.

As far as America's Ivy League nation-builders are concerned, you can set up an independent central bank, reform the tax code, liberalize prices and privatize the major utilities—and be home in time for the first reunion. . . .

What, then, about the much-vaunted role of nongovernmental organizations? Might they provide the men and women on the ground who are so conspicuously hard to find in government service?

It is true that a substantial number of Americans are currently working overseas for NGO's. An American friend of mine recently startled his friends—not to mention his wife—by quitting his artist's studio and his teaching job in London, where he has spent much of the last 20 years, to take a position with a French-run aid agency in one of the most dysfunctional of Central Africa's wretched republics. Perhaps he will find the new life he seeks there. But most Americans who do this kind of thing start younger and spend little more than a year overseas. For many it is not much more than a politically correct "gap year" before starting at graduate school. . . .

The dilemma is perhaps insoluble. Americans yearn for the quiet life at home. But since 9/11 they have felt impelled to grapple with rogue regimes in the hope that their overthrow will do something to reduce the threat of future terrorist attacks. The trouble is that if they do not undertake these interventions with conviction and commitment, they are unlikely to achieve their stated goals. Anyone who thinks Iraq can become a stable democracy in a matter of months—whether 3, 6 or 24—is simply fantasizing.

Where, then, is the new imperial elite to come from? Not, I hope, exclusively from the reserve army of unemployed generals with good Pentagon connections. The work needs to begin, and swiftly, to encourage American students at the country's leading universities to think more seriously about careers overseas—and by overseas I do not mean in London. Are there, for example, enough good scholarships to attract undergraduates and graduates to study Arabic? How many young men and women currently graduate with a functioning grasp of Chinese? That, after all, is the language of this country's nearest imperial rival, and the power President Bush urgently needs to woo if he is to deal effectively with North Korea.

After Kipling, John Buchan was perhaps the most readable writer produced by British imperialism. In his 1916 thriller "Greenmantle," he memorably personifies imperial Britain in the person of Sandy Arbuthnot—an Orientalist so talented that he can pass for a Moroccan in Mecca or a Pathan in Peshawar. Arbuthnot's antithesis is the dyspeptic American millionaire John Scantlebury Blenkiron: "a big fellow with a fat, sallow, clean-shaven face" and "a pair of full sleepy eyes, like a ruminating ox." These eyes have seen "nothing gorier than a presidential election," he tells Buchan's hero, Richard Hannay. The symbolism is a little crude, but it has something to it.

Well, now the Blenkirons have seen something gorier than an election. But will it whet their appetites for an empire in the British mode? Only, I think, if Americans radically rethink their attitude to the world beyond their borders. Until there are more Americans not just willing but eager to shoulder the "nation-builder's burden," adventures like the current occupation of

Iraq will lack a vital ingredient. For the lesson of Britain's imperial experience is clear: you simply cannot have an empire without imperialists—out there, on the spot—to run it.

Could Blenkiron somehow transform into Arbuthnot? Perhaps. After all, in the years after the Second World War, the generation that had just missed the fighting left Harvard and Yale with something like Buchan's zeal for global rule. Many of them joined the Central Intelligence Agency and devoted their lives to fighting Communism in far-flung lands from Cuba to Cambodia. Yet—as Graham Greene foresaw in "The Quiet American"—their efforts at what the British would have called "indirect rule" were constrained by the need to shore up the local potentates more or less covertly. (The low quality of the locals backed by the United States didn't help, either.) Today, the same fiction that underpinned American strategy in Vietnam—that the United States was not trying to resurrect French colonial rule in Indochina—is peddled in Washington to rationalize what is going on in Iraq. Sure, it may look like the resurrection of British colonial rule in Iraq, but honestly, all we want to do is give the Iraqi people democracy and then go home.

So long as the American empire dare not speak its own name—so long as it continues this tradition of organized hypocrisy—today's ambitious young men and women will take one look at the prospects for postwar Iraq and say with one voice, "Don't even go there."

Americans need to go there. If the best and brightest insist on staying home, today's unspoken imperial project may end—unspeakably—tomorrow.

Strategic Choice

Unilateralism or Multilateralism?

OVERVIEW

Should the United States exercise leadership in a multilateral fashion, working to build strong international institutions in cooperation with likeminded states? Or should the United States seek to maximize its autonomy and sovereignty, acting independently of other states when its interests so dictate? These have become crucial questions in recent years. American allies in Europe and elsewhere have expressed growing dismay at what is often characterized as the increasingly unilateralist character of U.S. foreign policy. The choice between unilateralism and multilateralism has also become a key subject for domestic debate within the United States.

The chapters contained in this part address this debate. How sharp a break is the "new unilateralism" from past practice? Would U.S. interests be better served by a more multilateralist foreign policy? Is the new unilateralism a temporary aberration or will it prove more lasting?

The Tradeoff: Cooperation versus Autonomy

The term *multilateralism* refers to the process by which three or more states coordinate their policies through international treaties, international organizations, or regularized consultation in order to achieve common objectives. Unilateralism, by contrast, refers to the practice of conducting a state's foreign policies independent of such constraints. Between these extremes lie intermediate options, including short-term collaboration among ad hoc and shifting combinations of states.

In deciding whether to cooperate with other states or go it alone, policymakers must consider the tradeoffs involved. Multilateralism allows groups of states to achieve common aims that none could accomplish alone. It also, however, entails commitments that bind a state's future behavior and limit available policy options. Policymakers are typically willing to endure the loss of autonomy that results from multilateral commitments only if such arrangements lead to desirable changes in the behavior of other states. Multilateralism thus rests upon a process of reciprocity that mutually constrains the autonomy of participating states.

Historical Patterns

Through much of its history, the United States has prized autonomy over collaboration with other states. In his presidential farewell address, George Washington warned his fellow citizens against becoming entrapped by "entangling alliances" with the old world powers of Europe. Surrounded by two oceans and weak or friendly neighbors, American policymakers saw little reason to depart from Washington's advice for more than a century.

As World War I progressed, however, U.S. officials began to perceive a stake in the outcome of that epochal struggle. Seeking to prevent German domination of the European continent—an outcome considered potentially dangerous to America's own future security—Woodrow Wilson committed the United States to war on the side of Great Britain, France, and the other allied powers. The war convinced Wilson and many others that the United States could no longer afford a stance of isolationism and unilateralism.

In the wake of allied victory, Wilson championed an American blueprint for a new world order built around the principles of democracy and self-determination within nations and multilateral cooperation and international law among nations. Wilson's vision was, however, too sharp a break with American traditions to win acceptance at home. The U.S. Senate refused to ratify U.S. entrance to Wilson's cherished League of Nations. With some exceptions, the United States retreated into isolationism for much of the following two decades.

World War II finally brought about a domestic consensus in favor of international engagement and American leadership abroad. Following this war, the United States helped to create and support a host of important multilateral institutions, including the United Nations, the North Atlantic Treaty Organization, the International Monetary Fund, the World Bank, and the General Agreement on Tariffs and Trade. Through the Marshall Plan, the United States helped launch the process of European integration, leading to the present-day European Union. Regional security alliances were created in

the Americas, the Middle East, and East Asia in support of U.S. cold war policy. Economic cooperation deepened through consultation among members
of the Group of Seven (G7) and the Organisation for Economic Co-opera-
tion and Development. In general, the United States cemented a Western
order by providing important public goods, including security, postwar reconstruction, economic openness, and support for democratization. These
policies provided powerful incentives for other states to follow American
leadership.

This golden age of American-led institution building was spurred in part
by the desire of U.S. leaders to create a broad coalition of friendly countries that could successfully resist Soviet expansionism and the spread of
communism during the cold war. Yet even during the decades following
World War II, America's commitment to multilateralism was highly conditional. While the United States sought to constrain the behavior of other
states through multilateral rules and institutions, American policymakers
often insisted upon special prerogatives for the United States that preserved
American freedom of action.

Along with four other major powers, for instance, the United States enjoyed a veto over decisions of the UN Security Council. Weighted voting
schemes gave the United States effective control over the International Monetary Fund and the World Bank. U.S. policymakers periodically invoked escape clause and antidumping provisions of the General Agreement on Tariffs and Trade as grounds for the imposition of import restrictions, and the
Congress regularly attached conditions to U.S. ratification of major international human rights accords that effectively preempted their enforcement
against the U.S. government or its citizens. The United States repeatedly intervened abroad in ventures of dubious international legitimacy (for example, military or covert interventions in Indonesia, Vietnam, the Dominican
Republic, Cuba, Central America, Iran, and Chile).

Despite this inconsistent record, American investment in a multilateral
order built around a set of innovative rules and institutions was considerable. U.S. financial and political support for this Western order served to legitimize American power and generate deference to U.S. leadership on the
part of allied states. With significant exceptions, this multilateralist system
produced relative peace, growing prosperity, and the spread of political
democracy in much of the noncommunist world.

The Unilateralist Turn

Nevertheless, the end of the cold war has weakened America's already conditional embrace of multilateralism while also undermining the willingness
of other states to tolerate special U.S. prerogatives. In recent years, the
United States has rejected a series of major international treaties and agreements, including the Kyoto Protocol on Climate Change, the Rome Statute

of the International Criminal Court, the Ottawa Treaty to ban landmines, the Comprehensive Nuclear Test Ban Treaty, the Programme of Action on Illicit Trade in Small Arms and Light Weapons, the Anti-Ballistic Missile Treaty, and a new protocol designed to verify compliance with the Biological Weapons Convention. The United States has also fallen into arrears on its financial commitments to the United Nations and other international agencies. The American decision to launch war against Iraq despite the lack of an explicit mandate from the UN Security Council and without the support of many key allies is the most dramatic manifestation of growing American unilateralism.

U.S. allies have become less deferent to U.S. leadership and less willing to grant the United States exemptions from the multilateral rules that bind other states. For instance, other parties to the negotiations rejected U.S. demands that the landmine ban treaty be amended to permit the continued deployment of U.S. mines along the border between North Korea and South Korea. Similarly, U.S. proposals that would have given the United States an effective veto over prosecutions by the International Criminal Court were also rebuffed. Absent the overarching common interests once provided by the Soviet threat, the United States and many of its longtime allies are less willing to make the key compromises that once buttressed the cold war bargain.

The Debate

Whether the growing rift between the United States and its allies is to be welcomed or lamented is a matter of some dispute. Charles Krauthammer offers a defense of unilateralism in U.S. foreign policy. In Krauthammer's view, international institutions and international law are incapable of spreading democracy and countering aggression. Only American power can accomplish these crucial objectives. Advocates of multilateralism would, according to Krauthammer, subordinate American power and interests to the ephemeral whims of an imaginary international community. By handcuffing U.S. freedom of action in the name of a utopian vision, multilateralists would weaken the ability of the United States to secure not only its own interests but also those of the peoples and states that depend upon American power for their own security and prosperity. Krauthammer blends a realist emphasis on international power with a willingness to use American strength, unfettered by international institutions, for the purposes of implanting democracy and defending U.S. values abroad.

Francis Fukuyama's chapter was written as a critique of neoconservative ideas and policies, such as those advocated by Krauthammer. Fukuyama criticizes neoconservatives for underestimating the costs and difficulties of implanting democracy abroad through force and for ignoring the price that the United States pays when unilateral action prompts other states to question the legitimacy of American leadership. Fukuyama calls for a U.S. foreign policy that seeks to strengthen international institutions, especially those built around cooperation among democratic allies.

Like Fukuyama, Ralph G. Carter argues that American unilateralism has proven costly to U.S. interests and threatens the ability of the international community to effectively mount collective responses to common problems. America's unwillingness to engage in genuine international consultation, its rejection of cooperative efforts that enjoy broad international support, and its predilection for the use of military force have generated resentment and resistance in many parts of the world. Since even a country as powerful as the United States needs the assistance of other states in dealing with such problems as terrorism, weapons proliferation, and global environmental challenges, Carter considers the recent unilateralist turn in U.S. foreign policy to be shortsighted and counterproductive.

G. John Ikenberry contends that the new unilateralism is likely to prove less profound or lasting in its consequences for U.S. foreign policy than either its advocates or detractors have suggested. While Ikenberry concedes that many top officials in the Bush administration are skeptical about the value of multilateral agreements and institutions, he argues that even Bush's unilateralist leanings have not undermined the "foundational" sources of multilateral cooperation among the United States, Japan, and Europe. These regions remain tied together by economic openness, enduring security relationships, and a common commitment to democratic values.

These deeper sources of multilateral cooperation are likely to survive recent differences arising from the Bush administration's rejection of a series of global treaties or its decision to use force in Iraq without authorization from the UN Security Council. In the longer term, Ikenberry rejects the notion that American dominance alone leads inevitably to a unilateralist foreign policy. He argues that the incentives for the United States to engage in multilateral cooperation remain strong. These include the desire to manage and preserve global economic interdependence, the need to institutionalize American international preferences, and the underlying support of the American people for multilateral engagement.

Conclusion

Debates over the sources of the new unilateralism, its consequences, and its future are critical to understanding the present era in U.S. foreign policy. Given the central role that the United States plays in world politics, a long-term shift away from cooperative engagement with the current constellation of international institutions could have profound consequences. Subsequent parts of this book examine American and foreign attitudes toward the U.S. global role and the strategic orientation of the administration of President George W. Bush.

DISCUSSION QUESTIONS

1. What are the sources of unilateralism in U.S. foreign policy? Is unilateralism a necessary consequence of America's superpower status?

2. What are the costs and benefits of unilateralism from a U.S. perspective?

3. What is the likelihood that future U.S. foreign policy will swing back in a multilateralist direction?

4. Which domestic interests benefit from multilateralist foreign policy initiatives and which tend to oppose such initiatives?

SUGGESTED READINGS

Foot, Rosemary, S. Neil MacFarlane, and Michael Mastanduno, eds. *U.S. Hegemony and International Organizations: The United States and Multilateralist Institutions.* New York: Oxford University Press, 2003.

Lake, David A. *Entangling Relations: American Foreign Policy in Its Century.* Princeton, N.J.: Princeton University Press, 1999.

Malone, David M., and Yuen Foong Khong, eds. *Unilateralism and U.S. Foreign Policy: International Perspectives.* Boulder, Colo.: Lynne Rienner, 2003.

Patrick, Stewart, and Shepard Forman, eds. *Multilateralism and U.S. Foreign Policy: Ambivalent Engagement.* Boulder, Colo.: Lynne Rienner, 2002.

Prestowitz, Clyde. *Rogue Nation: American Unilateralism and the Failure of Good Intentions.* New York: Basic Books, 2003.

Prins, Gwyn, ed. *Understanding Unilateralism in American Foreign Relations.* London: Royal Institute of International Affairs, 2000.

12

Democratic Realism

An American Foreign Policy for a Unipolar World

Charles Krauthammer

A UNIPOLAR WORLD

Americans have a healthy aversion to foreign policy. It stems from a sense of thrift: Who needs it? We're protected by two great oceans. We have this continent practically to ourselves. And we share it with just two neighbors, both friendly, one so friendly that its people seem intent upon moving in with us.

It took three giants of the twentieth century to drag us into its great battles: Wilson into World War I, Roosevelt into World War II, Truman into the Cold War. And then it ended with one of the great anticlimaxes in history. Without a shot fired, without a revolution, without so much as a press release, the Soviet Union simply gave up and disappeared.

It was the end of everything—the end of communism, of socialism, of the Cold War, of the European wars. But the end of everything was also a beginning. On December 26, 1991, the Soviet Union died and something new was born, something utterly new: a unipolar world dominated by a single superpower unchecked by any rival and with decisive reach in every corner of the globe.

This is a staggering new development in history, not seen since the fall of Rome. It is so new, so strange, that we have no idea how to deal with it. Our first reaction—the 1990s—was utter confusion. The next reaction was awe. When Paul Kennedy, who had once popularized the idea of

American decline, saw what America did in the Afghan war—a display of fully mobilized, furiously concentrated unipolar power at a distance of 8,000 miles—he not only recanted, he stood in wonder: "Nothing has ever existed like this disparity of power," he wrote, "nothing. . . . No other nation comes close. . . . Charlemagne's empire was merely western European in its reach. The Roman empire stretched farther afield, but there was another great empire in Persia, and a larger one in China. There is, therefore, no comparison."

Even Rome is no model for what America is today. First, because we do not have the imperial culture of Rome. We are an Athenian republic, even more republican and infinitely more democratic than Athens. And this American Republic has acquired the largest seeming empire in the history of the world—acquired it in a fit of absent-mindedness greater even than Britain's. And it was not just absent-mindedness; it was sheer inadvertence. We got here because of Europe's suicide in the world wars of the twentieth century, and then the death of its Eurasian successor, Soviet Russia, for having adopted a political and economic system so inhuman that, like a genetically defective organism, it simply expired in its sleep. Leaving us with global dominion.

Second, we are unlike Rome, unlike Britain and France and Spain and the other classical empires of modern times, in that *we do not hunger for territory*. The use of the word "empire" in the American context is ridiculous. It is absurd to apply the word to a people whose first instinct upon arriving on anyone's soil is to demand an exit strategy. I can assure you that when the Romans went into Gaul and the British into India, they were not looking for exit strategies. They were looking for entry strategies.

In David Lean's *Lawrence of Arabia,* King Faisal says to Lawrence: "I think you are another of these desert-loving English. . . . The English have a great hunger for desolate places." Indeed, for five centuries, the Europeans did hunger for deserts and jungles and oceans and new continents.

Americans do not. We like it here. We like our McDonald's. We like our football. We like our rock-and-roll. We've got the Grand Canyon and Graceland. We've got Silicon Valley and South Beach. We've got everything. And if that's not enough, we've got Vegas—which is a facsimile of everything. What could we possibly need anywhere else? We don't like exotic climates. We don't like exotic languages—lots of declensions and moods. We don't even know what a mood is. We like Iowa corn and New York hot dogs, and if we want Chinese or Indian or Italian, we go to the food court. We don't send the Marines for takeout.

That's because we are not an imperial power. We are a commercial republic. We don't take food; we trade for it. Which makes us something unique in history, an anomaly, a hybrid: a commercial republic with overwhelming global power. A commercial republic that, by pure accident of history, has been designated custodian of the international system. The eyes of every supplicant from East Timor to Afghanistan, from Iraq to Liberia; Arab and Israeli, Irish and British, North and South Korean are upon us.

That is who we are. That is where we are.

Now the question is: What do we do? What is a unipolar power to do?

ISOLATIONISM

The oldest and most venerable answer is to hoard that power and retreat. This is known as isolationism. Of all the foreign policy schools in America, it has the oldest pedigree, not surprising in the only great power in history to be isolated by two vast oceans.

Isolationism originally sprang from a view of America as spiritually superior to the Old World. We were too good to be corrupted by its low intrigues, entangled by its cynical alliances.

Today, however, isolationism is an ideology of fear. Fear of trade. Fear of immigrants. Fear of the Other. Isolationists want to cut off trade and immigration, and withdraw from our military and strategic commitments around the world. . . .

They are for a radical retrenchment of American power—for pulling up the drawbridge to Fortress America.

Isolationism is an important school of thought historically, but not today. Not just because of its brutal intellectual reductionism, but because it is so obviously inappropriate to the world of today—a world of export-driven economies, of massive population flows, and of 9/11, the definitive demonstration that the combination of modern technology and transnational primitivism has erased the barrier between "over there" and over here. . . . Classic isolationism is moribund and marginalized.

Who then rules America?

LIBERAL INTERNATIONALISM

In the 1990s, it was liberal internationalism. Liberal internationalism is the foreign policy of the Democratic Party and the religion of the foreign policy elite. It has a peculiar history. It traces its pedigree to Woodrow Wilson's utopianism, Harry Truman's anticommunism, and John Kennedy's militant universalism. But after the Vietnam War, it was transmuted into an ideology of passivity, acquiescence and almost reflexive anti-interventionism.

Liberals today proudly take credit for Truman's and Kennedy's roles in containing communism, but they prefer to forget that, for the last half of the Cold War, liberals used "cold warrior" as an epithet. In the early 1980s, they gave us the nuclear freeze movement, a form of unilateral disarmament in the face of Soviet nuclear advances. Today, John Kerry boasts of opposing, during the 1980s, what he calls Ronald Reagan's "illegal war in Central America"—and oppose he did what was, in fact, an indigenous anticommunist rebellion that ultimately succeeded in bringing down Sandinista rule and ushering in democracy in all of Central America.

That boast reminds us how militant was liberal passivity in the last half of the Cold War. But that passivity outlived the Cold War. When Kuwait was invaded, the question was: Should the United States go to war to prevent the Persian Gulf from falling into hostile hands? The Democratic Party joined the Buchananite isolationists in saying No. The Democrats voted No overwhelmingly—two to one in the House, more than four to one in the Senate.

And yet, quite astonishingly, when liberal internationalism came to power just two years later in the form of the Clinton administration, it turned almost hyperinterventionist. It involved us four times in military action: deepening intervention in Somalia, invading Haiti, bombing Bosnia, and finally going to war over Kosovo. .

How to explain the amazing transmutation of Cold War and Gulf War doves into Haiti and Balkan hawks? The crucial and obvious difference is this: Haiti, Bosnia and Kosovo were humanitarian ventures—fights for right and good, *devoid of raw national interest.* And only humanitarian interventionism—disinterested interventionism devoid of national interest—is morally pristine enough to justify the use of force. The history of the 1990s refutes the lazy notion that liberals have an aversion to the use of force. They do not. They have an aversion to using force for reasons of pure national interest.

And by national interest I do not mean simple self-defense. Everyone believes in self-defense, as in Afghanistan. I am talking about national interest as defined by a Great Power: shaping the international environment by projecting power abroad to secure economic, political, and strategic goods. Intervening militarily for *that* kind of national interest, liberal internationalism finds unholy and unsupportable. It sees that kind of national interest as merely self-interest writ large, in effect, a form of grand national selfishness. Hence Kuwait, no; Kosovo, yes.

The other defining feature of the Clinton foreign policy was multilateralism, which expressed itself in a mania for treaties. The Clinton administration negotiated a dizzying succession of parchment promises on bioweapons, chemical weapons, nuclear testing, carbon emissions, antiballistic missiles, etc.

Why? No sentient being could believe that, say, the chemical or biological weapons treaties were anything more than transparently useless. Senator Joseph Biden once defended the Chemical Weapons Convention, which even its proponents admitted was unenforceable, on the grounds that it would "provide us with a valuable tool"—the "moral suasion of the entire international community."

Moral suasion? Was it moral suasion that made Qaddafi see the wisdom of giving up his weapons of mass destruction? Or Iran agree for the first time to spot nuclear inspections? It was the suasion of the bayonet. It was the ignominious fall of Saddam—and the desire of interested spectators not to be next on the list. The whole point of this treaty was to keep *rogue states* from developing chemical weapons. Rogue states are, by definition, impervious to moral suasion.

Moral suasion is a farce. Why then this obsession with conventions, protocols, legalisms? Their obvious net effect is to temper American power. Who, after all, was really going to be most constrained by these treaties? The ABM amendments were aimed squarely at American advances and strategic defenses, not at Russia, which lags hopelessly behind. The Kyoto Protocol exempted India and China. The nuclear test ban would have seriously degraded the American nuclear arsenal. And the landmine treaty (which the Clinton administration spent months negotiating but, in the end, met so much Pentagon resistance that even Clinton could not initial it) would have had a devastating impact on U.S. conventional forces, particularly at the DMZ in Korea.

But that, you see, is the whole point of the multilateral enterprise: To reduce American freedom of action by making it subservient to, dependent on, constricted by the will—and interests—of other nations. To tie down Gulliver with a thousand strings. To domesticate the most undomesticated, most outsized, national interest on the planet—ours.

Today, multilateralism remains the overriding theme of liberal internationalism. When in power in the 1990s, multilateralism expressed itself as a mania for treaties. When out of power in this decade, multilateralism manifests itself in the slavish pursuit of "international legitimacy"—and opposition to any American action undertaken without universal foreign blessing.

Which is why the Democratic critique of the war in Iraq is so peculiarly one of process and not of policy. The problem was that we did not have the permission of the UN; we did not have a large enough coalition; we did not have a second Security Council resolution. Kofi Annan was unhappy and the French were cross.

The Democratic presidential candidates all say that we should have internationalized the conflict, brought in the UN, enlisted the allies. Why? Two reasons: assistance and legitimacy. First, they say, we could have used these other countries to help us in the reconstruction. . . .

Of course it would be nice if we had more allies rather than fewer. It would also be nice to be able to fly. But when some nations are not with you on your enterprise, including them in your coalition is not a way to broaden it; it's a way to abolish it.

At which point, liberal internationalists switch gears and appeal to legitimacy—on the grounds that multilateral action has a higher moral standing. I have always found this line of argument incomprehensible. By what possible moral calculus does an American intervention to liberate 25 million people forfeit moral legitimacy because it lacks the blessing of the butchers of Tiananmen Square or the cynics of the Quai d'Orsay?

Which is why it is hard to take these arguments at face value. Look: We know why liberal internationalists demanded UN sanction for the war in Iraq. It was a way to stop the war. It was the Gulliver effect. Call a committee meeting of countries with hostile or contrary interests—i.e., the Security Council—and you have guaranteed yourself another twelve years of inaction.

Historically, multilateralism is a way for weak countries to multiply their power by attaching themselves to stronger ones. But multilateralism imposed on Great Powers, and particularly on a unipolar power, is intended to *restrain* that power. Which is precisely why France is an ardent multilateralist. But why should America be?

Why, in the end, *does* liberal internationalism want to tie down Gulliver, to blunt the pursuit of American national interests by making them subordinate to a myriad of other interests?

In the immediate post-Vietnam era, this aversion to national interest might have been attributed to self-doubt and self-loathing. I don't know. What I do know is that today it is a mistake to see liberal foreign policy as deriving from anti-Americanism or lack of patriotism or a late efflorescence of 1960s radicalism.

On the contrary. The liberal aversion to national interest stems from an idealism, a larger vision of country, a vision of some ambition and nobility— the ideal of a true international community. And that is: To transform the international system from the Hobbesian universe into a Lockean universe. To turn the state of nature into a norm-driven community. To turn the law of the jungle into the rule of law—of treaties and contracts and UN resolutions. In short, to remake the international system in the image of domestic civil society.

They dream of a new world, a world described in 1943 by Cordell Hull, FDR's secretary of state—a world in which "there will no longer be need for spheres of influence, for alliances, for balance of power, or any other of the special arrangements by which, in the unhappy past, the nations strove to safeguard their security or promote their interests."

And to create such a true international community, you have to temper, transcend, and, in the end, abolish the very idea of state power and national interest. Hence the antipathy to American hegemony and American power. If you are going to break the international arena to the mold of domestic society, you have to domesticate its single most powerful actor. You have to abolish American dominance, not only as an affront to fairness, but also as the greatest obstacle on the whole planet to a democratized international system where all live under self-governing international institutions and self-enforcing international norms.

REALISM

This vision is all very nice. All very noble. And all very crazy. Which brings us to the third great foreign policy school: realism.

The realist looks at this great liberal project and sees a hopeless illusion. Because turning the Hobbesian world that has existed since long before the Peloponnesian Wars into a Lockean world, turning a jungle into a suburban subdivision, requires a revolution in human nature. Not just an erector set of new institutions, but a revolution in human nature. And realists do not believe in revolutions in human nature, much less stake their future, and the future of their nation, on them.

Realism recognizes the fundamental fallacy in the whole idea of the international system being modeled on domestic society.

First, what holds domestic society together is a supreme central authority wielding a monopoly of power and enforcing norms. In the international arena there is no such thing. Domestic society may look like a place of self-regulating norms, but if somebody breaks into your house, you call 911, and the police arrive with guns drawn. That's not exactly self-enforcement. That's law enforcement.

Second, domestic society rests on the shared goodwill, civility and common values of its individual members. What values are shared by, say, Britain, Cuba, Yemen and Zimbabwe—all nominal members of this fiction we call the "international community"? . . .

The realist believes the definition of peace Ambrose Bierce offered in *The Devil's Dictionary:* "Peace: *noun,* in international affairs, a period of cheating between two periods of fighting."

Hence the realist axiom: The "international community" is a fiction. It is not a community, it is a cacophony—of straining ambitions, disparate values and contending power.

What does hold the international system together? What keeps it from degenerating into total anarchy? Not the phony security of treaties, not the best of goodwill among the nicer nations. In the unipolar world we inhabit, what stability we do enjoy today is owed to the overwhelming power and deterrent threat of the United States.

If someone invades your house, you call the cops. Who do you call if someone invades your country? You dial Washington. In the unipolar world, the closest thing to a centralized authority, to an enforcer of norms, is America—American power. And ironically, American power is precisely what liberal internationalism wants to constrain and tie down and subsume in pursuit of some brave new Lockean world. . . .

The land mine that protects civilization from barbarism is not parchment but power, and in a unipolar world, American power—wielded, if necessary, unilaterally. If necessary, preemptively. Now, those uneasy with American power have made these two means of wielding it—preemption and unilateralism—the focus of unrelenting criticism. The doctrine of preemption, in particular, has been widely attacked for violating international norms.

What international norm? The one under which Israel was universally condemned—even the Reagan administration joined the condemnation at the Security Council—for preemptively destroying Iraq's Osirak nuclear reactor in 1981? Does anyone today doubt that it was the right thing to do, both strategically and morally?

In a world of terrorists, terrorist states and weapons of mass destruction, the option of preemption is especially necessary. In the bipolar world of the Cold War, with a stable nonsuicidal adversary, deterrence could work. Deterrence does not work against people who ache for heaven. It does not work against *undeterrables*. And it does not work against undetectables: nonsuicidal enemy regimes that might attack through clandestine means—a suitcase nuke or anonymously delivered anthrax. Against both undeterrables and undetectables, preemption is the only possible strategy.

Moreover, the doctrine of preemption against openly hostile states pursuing weapons of mass destruction is an improvement on classical deterrence. Traditionally, we deterred the use of WMDs by the threat of retaliation after we'd been attacked—and that's too late; the point of preemption is to deter the very acquisition of WMDs in the first place.

Whether or not Iraq had large stockpiles of WMDs, the very fact that the United States overthrew a hostile regime that repeatedly refused to come clean on its weapons has had precisely this deterrent effect. We are safer today not just because Saddam is gone, but because Libya and any others contemplating trafficking with WMDs have—for the first time—seen that it carries a cost, a very high cost.

Yes, of course, imperfect intelligence makes preemption problematic. But that is not an objection on principle, it is an objection in practice. Indeed, the objection concedes the principle. We need good intelligence. But we remain defenseless if we abjure the option of preemption.

The other great objection to the way American unipolar power has been wielded is its unilateralism. I would dispute how unilateralist we have in fact been. Constructing ad hoc "coalitions of the willing" hardly qualifies as unilateralism just because they do not have a secretariat in Brussels or on the East River.

Moreover, unilateralism is often the very road to multilateralism. As we learned from the Gulf War, it is the leadership of the United States—indeed, its willingness to act unilaterally if necessary—that galvanized the Gulf War coalition into existence.

Without the president of the United States declaring "This will not stand" about the invasion of Kuwait—and making it clear that America would go it alone if it had to—there never would have been the great wall-to-wall coalition that is now so retroactively applauded and held up as a model of multilateralism.

Of course one acts in concert with others if possible. It is nice when others join us in the breach. No one seeks to be unilateral. Unilateralism simply means that one does not allow oneself to be held hostage to the will of others. . . .

Irving Kristol once explained that he preferred the Organization of American States to the United Nations because in the OAS we can be voted down in only three languages, thereby saving translators' fees. Realists choose not to be Gulliver. In an international system with no sovereign, no police, no protection—where power is the ultimate arbiter and history has bequeathed us unprecedented power—we should be vigilant in preserving that power. And our freedom of action to use it.

But here we come up against the limits of realism: You cannot live by power alone. Realism is a valuable antidote to the woolly internationalism of the 1990s. But realism can only take you so far.

Its basic problem lies in its definition of national interest as classically offered by its great theorist, Hans Morgenthau: interest defined as power. Morgenthau postulated that what drives nations, what motivates their foreign policy, is the will to power—to keep it and expand it.

For most Americans, will to power might be a correct description of the world—of what motivates other countries—but it cannot be a prescription for America. It cannot be our purpose. America cannot and will not live by realpolitik alone. Our foreign policy must be driven by something beyond power. Unless conservatives present ideals to challenge the liberal ideal of a domesticated international community, they will lose the debate.

Which is why among American conservatives, another, more idealistic, school has arisen that sees America's national interest as an expression of values.

DEMOCRATIC GLOBALISM

It is this fourth school that has guided U.S. foreign policy in this decade. This conservative alternative to realism is often lazily and invidiously called neoconservatism, but that is a very odd name for a school whose major proponents in the world today are George W. Bush and Tony Blair—if they are neoconservatives, then Margaret Thatcher was a liberal. There's nothing neo about Bush, and there's nothing con about Blair.

Yet they are the principal proponents today of what might be called democratic globalism, a foreign policy that defines the national interest not as power but as values, and that identifies one supreme value, what John Kennedy called "the success of liberty." As President Bush put it in his speech at Whitehall last November: "The United States and Great Britain share a mission in the world beyond the balance of power or the simple pursuit of interest. We seek the advance of freedom and the peace that freedom brings."

Beyond power. Beyond interest. Beyond interest defined as power. That is the credo of democratic globalism. Which explains its political appeal: America is a nation uniquely built not on blood, race or consanguinity, but on a proposition—to which its sacred honor has been pledged for two centuries. . . .

Democratic globalism sees as the engine of history not the will to power but the will to freedom. And while it has been attacked as a dreamy, idealistic innovation, its inspiration comes from the Truman Doctrine of 1947, the Kennedy inaugural of 1961, and Reagan's "evil empire" speech of 1983. They all sought to recast a struggle for power between two geopolitical titans into a struggle between freedom and unfreedom, and yes, good and evil.

. . . Today, post-9/11, we find ourselves in a similar existential struggle but with a different enemy: not Soviet communism, but Arab-Islamic totalitarianism, both secular and religious. Bush and Blair are similarly attacked for naively and crudely casting this struggle as one of freedom versus unfreedom, good versus evil.

Now, given the way not just freedom but human decency were suppressed in both Afghanistan and Iraq, the two major battles of this new war, you would have to give Bush and Blair's moral claims the decided advantage of being obviously true.

Nonetheless, something can be true and still be dangerous. Many people are deeply uneasy with the Bush-Blair doctrine—many conservatives in particular. When Blair declares in his address to Congress: "The spread of freedom is . . . our last line of defense and our first line of attack," they see a dangerously expansive, aggressively utopian foreign policy. In short, they see Woodrow Wilson.

Now, to a conservative, Woodrow Wilson is fightin' words. Yes, this vision is expansive and perhaps utopian. But it ain't Wilsonian. Wilson envisioned the spread of democratic values through as-yet-to-be invented international institutions. He could be forgiven for that. In 1918, there was no way to know how utterly corrupt and useless those international institutions would turn out to be. Eight decades of bitter experience later—with Libya chairing the UN Commission on Human Rights—there is no way *not* to know.

Democratic globalism is not Wilsonian. Its attractiveness is precisely that it shares realism's insights about the centrality of power. Its attractiveness is precisely that it has appropriate contempt for the fictional legalisms of liberal internationalism.

Moreover, democratic globalism is an improvement over realism. What it can teach realism is that the spread of democracy is not just an end but a means, an indispensable means for securing American interests. The reason is simple. Democracies are inherently more friendly to the United States, less belligerent to their neighbors, and generally more inclined to peace. Realists are right that to protect your interests you often have to go around the world bashing bad guys over the head. But that technique, no matter how satisfying, has its limits. At some point, you have to implant something, something organic and self-developing. And that something is democracy.

But where? The danger of democratic globalism is its universalism, its open-ended commitment to human freedom, its temptation to plant the flag of democracy everywhere. It must learn to say no. And indeed, it does say no. But when it says no to Liberia, or Congo, or Burma, or countenances alliances with authoritarian rulers in places like Pakistan or, for that matter, Russia, it stands accused of hypocrisy. Which is why we must articulate criteria for saying yes.

Where to intervene? Where to bring democracy? Where to nation-build? I propose a single criterion: where it counts.

Call it democratic *realism*. And this is its axiom: *We will support democracy everywhere, but we will commit blood and treasure only in places where there is a strategic necessity—meaning, places central to the larger war against the existential enemy, the enemy that poses a global mortal threat to freedom.*

Where does it count? Fifty years ago, Germany and Japan counted. Why? Because they were the seeds of the greatest global threat to freedom in midcentury—fascism—and then were turned, by nation building, into bulwarks against the next great threat to freedom, Soviet communism.

Where does it count today? Where the overthrow of radicalism and the beginnings of democracy can have a decisive effect in the war against the new global threat to freedom, the new existential enemy, the Arab-Islamic totalitarianism that has threatened us in both its secular and religious forms for the quarter-century since the Khomeini revolution of 1979.

Establishing civilized, decent, nonbelligerent, pro-Western polities in Afghanistan and Iraq and ultimately their key neighbors would, like the flipping of Germany and Japan in the 1940s, change the strategic balance in the fight against Arab-Islamic radicalism.

Yes, it may be a bridge too far. Realists have been warning against the hubris of thinking we can transform an alien culture because of some postulated natural and universal human will to freedom. And they may yet be right. But how do they know in advance? Half a century ago, we heard the same confident warnings about the imperviousness to democracy of Confucian culture. That proved stunningly wrong. Where is it written that Arabs are incapable of democracy?

Yes, as in Germany and Japan, the undertaking is enormous, ambitious and arrogant. It may yet fail. But we cannot afford not to try. There is not a single, remotely plausible, alternative strategy for attacking the monster behind 9/11. It's not Osama bin Laden; it is the cauldron of political oppression, religious intolerance, and social ruin in the Arab-Islamic world—oppression transmuted and deflected by regimes with no legitimacy into virulent, murderous anti-Americanism. It's not one man; it is a condition. It will be nice to find that man and hang him, but that's the cops-and-robbers law-enforcement model of fighting terrorism that we tried for twenty years and that gave us 9/11. This is war, and in war arresting murderers is nice. But you win by taking territory—and leaving something behind.

SEPTEMBER 11

We are the unipolar power and what do we do?

. . . [O]ur problem is 9/11 and the roots of Arab-Islamic nihilism. September 11 felt like a new problem, but for all its shock and surprise, it is an old problem with a new face. September 11 felt like the initiation of a new history, but it was a return to history, the twentieth-century history of radical ideologies and existential enemies.

The anomaly is not the world of today. The anomaly was the 1990s, our holiday from history. It felt like peace, but it was an interval of dreaming between two periods of reality.

From which 9/11 awoke us. It startled us into thinking everything was new. It's not. What is new is what happened not on 9/11 but ten years earlier on December 26, 1991: the emergence of the United States as the world's unipolar power. What is unique is our advantage in this struggle, an advantage we did not have during the struggles of the twentieth century. The question for our time is how to press this advantage, how to exploit our unipolar power, how to deploy it to win the old/new war that exploded upon us on 9/11.

What is the unipolar power to do?

Four schools, four answers.

The isolationists want simply to ignore unipolarity, pull up the drawbridge, and defend Fortress America. Alas, the Fortress has no moat—not after the airplane, the submarine, the ballistic missile—and as for the drawbridge, it was blown up on 9/11.

Then there are the liberal internationalists. They like to dream, and to the extent they are aware of our unipolar power, they don't like it. They see its use for anything other than humanitarianism or reflexive self-defense as an expression of national selfishness. And they don't just want us to ignore our unique power, they want us to yield it piece by piece, by subsuming our-

selves in a new global architecture in which America becomes not the arbiter of international events, but a good and tame international citizen.

Then there is realism, which has the clearest understanding of the new
unipolarity and its uses—unilateral and preemptive if necessary. But in the
end, it fails because it offers no vision. It is all means and no ends. It cannot adequately define our mission.

Hence, the fourth school: democratic globalism. It has, in this decade,
rallied the American people to a struggle over values. It seeks to vindicate
the American idea by making the spread of democracy, the success of liberty, the ends and means of American foreign policy.

I support that. I applaud that. But I believe it must be tempered in its universalistic aspirations and rhetoric from a democratic globalism to a democratic realism. It must be targeted, focused and limited. We are friends to all,
but we come ashore only where it really counts. And where it counts today
is that Islamic crescent stretching from North Africa to Afghanistan. . . .

13

After Neoconservatism

Francis Fukuyama

As we approach the third anniversary of the onset of the Iraq war, it seems very unlikely that history will judge either the intervention itself or the ideas animating it kindly. By invading Iraq, the Bush administration created a self-fulfilling prophecy: Iraq has now replaced Afghanistan as a magnet, a training ground and an operational base for jihadist terrorists, with plenty of American targets to shoot at. The United States still has a chance of creating a Shiite-dominated democratic Iraq, but the new government will be very weak for years to come; the resulting power vacuum will invite outside influence from all of Iraq's neighbors, including Iran. There are clear benefits to the Iraqi people from the removal of Saddam Hussein's dictatorship, and perhaps some positive spillover effects in Lebanon and Syria. But it is very hard to see how these developments in themselves justify the blood and treasure that the United States has spent on the project to this point.

The so-called Bush Doctrine that set the framework for the administration's first term is now in shambles. The doctrine (elaborated, among other places, in the 2002 National Security Strategy of the United States) argued that, in the wake of the Sept. 11 attacks, America would have to launch periodic preventive wars to defend itself against rogue states and terrorists with weapons of mass destruction; that it would do this alone, if necessary; and that it would work to democratize the greater Middle East as a long-term solution to the terrorist problem. But successful pre-emption depends on the ability to predict the future accurately and on good intelligence, which was not forthcoming, while America's perceived unilateralism has isolated it as never before. It is not surprising that in its second term, the administration has been distancing itself from these policies and is in the process of rewriting the National Security Strategy document.

But it is the idealistic effort to use American power to promote democracy and human rights abroad that may suffer the greatest setback. Perceived failure in Iraq has restored the authority of foreign policy "realists" in the tradition of Henry Kissinger. Already there is a host of books and articles decrying America's naive Wilsonianism and attacking the notion of trying to democratize the world. The administration's second-term efforts to push for greater Middle Eastern democracy, introduced with the soaring rhetoric of Bush's second Inaugural Address, have borne very problematic fruits. The Islamist Muslim Brotherhood made a strong showing in Egypt's parliamentary elections in November and December. While the holding of elections in Iraq this past December was an achievement in itself, the vote led to the ascendance of a Shiite bloc with close ties to Iran (following on the election of the conservative Mahmoud Ahmadinejad as president of Iran in June). But the clincher was the decisive Hamas victory in the Palestinian election last month, which brought to power a movement overtly dedicated to the destruction of Israel. In his second inaugural, Bush said that "America's vital interests and our deepest beliefs are now one," but the charge will be made with increasing frequency that the Bush administration made a big mistake when it stirred the pot, and that the United States would have done better to stick by its traditional authoritarian friends in the Middle East. . . .

The reaction against democracy promotion and an activist foreign policy may not end there. Those whom Walter Russell Mead labels Jacksonian conservatives—red-state Americans whose sons and daughters are fighting and dying in the Middle East—supported the Iraq war because they believed that their children were fighting to defend the United States against nuclear terrorism, not to promote democracy. They don't want to abandon the president in the middle of a vicious war, but down the road the perceived failure of the Iraq intervention may push them to favor a more isolationist foreign policy, which is a more natural political position for them. A recent Pew poll indicates a swing in public opinion toward isolationism; the percentage of Americans saying that the United States "should mind its own business" has never been higher since the end of the Vietnam War.

More than any other group, it was the neoconservatives both inside and outside the Bush administration who pushed for democratizing Iraq and the broader Middle East. They are widely credited (or blamed) for being the decisive voices promoting regime change in Iraq, and yet it is their idealistic agenda that in the coming months and years will be the most directly threatened. Were the United States to retreat from the world stage, following a drawdown in Iraq, it would in my view be a huge tragedy, because

American power and influence have been critical to the maintenance of an open and increasingly democratic order around the world. The problem with neoconservatism's agenda lies not in its ends, which are as American as apple pie, but rather in the overmilitarized means by which it has sought to accomplish them. What American foreign policy needs is not a return to a narrow and cynical realism, but rather the formulation of a "realistic Wilsonianism" that better matches means to ends.

THE NEOCONSERVATIVE LEGACY

How did the neoconservatives end up overreaching to such an extent that they risk undermining their own goals? The Bush administration's first-term foreign policy did not flow ineluctably from the views of earlier generations of people who considered themselves neoconservatives, since those views were themselves complex and subject to differing interpretations. Four common principles or threads ran through much of this thought up through the end of the cold war: a concern with democracy, human rights and, more generally, the internal politics of states; a belief that American power can be used for moral purposes; a skepticism about the ability of international law and institutions to solve serious security problems; and finally, a view that ambitious social engineering often leads to unexpected consequences and thereby undermines its own ends.

The problem was that two of these principles were in potential collision. The skeptical stance toward ambitious social engineering—which in earlier years had been applied mostly to domestic policies like affirmative action, busing and welfare—suggested a cautious approach toward remaking the world and an awareness that ambitious initiatives always have unanticipated consequences. The belief in the potential moral uses of American power, on the other hand, implied that American activism could reshape the structure of global politics. By the time of the Iraq war, the belief in the transformational uses of power had prevailed over the doubts about social engineering.

In retrospect, things did not have to develop this way. The roots of neoconservatism lie in a remarkable group of largely Jewish intellectuals who attended City College of New York (C.C.N.Y.) in the mid- to late 1930's and early 1940's, a group that included Irving Kristol, Daniel Bell, Irving Howe, Nathan Glazer and, a bit later, Daniel Patrick Moynihan. The story of this group has been told in a number of places, most notably in a documentary film by Joseph Dorman called "Arguing the World." The most important inheritance from the C.C.N.Y. group was an idealistic belief in social progress and the universality of rights, coupled with intense anti-Communism. . . .

If there was a single overarching theme to the domestic social policy critiques issued by those who wrote for the neoconservative journal "The

Public Interest," founded by Irving Kristol, Nathan Glazer and Daniel Bell in 1965, it was the limits of social engineering. Writers like Glazer, Moynihan and, later, Glenn Loury argued that ambitious efforts to seek social justice often left societies worse off than before because they either required massive state intervention that disrupted pre-existing social relations (for example, forced busing) or else produced unanticipated consequences (like an increase in single-parent families as a result of welfare). . . .

How, then, did a group with such a pedigree come to decide that the "root cause" of terrorism lay in the Middle East's lack of democracy, that the United States had both the wisdom and the ability to fix this problem and that democracy would come quickly and painlessly to Iraq? Neoconservatives would not have taken this turn but for the peculiar way that the cold war ended.

Ronald Reagan was ridiculed by sophisticated people on the American left and in Europe for labeling the Soviet Union and its allies an "evil empire" and for challenging Mikhail Gorbachev not just to reform his system but also to "tear down this wall." . . . That community felt that the Reaganites were dangerously utopian in their hopes for actually winning, as opposed to managing, the cold war.

And yet total victory in the cold war is exactly what happened in 1989–91. Gorbachev accepted . . . deep cuts in conventional forces, and then failed to stop the Polish, Hungarian and East German defections from the empire. Communism collapsed within a couple of years because of its internal moral weaknesses and contradictions, and with regime change in Eastern Europe and the former Soviet Union, the Warsaw Pact threat to the West evaporated.

The way the cold war ended shaped the thinking of supporters of the Iraq war, including younger neoconservatives like William Kristol and Robert Kagan, in two ways. First, it seems to have created an expectation that all totalitarian regimes were hollow at the core and would crumble with a small push from outside. The model for this was Romania under the Ceauşescus: once the wicked witch was dead, the munchkins would rise up and start singing joyously about their liberation. As Kristol and Kagan put it in their 2000 book "Present Dangers": "To many the idea of America using its power to promote changes of regime in nations ruled by dictators rings of utopianism. But in fact, it is eminently realistic. There is something perverse in declaring the impossibility of promoting democratic change abroad in light of the record of the past three decades."

This overoptimism about postwar transitions to democracy helps explain the Bush administration's incomprehensible failure to plan adequately for the insurgency that subsequently emerged in Iraq. The war's supporters seemed to think that democracy was a kind of default condition to which societies reverted once the heavy lifting of coercive regime change occurred, rather than a long-term process of institution-building and reform. While they now assert that they knew all along that the democratic transformation of Iraq would be long and hard, they were clearly taken by surprise. . . .

By the 1990's, neoconservatism had been fed by several other intellectual streams. One came from the students of the German Jewish political theorist Leo Strauss, who . . . was a serious reader of philosophical texts who did not express opinions on contemporary politics or policy issues. Rather, he was concerned with the "crisis of modernity" brought on by the relativism of Nietzsche and Heidegger, as well as the fact that neither the claims of religion nor deeply held opinions about the nature of the good life could be banished from politics, as the thinkers of the European Enlightenment had hoped. Another stream came from Albert Wohlstetter, a Rand Corporation strategist who was the teacher of Richard Perle, Zalmay Khalilzad (the current American ambassador to Iraq) and Paul Wolfowitz (the former deputy secretary of defense), among other people. Wohlstetter was intensely concerned with the problem of nuclear proliferation and the way that the 1968 Nonproliferation Treaty left loopholes, in its support for "peaceful" nuclear energy, large enough for countries like Iraq and Iran to walk through.

I have numerous affiliations with the different strands of the neoconservative movement. I was a student of Strauss's protege Allan Bloom, who wrote the bestseller "The Closing of the American Mind"; worked at Rand and with Wohlstetter on Persian Gulf issues; and worked also on two occasions for Wolfowitz. Many people have also interpreted my book "The End of History and the Last Man" (1992) as a neoconservative tract, one that argued in favor of the view that there is a universal hunger for liberty in all people that will inevitably lead them to liberal democracy, and that we are living in the midst of an accelerating, transnational movement in favor of that liberal democracy. This is a misreading of the argument. "The End of History" is in the end an argument about modernization. What is initially universal is not the desire for liberal democracy but rather the desire to live in a modern—that is, technologically advanced and prosperous—society, which, if satisfied, tends to drive demands for political participation. Liberal democracy is one of the byproducts of this modernization process, something that becomes a universal aspiration only in the course of historical time.

"The End of History," in other words, presented a kind of Marxist argument for the existence of a long-term process of social evolution, but one that terminates in liberal democracy rather than communism. In the formulation of the scholar Ken Jowitt, the neoconservative position articulated by people like Kristol and Kagan was, by contrast, Leninist; they believed that history can be pushed along with the right application of power and will. Leninism was a tragedy in its Bolshevik version, and it has returned as farce when practiced by the United States. Neoconservatism, as both a political symbol and a body of thought, has evolved into something I can no longer support.

THE FAILURE OF BENEVOLENT HEGEMONY

The Bush administration and its neoconservative supporters did not simply underestimate the difficulty of bringing about congenial political outcomes in places like Iraq; they also misunderstood the way the world would react to the use of American power. Of course, the cold war was replete with instances of what the foreign policy analyst Stephen Sestanovich calls American maximalism, wherein Washington acted first and sought legitimacy and support from its allies only after the fact. But in the post-cold-war period, the structural situation of world politics changed in ways that made this kind of exercise of power much more problematic in the eyes of even close allies. After the fall of the Soviet Union, various neoconservative authors like Charles Krauthammer, William Kristol and Robert Kagan suggested that the United States would use its margin of power to exert a kind of "benevolent hegemony" over the rest of the world, fixing problems like rogue states with W.M.D., human rights abuses and terrorist threats as they came up. Writing before the Iraq war, Kristol and Kagan considered whether this posture would provoke resistance from the rest of the world, and concluded, "It is precisely because American foreign policy is infused with an unusually high degree of morality that other nations find they have less to fear from its otherwise daunting power."

It is hard to read these lines without irony in the wake of the global reaction to the Iraq war, which succeeded in uniting much of the world in a frenzy of anti-Americanism. The idea that the United States is a hegemon more benevolent than most is not an absurd one, but there were warning signs that things had changed in America's relationship to the world long before the start of the Iraq war. The structural imbalance in global power had grown enormous. America surpassed the rest of the world in every dimension of power by an unprecedented margin, with its defense spending nearly equal to that of the rest of the world combined. Already during the Clinton years, American economic hegemony had generated enormous hostility to an American-dominated process of globalization, frequently on the part of close democratic allies who thought the United States was seeking to impose its antistatist social model on them.

There were other reasons as well why the world did not accept American benevolent hegemony. In the first place, it was premised on American exceptionalism, the idea that America could use its power in instances where others could not because it was more virtuous than other countries. The doctrine of pre-emption against terrorist threats contained in the 2002 National Security Strategy was one that could not safely be generalized through the international system; America would be the first country to object if Russia, China, India or France declared a similar right of unilateral action. The United States was seeking to pass judgment on others while being unwilling to have its own conduct questioned in places like the International Criminal Court.

Another problem with benevolent hegemony was domestic. There are sharp limits to the American people's attention to foreign affairs and willingness to finance projects overseas that do not have clear benefits to American interests. Sept. 11 changed that calculus in many ways, providing popular support for two wars in the Middle East and large increases in defense spending. But the durability of the support is uncertain: although most Americans want to do what is necessary to make the project of rebuilding Iraq succeed, the aftermath of the invasion did not increase the public appetite for further costly interventions. Americans are not, at heart, an imperial people. Even benevolent hegemons sometimes have to act ruthlessly, and they need a staying power that does not come easily to people who are reasonably content with their own lives and society.

Finally, benevolent hegemony presumed that the hegemon was not only well intentioned but competent as well. Much of the criticism of the Iraq intervention from Europeans and others was not based on a normative case that the United States was not getting authorization from the United Nations Security Council, but rather on the belief that it had not made an adequate case for invading Iraq in the first place and didn't know what it was doing in trying to democratize Iraq. In this, the critics were unfortunately quite prescient.

The most basic misjudgment was an overestimation of the threat facing the United States from radical Islamism. Although the new and ominous possibility of undeterrable terrorists armed with weapons of mass destruction did indeed present itself, advocates of the war wrongly conflated this with the threat presented by Iraq and with the rogue state/proliferation problem more generally. The misjudgment was based in part on the massive failure of the American intelligence community to correctly assess the state of Iraq's W.M.D. programs before the war. But the intelligence community never took nearly as alarmist a view of the terrorist/W.M.D. threat as the war's supporters did. Overestimation of this threat was then used to justify the elevation of preventive war to the centerpiece of a new security strategy, as well as a whole series of measures that infringed on civil liberties, from detention policy to domestic eavesdropping.

WHAT TO DO

Now that the neoconservative moment appears to have passed, the United States needs to reconceptualize its foreign policy in several fundamental ways. In the first instance, we need to demilitarize what we have been calling the global war on terrorism and shift to other types of policy instruments. We are fighting hot counterinsurgency wars in Afghanistan and Iraq and against the international jihadist movement, wars in which we need to prevail. But "war" is the wrong metaphor for the broader struggle, since wars are fought at full intensity and have clear beginnings and endings. Meeting the jihadist challenge is more of a "long, twilight struggle" whose core is not a military campaign but a political contest for the hearts and minds of ordinary Muslims around the world. . . .

The United States needs to come up with something better than "coalitions of the willing" to legitimate its dealings with other countries. The world today lacks effective international institutions that can confer legitimacy on collective action; creating new organizations that will better balance the dual requirements of legitimacy and effectiveness will be the primary task for the coming generation. As a result of more than 200 years of political evolution, we have a relatively good understanding of how to create institutions that are rulebound, accountable and reasonably effective in the vertical silos we call states. What we do not have are adequate mechanisms of horizontal accountability among states.

The conservative critique of the United Nations is all too cogent: while useful for certain peacekeeping and nation-building operations, the United Nations lacks both democratic legitimacy and effectiveness in dealing with serious security issues. The solution is not to strengthen a single global body, but rather to promote what has been emerging in any event, a "multimultilateral world" of overlapping and occasionally competing international institutions that are organized on regional or functional lines. Kosovo in 1999 was a model: when the Russian veto prevented the Security Council from acting, the United States and its NATO allies simply shifted the venue to NATO, where the Russians could not block action.

The final area that needs rethinking, and the one that will be the most contested in the coming months and years, is the place of democracy promotion in American foreign policy. The worst legacy that could come from the Iraq war would be an anti-neoconservative backlash that coupled a sharp turn toward isolation with a cynical realist policy aligning the United States with friendly authoritarians. Good governance, which involves not just democracy but also the rule of law and economic development, is critical to a host of outcomes we desire, from alleviating poverty to dealing with pandemics to controlling violent conflicts. A Wilsonian policy that pays attention to how rulers treat their citizens is therefore right, but it needs to be informed by a certain realism that was missing from the thinking of the Bush administration in its first term and of its neoconservative allies.

We need in the first instance to understand that promoting democracy and modernization in the Middle East is not a solution to the problem of jihadist terrorism; in all likelihood it will make the short-term problem worse, as we have seen in the case of the Palestinian election bringing

Hamas to power. Radical Islamism is a byproduct of modernization itself, arising from the loss of identity that accompanies the transition to a modern, pluralist society. . . . More democracy will mean more alienation, radicalization and—yes, unfortunately—terrorism.

But greater political participation by Islamist groups is very likely to occur whatever we do, and it will be the only way that the poison of radical Islamism can ultimately work its way through the body politic of Muslim communities around the world. The age is long since gone when friendly authoritarians could rule over passive populations and produce stability indefinitely. New social actors are mobilizing everywhere, from Bolivia and Venezuela to South Africa and the Persian Gulf. A durable Israeli-Palestinian peace could not be built upon a corrupt, illegitimate Fatah that constantly had to worry about Hamas challenging its authority. Peace might emerge, sometime down the road, from a Palestine run by a formerly radical terrorist group that had been forced to deal with the realities of governing.

If we are serious about the good governance agenda, we have to shift our focus to the reform, reorganization and proper financing of those institutions of the United States government that actually promote democracy, development and the rule of law around the world, organizations like the State Department, U.S.A.I.D., the National Endowment for Democracy and the like. The United States has played an often decisive role in helping along many recent democratic transitions, including in the Philippines in 1986; South Korea and Taiwan in 1987; Chile in 1988; Poland and Hungary in 1989; Serbia in 2000; Georgia in 2003; and Ukraine in 2004–5. But the overarching lesson that emerges from these cases is that the United States does not get to decide when and where democracy comes about. By definition, outsiders can't "impose" democracy on a country that doesn't want it; demand for democracy and reform must be domestic. Democracy promotion is therefore a long-term and opportunistic process that has to await the gradual ripening of political and economic conditions to be effective.

The Bush administration has been walking—indeed, sprinting—away from the legacy of its first term, as evidenced by the cautious multilateral approach it has taken toward the nuclear programs of Iran and North Korea. Condoleezza Rice gave a serious speech in January about "transformational diplomacy" and has begun an effort to reorganize the nonmilitary side of the foreign-policy establishment, and the National Security Strategy document is being rewritten. All of these are welcome changes, but the legacy of the Bush first-term foreign policy and its neoconservative supporters has been so polarizing that it is going to be hard to have a reasoned debate about how to appropriately balance American ideals and interests in the coming years. The reaction against a flawed policy can be as damaging as the policy itself, and such a reaction is an indulgence we cannot afford, given the critical moment we have arrived at in global politics.

Neoconservatism, whatever its complex roots, has become indelibly associated with concepts like coercive regime change, unilateralism and American hegemony. What is needed now are new ideas, neither neoconservative nor realist, for how America is to relate to the rest of the world—ideas that retain the neoconservative belief in the universality of human rights, but without its illusions about the efficacy of American power and hegemony to bring these ends about.

14

Leadership at Risk

The Perils of Unilateralism

Ralph G. Carter

Many of America's longtime allies are increasingly frustrated, if not down-right angry, with the recent behavior of the United States. On the 57th anniversary of the Hiroshima bombing, Hiroshima Mayor Tadatoshi Akiba lashed out at the American response to the September 11th terrorist attack. . . . As he put it, "The United States government has no right to force Pax Americana on the rest of us, or to unilaterally determine the fate of the world."

Sadly, the mayor's feelings are not unique. The September 11th attacks are the worst-case illustration of "a deep vein of global anti-American resentment." While such resentment might be expected from those who do not share American values, it is more surprising when it comes from those who do share those same values. Such resentments have become a global phenomenon. According to the PEW Research Center, the United States is globally perceived as "Too big, too powerful, too willing to go it alone in the world." According to the Council on Foreign Relations, "Around the world, from Western Europe to the Far East, many see the United States as arrogant, hypocritical, self-absorbed, self-indulgent, and contemptuous of others." The problem is severe enough to warrant the Bush Administration's creation of an Office on Global Communications, designed to polish the American image around the globe.

Image-polishing, spin-doctoring, and other public relations approaches may be helpful, but they can only go so far. The real problem lies in U.S.

unilateralist policies, the list of which is quite long. U.S. rejections of policies endorsed by the rest of the international community include the Ottawa Convention banning land mines, the Comprehensive Test Ban Treaty, the Kyoto Protocol on global warming, the verification protocol for the 1972 Biological Weapons Convention, and the new International Criminal Court. The current Bush Administration went further to "nullify" the prior U.S. signature on the International Criminal Court Treaty, an unprecedented step that raises troubling questions about other prior U.S. commitments. In multiple international venues, the administration continues to advance the exception of U.S. forces from any future prosecution before the ICC, threatening the withdrawal of U.S. funding for global peacekeeping operations if its demands are not met. In bilateral talks, the administration has reportedly threatened to suspend military aid to allies unless they agree to exempt U.S. forces from ICC prosecution.

Other illustrations of unilateralist behavior abound. For over a decade, the United States has withheld either its UN dues payments, or payments on its arrearages, until the UN satisfied U.S. concerns. The United States recently forced the ouster of the executive director of the Organization for the Prohibition of Chemical Weapons, because he was not anti-Iraqi enough to satisfy the Bush Administration. In a move surely to be seen as hypocritical, in 2001 the Bush Administration called on the World Bank to invest more money in education in the developing world but then, in 2002, chose not to provide any funds for the World Bank's education projects. At the 2002 UN General Assembly special session on children, the U.S. delegation insisted upon (and got) a provision exempting the United States from any requirement barring the imposition of the death penalty or life imprisonment for those under the age of 18. Only the United States and Somalia have not ratified the Convention on the Rights of the Child, and the United States is the only advanced industrialized state not to ratify the Convention on the Elimination of Discrimination Against Women. U.S. opposition alone killed a proposed UN convention to limit global trafficking in small arms. Finally, according to one summary, over the past decade the United States has either threatened or imposed unilateral economic sanctions on 35 countries representing over 40% of the global population. Such widespread use of economic sanctions has been called a form of "hyper-unilateralism."

It is one thing to offend one's opponents but quite another to offend one's friends. Behavior such as this creates real tensions with key allies in Western Europe. European allies resent that the United States chooses not to pay its full UN dues, provides less development aid per GDP than do 16 other countries, and fails to ratify treaties that it encourages others to ratify. Many in Europe do not care for U.S. strategic values or instrumental tactics. In their view, Americans tend to act unilaterally and without authorization by others, while Europeans prefer multilateral approaches that respect international institutions and international law. They also see an American preference for violent and confrontational instruments while they prefer diplomatic instruments that emphasize engagement. . . .

High-handed moralism and expressions of American exceptionalism combine to make such policy disputes increasingly difficult to resolve. As a member of the British House of Lords put it, Americans want to be either in charge or not involved. Further, they "like to think that their own country is the uniquely godly power in a world of fallen angels and their ways of thinking are genuinely good for everyone. They are startled and annoyed when others disagree." . . .

Beyond unpopularity, unilateralist actions and appearances have consequences. Even if not used, American power alone elicits anxiety and dread on the part of others. No less than two-thirds of the world's population feels the United States is the greatest single threat their nations face. Countries like France, Russia, China, and India—all of whom prefer a multipolar world of regional powers—can be expected to oppose the United States whenever possible. Consider a recent example. In 2001, following the early actions by the Bush Administration, the United States was voted off as a member of the UN Human Rights Commission. This act was shocking in two ways. First, the United States had been a member of the Commission since its inception. Second, two regimes with records of noted human rights abuses—Sierra Leone and Sudan—were elected to the Commission at the same time. The international community was sending the United States a message. More recently, throughout 2002 the Bush Administration sought international cooperation for its efforts to punish Iraq as a supporter of terrorism and a producer of weapons of mass destruction but got little support—either from its friends in Europe or "moderate" Arab regimes considered allies.

As Stanley Hoffmann points out, "Washington has yet to understand that nothing is more dangerous for a 'hyperpower' than the temptation of unilateralism." Those who do not agree with U.S. actions or attitudes are not required to either follow U.S. wishes or reward U.S. behavior. A troubling example of this comes in the "war on terrorism." President Bush "does not appear to have convinced European publics that the war on terrorism is their war," because they do not feel the United States is waging the war in their interests or the interests of "humanity in general." The U.S. actions seem to reflect a unilateral U.S. agenda, not a widely shared one. Moreover, Bush's attempt to broaden the "war on terrorism" by characterizing Iran, Iraq, and North Korea as an "Axis of Evil" produced strong opposition in Europe, by both publics and leaders. Others know the United States does not like these three regimes, but, with the possible exception of Britain's Tony Blair, they do not feel the United States has produced any evidence to link these regimes with the events on September 11th. . . .

. . . [A]s the terrorist attacks of September 11, 2001 attest, retaliations against American unilateralism may continue to be violent as well. While some terrorists are motivated by who and what Americans *are*, others are motivated by what the U.S. government *does*. When multiple states engage in actions that could inflame potential terrorists, the choice of where and against whom to retaliate becomes muddled. But when the United States takes unilateral actions perceived by potential terrorists to be against Islam . . . it becomes an inviting target for retaliation. In fact, U.S. actions promote anti-American sentiments that help potential terrorists in two ways: by generating both recruits and abettors willing to provide them shelter or assistance.

Unilateralist choices thus risk high costs. The choice to participate in only the international issues the United States cares about and to insist on only U.S.-preferred solutions to those issues may be "good politics" back home, but such behaviors are typically viewed abroad as hegemonic or imperial acts. Over time, it is natural to resent the dominant power, and such resentments arise on the part of both friends and foes. Worse still, such resentments can last for decades. . . . Given U.S. actions in the Mideast, one can only wonder how long anti-U.S. sentiments will last in the broader Arab and Muslim communities. However, regardless of whom the U.S. actions are directed against, unilateralism breeds resentments that linger. "Unilateralism may produce results in the short term, but it is apt to reduce the pool of voluntary help from other countries that the United States can draw on down the road, and thus in the end to make life more difficult rather than less." In short, unilateralism is counterproductive.

The way to avoid these costs is for the United States to pursue its foreign policy goals in a multilateral fashion wherever possible. Current policy makers seem to have forgotten that multilateral approaches have been very successful before. For many, the "heyday" of American leadership in world affairs was the 15 years following the end of the Second World War. At a time of unparalleled relative power, the United States chose *not* to act like a hegemon. Instead, it chose to work with others to build an international architecture of multilayered institutions that created order and dispensed benefits for all those who chose to participate. Such institutions (like the United Nations, the World Bank, the International Monetary Fund, NATO, etc.) helped empower others while addressing American political, national security, and economic objectives. The system lasted, in part, because its participants saw it as legitimate.

Current times seem to demand multilateral foreign policy approaches. As Ikenberry notes, "at key historical turning points, U.S. officials have resorted to multilateral institutional agreements that were related to the basic organization of international relations, using these commitments to advance the goals of grand strategy." The ending of the Cold War and the beginning of a new era certainly qualify as one of those "key historical turning points." As Nye argued over a decade ago, "Americans need to develop better approaches to multilateral burden sharing to deal with issues arising out of the diffusion of power. Yet the United States is the largest country in the international system in both hard and soft power resources, and if the largest power does not lead in organizing multilateral action, no one will."

That lesson is even truer now. The United States may be a unipolar power in military terms, but there are still other major regional military or nuclear powers. Moreover, many of the problems facing the United States cannot be resolved either by military instruments or by the United States acting alone. They require cooperation and economic instruments, and there is no unipolar power in the international economic system. Other major powers can be expected to resist U.S. unilateralist initiatives through counterbalancing strategies wherever possible. Multilateral approaches can help overcome the resentments and concerns of these other powers. "It is here—in the attempt to stabilize world political order during an era of extraordinary power disparities—that multilateral institutions can be most fully justified in the pursuit of the nation's core strategic interests." . . .

The bottom line is that we live in a *quid pro quo* world. If the United States hopes for international cooperation on the issues it cares about, then its leaders should be prepared to cooperate on the issues others care about. Certainly, U.S. leaders should not compromise core societal values, but otherwise U.S. leaders and citizens should expect that, in order to get something, they might have to give something up. To most world governments, a small compromise on sovereignty is a reasonable trade-off if it helps solve global problems. The United States should adopt this approach. Insisting on unfettered U.S. sovereignty at all costs is not only irresponsible in a global community, it ignores the fact that accommodating the interests of others brings benefits to all. . . .

The current international setting is ripe for the promotion of a U.S. foreign policy agenda featuring multilateral approaches to major problems, and prior administrations made some effort in this direction. The creation of NAFTA, APEC, and the WTO on the economic front, as well as the enlargement of NATO on the political-military front, are all examples of such efforts. However, as the litany of unilateralist actions from the mid-1990s on noted earlier indicates, more multilateral efforts can be made.

Current U.S. foreign policy makers ignore the fact that the American public supports multilateralist foreign policy approaches and has done so for a long time. For decades, Americans opposed by a two-to-one margin the argument that "we should go our own way in international matters, not worrying too much about whether other countries agree with us or not." More recently, working through the UN and NATO was endorsed by over 90% of Americans in 1998 and 1999. In 2000, the public was asked: "As a general rule, when it becomes necessary to use military force, do you think it is best for the U.S. to act on its own, to act as part of a United Nations operation, or to act as part of a NATO operation?" Forty-nine percent favored the use of force through the UN, 26% through NATO, and only 17%

favored unilateral uses of force. In 1999, 65% said "yes" when asked: "If another country files a complaint with the World Trade Organization and it rules against the U.S., as a general rule, should the U.S. comply with that decision?" Finally in 2000, 72% thought "the U.S. should do its share in efforts to solve international problems together with other countries." As [Steven] Kull summarizes, "contrary to widespread assumptions among the U.S. policy elite, the American public is not only amenable to multilateral engagement, but indeed strongly prefers it over other options . . . the American public shows strong support for the UN, multilateral use of force, international environmental regimes, international economic institutions, and international legal structures."

. . . While unilateralist initiatives may "feel good" at some emotional level and seem easy to understand and to explain within the borders of the United States, they will not help the United States effectively achieve its foreign policy goals in the near-term future. . . . Working with others to address shared problems is imminently preferable to trying to either "go it alone" or impose the U.S. will on the rest of the world. As Sam Rayburn put it long ago, "You cannot be a leader, and ask other people to follow you, unless you know how to follow, too." . . .

15

Is American Multilateralism in Decline?

G. John Ikenberry

American foreign policy appears to have taken a sharp unilateral turn. A half century of U.S. leadership in constructing an international order around multilateral institutions, rule-based agreements, and alliance partnerships seems to be giving way to a new assertive—even defiant—unilateralism. Over the last several years, the Bush administration has signaled a deep skepticism of multilateralism in a remarkable sequence of rejections of pending international agreements and treaties. . . . More recently, spurred by its war on terrorism, the Bush administration has advanced new, provocative ideas about the American unilateral and preemptive use of force—and under this go-it-alone-if-necessary banner, it defied allies and world public opinion by launching a preventive war against Iraq. "When it comes to our security," President Bush proclaimed, "we really don't need anybody's permission."

Unilateralism, of course, is not a new feature of American foreign policy. In every historical era, the United States has shown a willingness to reject treaties, violate rules, ignore allies, and use military force on its own. But many observers see today's U.S. unilateralism as something much more sweeping—not an occasional ad hoc policy decision, but a new strategic orientation. Capturing this view, one pundit calls it the "new unilateralism". . . .

Indeed, Richard Holbrooke, former U.S. ambassador to the United Nations, has charged that the Bush administration threatens to make "a radical break with 55 years of a bipartisan tradition that sought international agreements and regimes of benefit to us."

America's "new unilateralism" has unsettled world politics. . . . As American power has grown, the rest of the world is confronted with a disturbing double bind. On the one hand, the United States is becoming more crucial to other countries in the realization of their economic and security goals; it is increasingly in a position to help or hurt other countries. But on the other hand, the growth of American power makes the United States less dependent on weaker states, and so it is easier for the United States to resist or ignore these states.

Does this Bush-style unilateralism truly represent a major turn away from the long postwar tradition of multilateralism in American foreign policy? It depends on whether today's American unilateralism is a product of deep structural shifts in the country's global position or if it reflects more contingent and passing circumstances. Does American unipolarity "select" for unilateralism? Do powerful states—when they get the chance—inevitably seek to disentangle themselves from international rules and institutions? Or are more complex considerations at work? The answers to these questions are relevant to determining whether the rise of American preeminence in the years since the end of the Cold War is ultimately consistent with or destined to undermine the post-1945 multilateral international order.

This article makes three arguments:

First, the new unilateralism is not an inevitable reaction to rising American power. The international system may give the United States more opportunities to act unilaterally, but the incentives to do so are actually complex and mixed. And arguably, these incentives make a multilateral approach more—not less—desirable for Washington in many areas of foreign policy.

Second, despite key officials' deep and ideologically driven skepticism about multilateralism, the Bush administration's opposition to multilateralism represents in practical terms an attack on specific types of multilateral agreements more than it does a fundamental assault on the "foundational" multilateralism of the postwar system. . . . In the past, the United States has embraced multilateralism because it provided ways to protect American freedom of action: escape clauses, weighted voting, and veto rights. The "new unilateralism" is in part a product of the "new multilateralism," which offers fewer opportunities for the United States to exercise political control over others and fewer ways to escape the binding obligations of the agreements.

Weaker states have responded to the rise of American unipolarity by seeking to embed the United States further in binding institutional relationships (in effect, to "tie Gulliver down"), while American officials attempt to get the benefits of a multilateral order without accepting greater encroachments on its policy autonomy. We are witnessing not an end to multilateralism but a struggle over its scope and character. A "politics of institutions" is being played out between the United States and the rest of the world within the United Nations, the North Atlantic Treaty Organization (NATO), the World Trade Organization (WTO), and other postwar multilateral fora.

Third, the circumstances that led the United States to engage in multilateral cooperation in the past are still present and, in some ways, have actually increased. In particular, there are three major sources of multilateralism: functional demands for cooperation . . . ; hegemonic power management, both to institutionalize power advantages and, by reducing the arbitrary and indiscriminate exercise of power, to make the hegemonic order more stable and legitimate; and the American legal-institutional political tradition of seeing this domestic rule-of-law orientation manifest in the country's approach to international order. . . .

WHAT IS MULTILATERALISM?

Multilateralism involves the coordination of relations among three or more states according to a set of rules or principles. . . . Multilateralism entails some reduction in policy autonomy, since the choices and actions of the participating states are—at least to some degree—constrained by the agreed-upon rules and principles.

Multilateralism can operate at three levels of international order: system multilateralism, ordering or foundational multilateralism, and contract multilateralism. At the most basic level, it is manifest in the Westphalian state system, where norms of sovereignty, formal equality, and legal-diplomatic practice prevail. . . . At a more intermediate level, multilateralism can refer to the political-economic organization of regional or international order. John Ruggie notes that "an 'open' and 'liberal' international economic order is multilateral in form." The overall organization of relations among the advanced industrial countries has this basic multilateral characteristic. . . . At the surface level, multilateralism also refers to specific intergovernmental treaties and agreements. These can be thought of as distinct "contracts" among states.

Multilateralism can also be understood in terms of the binding character of the rules and principles that guide interstate relations. In its loosest form, multilateralism can simply entail general consultations and informal adjustments among states. . . . This loose, nonbinding type of multilateralism can be found today in the Asia Pacific Economic Cooperation (APEC), which was established in the early 1990s to promote regional economic cooperation. The WTO and other multilateral economic institutions entail more formal, treaty-based agreements that specify certain commitments and obligations. But the binding character of these multilateral agreements is still qualified: escape clauses, weighted voting, opt-out agreements, and veto rights are all part of the major post-1945 multilateral agreements. The most binding multilateral agreements are ones where states actually cede sovereignty in specific areas to supranational authorities. The European Union is the most important manifestation of this sovereignty-transferring, legally binding multilateralism. . . .

When deciding whether to sign a multilateral agreement, a state faces a trade-off. In choosing to abide by the rules and norms of the agreement, the state must accept a reduction in its policy autonomy. That is, it must agree to some constraints on its freedom of action—or independence of policy making—in a particular area. But in exchange, it expects other states to do the same. The multilateral bargain will be attractive to a state if it concludes that the benefits that flow to it through the coordination of policies are greater than the costs of lost policy autonomy. In an ideal world, a state might want to operate in an international environment in which all other states are heavily rule-bound while leaving itself entirely unencumbered by rules and institutional restraints. But because all states are inclined in this way, the question becomes one of how much autonomy each must relinquish in order to get rule-based behavior out of the others.

A state's willingness to agree to a multilateral bargain will hinge on several factors that shape the ultimate cost-benefit calculation. One is whether the policy constraints imposed on other states (*states b, c*, and *d*) really matter to the first state (*state a*). If the "unconstrained" behavior of other states is judged to have no undesirable impact on *a*, then *a* will be unwilling to give up any policy autonomy of its own. It also matters if the participating states can credibly restrict their policy autonomy. If *a* is not convinced that *b, c*, and *d* can actually be constrained by multilateral rules and norms, it will not be willing to sacrifice its own policy autonomy. Likewise, if the agreement is to work, *a* will need to convince the other states that it too will be constrained. . . .

When multilateral bargains are made by states with highly unequal power, the considerations can be more complex. The more that a powerful state is capable of dominating or abandoning weaker states, the more the weaker states will care about constraints on the leading state's policy autonomy. In other words, they will be more eager to see some limits placed on the arbitrary and indiscriminate exercise of power by the leading state. Similarly, the more that the powerful state can restrain itself in a credible fashion, the more that weaker states will be interested in multilateral rules and norms that accomplish this end. When both these conditions hold—when the leading state can use its power to dominate and abandon, and when it can restrain and commit itself—the weaker states will be particularly eager for a deal. They will, of course, also care about the positive benefits that accrue from cooperation. . . .

VARIETIES OF MULTILATERALISM

In this light, it is easy to see why the United States sought to build a post-1945 order around multilateral economic and security agreements such as the Bretton Woods agreements on monetary and trade relations and the

NATO security pact. The United States ended World War II in an unprecedented power position, so the weaker European states attached a premium
to taming and harnessing this newly powerful state. Britain, France, and
other major states were willing to accept multilateral agreements to the extent that they also constrained and regularized U.S. economic and security
actions. American agreement to operate within a multilateral economic
order and make an alliance-based security commitment to Europe was
worth the price: it ensured that Germany and the rest of Western Europe
would be integrated into a wider, American-centered international order. At
the same time, the actual restraints on U.S. policy were minimal. Convert-
ible currencies and open trade were in the United States' basic national economic interest. The United States did make a binding security guarantee to
Western Europe, and this made American power more acceptable to Europeans, who were then more eager to cooperate with the United States in
other areas. But the United States did not forswear the right to unilaterally
use force elsewhere. It supported multilateral economic and security relations with Europe, and it agreed to operate economically and militarily
within multilateral institutions organized around agreed-upon rules and
principles. In return, it ensured that Western Europe would be firmly an-
chored in an Atlantic and global political order that advanced America's
long-term national interest. . . .

. . . [T]he international order that took shape after 1945 was decidedly
multilateral. A core objective of American postwar strategists was to ensure
that the world did not break apart into 1930s-style closed regions. An open
system of trade and investment—enshrined in the General Agreement on
Tariffs and Trade (GATT) and the Bretton Woods agreement—provided one
multilateral foundation to the postwar order. The alliance ties between the
United States and Europe provided another. NATO was not just a narrow security pact but was seen by its founders as an extension of the collective
self-defense provision of the UN Charter. The security of Europe and America are bound together; the parties thus have substantial consultative and decision-making obligations to each other. This indivisibility of economic and
security relations is what has given the Western-centered international order
a deep multilateral character. The United States makes commitments to other
participating states—that is, it provides security protection and access to its
markets, technology, and society in the context of an open international system. In exchange, other states agree to be stable political partners with the
United States and offer it economic, diplomatic, and logistical support. . . .

On top of this foundational multilateral order, a growing number and variety of multilateral agreements have been offered up and signed by states.
At a global level, between 1970 and 1997, the number of international
treaties more than tripled; and from 1985 through 1999 alone, the number
of international institutions increased by two-thirds. What this means is that
an expanding number of multilateral "contracts" is being proposed and

agreed to by states around the world. The United States has become party to more and more of these contracts. This is reflected in the fact that the number of multilateral treaties in force for the United States steadily grew during the twentieth century. There were roughly 150 multilateral treaties in force in 1950, 400 in 1980, and close to 600 in 2000. In the most recent five-year period, 1996 through 2000, the United States ratified roughly the same number of treaties as in earlier postwar periods. Other data . . . indicate an increase in bilateral treaties passed by the Congress and a slight decrease in the number of multilateral treaties from 1945 through 2000. Measured in these rough aggregate terms, the United States has not significantly backed away from what is a more and more dense web of international treaties and agreements.

Two conclusions follow from these observations. First, in the most general of terms, there has not been a dramatic decline in the propensity of the United States to enter into multilateral treaties. In fact, the United States continues to take on multilateral commitments at a steady rate. . . . Second, even if the United States does act unilaterally in opposing specific multilateral treaties that come along, it is important to distinguish these rejected "contracts" from the older foundational agreements that give the basic order its multilateral form. There is no evidence of "rollback" at this deeper level of order. But it is necessary to look more closely at the specific explanations for American multilateralism and the recent unilateral turn.

UNIPOLAR POWER AND MULTILATERALISM

The simplest explanation for the new unilateralism is that the United States has grown in power during the 1990s, thereby reducing its incentives to operate within a multilateral order. As one pundit has put it: "Any nation with so much power always will be tempted to go it alone. Power breeds unilateralism. It is as simple as that." This is a structural-realist explanation that says, in effect, that because of the shifting distribution of power in favor of the United States, the international system is increasingly "selecting" for unilateralism in its foreign policy. The United States has become so powerful that it does not need to sacrifice its autonomy or freedom of action within multilateral agreements. Unipolar power gives the United States the ability to act alone and do so without serious costs.

Today's international order, then, is at the early stage of a significant transformation triggered by what will be a continuous and determined effort by a unipolar America to disentangle itself from the multilateral restraints of an earlier era. It matters little who is president and what political party runs the government. The United States will exercise its power more directly—less mediated or constrained by international rules, institutions, or alliances. The result will be an international order that is more hegemonic than multilateral, more power-based than rule-based. The rest of the world will complain, but will not be able or willing to impose sufficient costs on the United States to alter its growing unilateral orientation.

This explanation for the decline of American multilateralism rests on several considerations. First, the United States has turned into a unipolar global power without historical precedent. The 1990s surprised the world. Many observers expected the end of the Cold War to usher in a multipolar order with increasingly equal centers of power in Asia, Europe, and America. Instead, the United States began the decade as the world's only superpower and proceeded to grow more powerful at the expense of the other major states. Between 1990 and 1998, the United States' gross national product grew 27 percent, Europe's 16 percent, and Japan's 7 percent. Today, the American economy is equal to the economies of Japan, the United Kingdom, and Germany combined. The United States' military capacity is even more in a league of its own. It spends as much on defense as the next 14 countries taken together. It has bases in 40 countries. Eighty percent of world military research and development takes place in the United States. What the 1990s wrought is a unipolar America that is more powerful than any other great state in history.

Second, these massive power advantages give the United States opportunities to resist entanglements in multilateral rules and institutions. Multilateralism can be a tool or expedient in some circumstances, but states will avoid or shed entanglements in rules and institutions when they can. This realist vision of multilateralism is captured by Robert Kagan, who argues that multilateralism is a "weapon of the weak." He adds: "When the United States was weak, it practiced the strategies of indirection, the strategies of weakness; now that the United States is powerful, it behaves as powerful nations do." . . .

According to this view, the American willingness to act multilaterally during the postwar era was an artifact of the bipolar struggle. The United States needed allies, and the construction of this "free world" coalition entailed some American willingness to agree to multilateral commitments and restraints. Yet even during the Cold War decades, realists note, multilateral economic and security commitments did not entail great compromises on American policy autonomy. Voting shares, veto power, and escape clauses have been integral to American multilateralism during this earlier era. Today, even these contingent multilateral commitments and restraints are unnecessary.

Third, the shifting power differentials have also created new divergent interests between the United States and the rest of the world, a fact that further reduces possibilities for multilateral cooperation. For example, the sheer size of the American economy—and a decade of growth unmatched by Europe, Japan, or the other advanced countries—means that U.S. obligations under the Kyoto Protocol would be vastly greater than those of other states. The United States has global interests and security threats that no other state has. Its troops are the ones most likely to be dispatched to distant battlefields, which means that it is more exposed than other states to the legal liabilities of the ICC. The United States must worry about threats to its interests in all major regions of the world. Such unipolar power is a unique target for terrorism. It is not surprising that Europeans and Asians make different assessments of terrorist threats and rogue states seeking weapons of mass destruction than American officials do. Since multilateralism entails working within agreed-upon rules and institutions about the use of force, this growing divergence will make multilateral agreements less easy to achieve—and less desirable in the view of the United States.

This structural-power perspective on multilateralism generates useful insights. One such insight is that the United States—as well as other states—has walked away from international rules and agreements when they did not appear to advance American interests. This helps to explain a lot about American foreign policy over many decades. . . .

But the more general claim about unipolarity and the decline of multilateralism is misleading. To begin with, at earlier moments of power preeminence, the United States did not shy away from multilateralism. As Fareed Zakaria notes:

> America was the most powerful country in the world when it proposed the creation of an international organization, the League of Nations, to manage international relations after the First World War. It was the dominant power at the end of the Second World War, when it founded the United Nations, created the Bretton Woods system of international economic cooperation, and launched most of the world's key international organizations.

During the 1990s, the United States again used its unrivaled position after the end of the Cold War to advance new multilateral agreements, including the WTO, NAFTA (the North American Free Trade Agreement), and APEC. There is no necessary or simple connection between a state's power position and its inclinations toward multilateralism, a tool that weak and strong alike can use.

What is most distinctive about American policy is its mixed record on multilateralism. The United States is not rolling back its commitments to foundational multilateralism, but it is picking and choosing among the variety of multilateral agreements being negotiated today. Power considerations—and American unipolar power—surely are part of the explanation for both the calculations that go into American decisions and the actions of other states. The United States has actively championed the WTO but is resisting a range of arms control treaties. One has to look beyond gross power distributions and identify more specific costs and incentives that inform state policy.

The chief problem with the structural-power explanation for America's new unilateralism is that it hinges on an incomplete accounting of the potential costs of unilateralism. The assumption is that the United States has become so powerful that other countries are unable to impose costs if it acts alone. On economic, environmental, and security issues, the rhetorical question that the United States can always ask when confronted with opposition to American unilateralism is this: they may not like it, but what are they going to do about it? According to this view, the United States is increasingly in the position that it was in East Asia during the early Cold War: it is so hegemonic that it has few incentives to tie itself to multilateral rules and institutions, and it can win on issues that it cares about by going it alone or bargaining individually with weaker states. This view—as we shall see below—is a very superficial reading of the situation.

UNIPOLARITY AND UNILATERALIST IDEOLOGIES

One source of the new unilateralism does follow—at least indirectly—from unipolar power. The United States is so powerful that the ideologies and policy views of a few key decision makers in Washington can have a huge impact on the global order, even if these views are not necessarily representative of the wider foreign policy community or of public opinion. In effect, the United States is so powerful that the structural pressures associated with anarchy—which lead to security competition and relative gains calculations—decline radically. The passing views of highly placed administration elites matter more than in other states or international structural circumstances.

Indeed, the Bush administration does have a large group of officials who have articulated deep intellectual reservations about international treaties and multilateral organizations. Many of America's recent departures from multilateralism are agreements dealing with arms control and proliferation. In this area, American policy elites are deeply divided on how to advance the nation's security—a division that dates back to right-wing opposition to American arms control diplomacy with the Soviet Union during the Nixon-Kissinger era. . . .

Some observers contend that the Bush administration has embraced a more ambitious unilateralist agenda aimed at rolling back and disentangling the United States from post-1945 foundational multilateral rules and institutions. Grand strategic ideas of this sort are circulating inside and outside the administration. One version of this thinking is simply old-style nationalism that sees international institutions and agreements as a basic threat to American sovereignty. Another version—increasingly influential in Washington—is advanced by the so-called neoconservative movement, which seeks to use American power to singlehandedly reshape entire countries, particularly in the Middle East, so as to make them more congenial with American interests. This is a neo-imperial vision of American order that requires the United States to unshackle itself from the norms and institutions of multilateral action (and from partners that reject the neo-imperial project).

It is possible that this neo-imperial agenda could undermine the wider and deeper multilateral order. Given sufficient time and opportunity, a small group of determined foreign policy officials could succeed in subverting multilateral agreements and alliance partnerships—even if such steps were opposed by the wider foreign policy community and the American public. This could be done intentionally or it could happen indirectly if, by violating core multilateral rules and norms, the credibility of American commitment to the wider array of agreements and norms becomes suspect and the entire multilateral edifice crumbles. . . .

It is extremely doubtful, however, that a neo-imperial foreign policy can be sustained at home or abroad. There is no evidence that the American people are eager for or willing to support such a transformed global role. It is not clear that the country will even be willing to bear the costs of re-building Iraq, let alone undertake a global neo-imperial campaign to over-turn and rebuild other countries in the region. Moreover, if the neoconservative agenda is really focused on promoting democracy in the Arab and Muslim world, the unilateral use of force will be of limited and diminishing importance, while the multilateral engagement of the region will be critical. In the end, a determined, ideologically motivated policy elite can push the United States in dramatic new directions, but electoral cycles and democratic politics make it difficult for costly and self-destructive policy orientations to be sustained over the long term. . . .

SOURCES OF MULTILATERALISM

The United States is not structurally destined to disentangle itself from the multilateral order and go it alone. Indeed, there continue to be deep underlying incentives for the United States to support multilateralism—incentives that in many ways are increasing. . . .

Interdependence and Functional Multilateralism

American support for multilateralism is likely to be sustained, even in the face of resistance and ideological challenges to multilateralism within the Bush administration, in part because of a simple logic: as global economic interdependence grows, so does the need for multilateral coordination of policies. The more economically interconnected states become, the more dependent they are on the actions of other states for the realization of objectives. . . .

One theoretical tradition, neoliberal institutionalism, provides an explanation for the rise of multilateral institutions under these circumstances. Institutions perform a variety of functions, such as reducing uncertainty and the costs of transactions between states. Mutually beneficial exchanges are missed in the absence of multilateral rules and procedures, which help states overcome collective action, asymmetrical information, and the fear that other states will cheat or act opportunistically. In effect, multilateral rules and institutions provide a contractual environment within which states can more easily pursue joint gains. Likewise, as the density of interactions between states increases, so will the demand for rules and institutions that facilitate these interactions. In this sense, multilateralism is self-reinforcing. . . .

This argument helps explain why a powerful state might support multilateral agreements, particularly in trade and other economic policy areas. . . . [T]he leading state has a major interest in inducing smaller states to open their economies and participate in an integrated world economy. . . . But to get weaker states to commit themselves to an open and increasingly elaborate rule-based regime, it must establish its own reliability. It must be willing to commit itself credibly to the same rules and institutions. It will be necessary for the dominant state to reduce its policy autonomy—and do so in a way that other states find credible. . . . The United States demands an expanding and ever-more complex international economic environment, but to get the support of other states, the United States must itself become more embedded in this system of rules and institutions. . . .

Hegemonic Power and Strategic Restraint

American support for multilateralism also stems from a grand strategic interest in preserving power and creating a stable and legitimate international order. This logic is particularly evident at major historical turning points—such as 1919, 1945, and after the Cold War—when the United States has faced choices about how to use power and organize interstate relations. The support for multilateralism is a way to signal restraint and commitment to other states, thereby encouraging the acquiescence and cooperation of weaker states. The United States has pursued this strategy to varying degrees across the twentieth century—and this reflects the remarkably durable and legitimate character of the existing international order. From this perspective, multilateralism—and the search for rule-based agreements—should increase rather than decrease with the rise of American unipolarity. . . .

This theoretical perspective begins by looking at the choices that dominant states face when they are in a position to shape the fundamental character of the international order. A state that wins a war, or through some other turn of events finds itself in a dominant global position, faces a choice: it can use its power to bargain and coerce other states in struggles over the distribution of gains, or, knowing that its power position will someday decline and that there are costs to enforcing its way within the order, it can move toward a more rule-based, institutionalized order in exchange for the acquiescence and compliant participation of weaker states.

In seeking a more rule-based order, the leading state is agreeing to engage in strategic restraint—it is acknowledging that there will be limits on the way in which it can exercise its power. Such an order, in effect, has "constitutional" characteristics. Limits are set on what a state within the order can do with its power advantages. Just as in constitutional polities, the implications of "winning" in politics are reduced. Weaker states realize that the implications of their inferior position are limited and perhaps temporary; operation within the order, despite their disadvantages, does not risk everything, nor will it give the dominant state a permanent advantage. . . .

Multilateralism becomes a mechanism by which a dominant state and weaker ones can reach a bargain over the character of international order. The dominant state reduces its "enforcement costs" and succeeds in establishing an order where weaker states will participate willingly rather than resist or balance against the leading power. It accepts some restrictions on how it can use its power. The rules and institutions that are created serve as an "investment" in the longer-run preservation of its power advantages. Weaker states agree to the order's rules and institutions. In return, they are assured that the worst excesses of the leading state—manifest as arbitrary and indiscriminate abuses of state power—will be avoided, and they gain institutional opportunities to work and help influence the leading state.

Arguably, this institutional bargain has been at the heart of the postwar Western order. After World War II, the United States launched history's most ambitious era of institution building. The UN, the IMF, the World Bank, GATT, NATO, and other institutions that emerged provided the most rule-based structure for political and economic relations in world history. The United States was deeply ambivalent about making permanent security commitments to other states or allowing its political and economic policies to be dictated by intergovernmental bodies. The Soviet threat during the Cold War was critical in overcoming these doubts. Networks and political relationships were built that made American power farther-reaching and durable but also more predictable and restrained. . . .

In its most extreme versions, today's new unilateralism appears to be a violation of this postwar bargain. Certainly this is the view of some Europeans and others around the world. But if the Bush administration's unilateral moves are seen as more limited—and not emerging as a basic challenge to the foundations of multilateralism—this observation might be incorrect. The problem with the argument about order built on an institutional bargain and strategic restraint is that it reflects judgments by decision makers about how much institutional restraint and commitment by the dominant state is necessary to secure how much participatory acquiescence and compliance by weaker states. The Bush administration might calculate that the order is sufficiently stable that the United States can resist an entire range of new multilateral agreements and still not trigger costly responses from its partners. It might also *miscalculate* in this regard and do great damage to the existing order. Yet if the thesis about the constitutional character of the postwar Western order is correct, a basic turn away from multilateralism should not occur. . . .

CONCLUSION

The rise of unipolarity is not an adequate explanation for recent unilateralism in American foreign policy. Nor is the United States doomed to shed its multilateral orientation. The dominant power position of the United States creates opportunities to go it alone, but the pressures and incentives that shape decisions about multilateral cooperation are quite varied and crosscutting. The sources of multilateralism—which can be traced to system, institutional, and domestic structural locations—still exist and continue to shape and restrain the Bush administration, unilateral inclinations notwithstanding.

Multilateralism can be manifest at the system, ordering, and contract levels of international order. The critical question is not whether the Bush administration is more inclined than previous administrations to reject specific multilateral treaties and agreements (in some instances, it is), but whether the accumulation of these refusals undermines the deeper organizational logic of multilateralism in the Western and global system. At the ordering or foundational level, multilateralism is manifest in what might be termed "indivisible" economic and security relations. The basic organization of the order is multilateral in that it is open and tied together through diffuse reciprocity and cooperative security. But there is little or no evidence that ordering multilateralism is eroding or under attack. . . .

IV

Attitudes toward American Power at Home and Abroad

OVERVIEW

Differences over the Iraq war created deep fissures in relations between the United States and several of its longtime European allies, especially France and Germany. In February 2005, President George W. Bush embarked on a fence-mending trip to Europe only one month into his second term of office. Speaking in Brussels, home of the European Union headquarters, Bush described what he saw as the common responsibility of the United States and its democratic allies in Europe: "We must be on the side of democratic reformers. We must encourage democratic movements. And we must support democratic transitions in practical ways. . . . Freedom is the direction of history, because freedom is the permanent hope of humanity" ("Bush's Speech in Brussels," *New York Times*, February 21, 2005).

Although Bush's meetings with European leaders did appear to ease tensions in transatlantic relations, Bush's challenge to Europe to join America in a campaign to secure democracy across the globe seemed unlikely to move a deeply skeptical European public. In an AP-Ipsos poll taken shortly before Bush's European trip, 84 percent of French respondents felt that the United States should not pursue democracy promotion as a central goal in its foreign policy; 80 percent of Germans and 66 percent of Britons took the same position, along with half of respondents in Spain and Italy. Interestingly, 53 percent of Americans also thought that the United States should not attempt to spread democracy abroad ("Poll Shows Doubts over Bush Democracy Push," *New York Times*, February 22, 2005).

The idealist strain that is evident in the foreign policy of the Bush administration is not new. Beginning with Woodrow Wilson, most U.S. presidents have proclaimed the desire to promote American values and institutions abroad. Just as often, idealistic rationales for America's international behavior have evoked a mixed response beyond U.S. borders. Some have admired America's willingness to assist oppressed peoples in freeing themselves from tyrannical rule. Others have viewed America's idealistic words and deeds as arrogant, hypocritical, or naive. This skepticism is at its most intense when American claims to promote democracy abroad are offered as justification for the use of military force, as in Vietnam during the 1960s and Iraq today.

The selections in this part of the book explore differences in the ways that political leaders and publics here and abroad view the purposes and values that drive U.S. foreign policy. The focus is on the United States and Europe, although the final chapter describes public opinion in the Middle East and other parts of the world as well. The authors of these chapters differ over a number of questions. How deep is the divide between American and European worldviews? Can disagreements over the Iraq war and other issues be attributed to fundamental differences in political culture, or do other factors, such as differing positions of power or recent historical experience, play more important roles? In Europe and in other parts of the world, does criticism of U.S. foreign policy also mean a rejection of core American values, such as support for democracy, political freedom, and market economics?

Explaining the Divide: Culture or Power?

Minxin Pei argues that America is a highly nationalistic society even though most Americans fail to acknowledge the role that nationalism plays in U.S. attitudes toward the world. In America, however, nationalism takes a different form than is typical in other parts of the world. America's "civic nationalism" revolves around a set of democratic ideals rather than ties of culture or ethnicity. In comparison with other nationalisms, American nationalism is universalistic rather than particular, triumphal rather than aggrieved, and forward-looking rather than backward-looking. Americans assume that their values and beliefs are applicable to all peoples and seek to spread these ideals by means of U.S. foreign policy. This makes it difficult for Americans to recognize, understand, and respond constructively to strong expressions of ethnic and cultural nationalism in other societies. In turn, America's insensitivity toward the collective identities of other societies and its moralistic, universalizing rhetoric generate resentment and resistance against U.S. power elsewhere in the world.

Robert Kagan rejects the view that recent strains between the United States and Europe can be attributed to underlying differences in political culture. Instead, he argues that relative power is a more important factor. As a global superpower, the United States naturally prefers the freedom of choice that accompanies a unilateralist approach to foreign policy and relies more heavily upon military means than other states. By virtue of its great power, the United States enjoys the options of acting alone or employing force when necessary. European countries, by contrast, are too weak to consider such options. Instead, European leaders prefer a strong system of international law and multilateral institutions that mask their own weakness and set predictable limits on the exercise of U.S. power.

A second source of differing U.S. and European perspectives, Kagan asserts, stems from recent historical experience. Western Europeans responded to the devastation of World War II by seeking political and economic unity under the umbrella of supranational institutions. The European Union served to avert a return to traditional patterns of military rivalry and promote a steady process of political and economic integration. Since the end of the cold war, many eastern European countries have joined this expanding European oasis of peace and prosperity. Based upon this experience, many Europeans seek to export this recipe for resolving international conflict by promoting the spread of international law and institutions on a global basis.

What Europeans sometimes forget, claims Kagan, is that Europe's pacific union was made possible only by virtue of the security guarantees provided by the United States in the context of the cold war. The United States, which bore the brunt of efforts to contain Soviet power around the world for half a century, learned the lesson that rules and institutions cannot substitute for power. As a result, American leaders are far more skeptical about the applicability of the European model to strife-torn regions in other parts of the world.

Comparing Public Attitudes

In contrast with Pei and Kagan, Todd S. Sechser's review of U.S. and European opinion on a range of issues casts doubt upon the common claim that American and European sentiments on foreign affairs are widely divergent. On several crucial dimensions—attitudes toward the use of military force, the nature of international threats, the willingness to engage in multilateral institutions, and interest in exercising global leadership—American and European public opinion share much in common. If the Bush administration's unilateralist foreign policies seem out of step with European opinion, they are perceived with similar skepticism at home. If Sechser is correct, then tensions between the United States and Europe may stem more from the style and policies of the current U.S. president than from deeper or more lasting sources.

A massive international survey project conducted by the PEW Global Attitudes Project offers a mixed picture of international opinion toward the United States. On the one hand, there is widespread support in most of the countries surveyed for broad political and economic objectives regularly championed by U.S. presidents, including democracy, free markets, and globalization. Yet large majorities in most countries also express opposition to the invasion of Iraq and many other aspects of U.S. foreign policy. This may signal skepticism about the professed motives of U.S. policymakers, about the means chosen to pursue U.S. objectives (e.g., military force), or about the gap between promised results and actual consequences. Regardless of which interpretation we choose, it appears that U.S. credibility abroad has taken a beating over recent years.

Responses to American Power

The final contribution to this part offers a look at the varied ways in which other states can and have responded to American power. Stephen M. Walt argues that political leaders in other countries have a variety of options, ranging from accommodation to balking to balancing, in dealing with the overriding reality of American dominance. To encourage more cooperative responses, the United States must exercise its power with restraint, with due consideration for the interests of others, and with close attention to the problem of international legitimacy.

Conclusion

International attitudes toward American power make a difference. Despite its enormous resources, the United States needs the cooperation of others in order to successfully fight terrorism or to achieve many of its other international goals. It will be difficult to obtain sustained cooperation from other governments if public opinion abroad is distrustful or even hostile toward the United States. Even where the United States has the power to impose its will, this is a far more costly method of exercising influence than providing a kind of global leadership that others willingly follow. As a first step toward closing the divide, it is important that Americans make the effort to examine the world and the U.S. role in it through the eyes of others.

DISCUSSION QUESTIONS

1. What are some common symbols or expressions of American nationalism (or patriotism) that we encounter in our daily lives?

2. Is America's foreign policy behavior abroad consistent with the ideals that America proclaims to uphold?

3. In what ways does American political culture and sense of national identity limit the ability of Americans to understand other forms of nationalism? Can you think of examples where this has undermined the effectiveness of U.S. foreign policy?

4. Are differences between the United States and Europe over multilateralism, international institutions, and the use of force due mainly to the gap in power between them or to other causes?

5. What do Sechser's findings on American and European opinion suggest about the prospects for improving U.S.-European relations over the long term?

6. Is rising anti-American sentiment abroad simply a short-term reaction to the Iraq war? Or do such attitudes have deeper and more fundamental sources?

SUGGESTED READINGS

Aspen Institute. *From Values to Advocacy: Activating the Public's Support for U.S. Engagement in an Interdependent World.* Washington, D.C.: Aspen Institute, 2002.

Brooks, Stephen. *America through Foreign Eyes: Classic Interpretations of American Political Life.* Don Mills, Ont.: Oxford University Press Canada, 2002.

Kagan, Robert. *Paradise and Power: America and Europe in the New World Order.* New York: Knopf, 2003.

Kull, Steven, and I. M. Destler. *Misreading the Public: The Myth of a New Isolationism.* Washington, D.C.: Brookings Institution Press, 1999.

Lieven, Anatol. *America Right or Wrong: An Anatomy of American Nationalism.* New York: Oxford University Press, 2004.

Page, Benjamin I., with Marshall M. Bouton. *The Foreign Policy Disconnect: What American Want from Our Leaders but Don't Get.* Chicago: University of Chicago Press, 2006.

Purdy, Jedediah. *Being America: Liberty, Commerce, and Violence in an American World,* rev. ed. New York: Vintage, 2004.

16

The Paradoxes of American Nationalism

Minxin Pei

As befits a nation of immigrants, American nationalism is defined not by notions of ethnic superiority, but by a belief in the supremacy of U.S. democratic ideals. This disdain for Old World nationalism creates a dual paradox in the American psyche: First, although the United States is highly nationalistic, it doesn't see itself as such. Second, despite this nationalistic fervor, U.S. policymakers generally fail to appreciate the power of nationalism abroad.

Nearly two years after the horrific terrorist attacks on the United States, international public opinion has shifted from heartfelt sympathy for Americans and their country to undisguised antipathy. The immediate catalyst for this shift is the United States' hard-line policy toward and subsequent war with Iraq. Yet today's strident anti-Americanism represents much more than a wimpy reaction to U.S. resolve or generic fears of a hegemon running amok. Rather, the growing unease with the United States should be seen as a powerful global backlash against the spirit of American nationalism that shapes and animates U.S. foreign policy.

Any examination of the deeper sources of anti-Americanism should start with an introspective look at American nationalism. But in the United States, this exercise, which hints at serious flaws in the nation's character, generates little enthusiasm. Moreover, coming to terms with today's growing animosity toward the United States is intellectually contentious because of the two paradoxes of American nationalism: First, although the United

States is a highly nationalistic country, it genuinely does not see itself as such. Second, despite the high level of nationalism in American society, U.S. policymakers have a remarkably poor appreciation of the power of nationalism in other societies and have demonstrated neither skill nor sensitivity in dealing with its manifestations abroad.

BLIND TO ONE'S VIRTUE

Nationalism is a dirty word in the United States, viewed with disdain and associated with Old World parochialism and imagined supremacy. Yet those who discount the idea of American nationalism may readily admit that Americans, as a whole, are extremely patriotic. When pushed to explain the difference between patriotism and nationalism, those same skeptics might concede, reluctantly, that there is a distinction, but no real difference. Political scientists have labored to prove such a difference, equating patriotism with allegiance to one's country and defining nationalism as sentiments of ethno-national superiority. In reality, however, the psychological and behavioral manifestations of nationalism and patriotism are indistinguishable, as is the impact of such sentiments on policy.

Polling organizations routinely find that Americans display the highest degree of national pride among Western democracies. Researchers at the University of Chicago reported that before the September 11, 2001, terrorist attacks, 90 percent of the Americans surveyed agreed with the statement "I would rather be a citizen of America than of any other country in the world"; 38 percent endorsed the view that "The world would be a better place if people from other countries were more like the Americans." (After the terrorist attacks, 97 and 49 percent, respectively, agreed with the same statements.) The World Values Survey reported similar results, with more than 70 percent of those surveyed declaring themselves "very proud" to be Americans. By comparison, the same survey revealed that less than half of the people in other Western democracies—including France, Italy, Denmark, Great Britain, and the Netherlands—felt "very proud" of their nationalities. . . .

Americans not only take enormous pride in their values but also regard them as universally applicable. According to the Pew Global Attitudes survey, 79 percent of the Americans polled agreed that "It's good that American ideas and customs are spreading around the world"; 70 percent said they "like American ideas about democracy." These views, however, are not widely shared, even in Western Europe, another bastion of liberalism and democracy. Pew found that, among the Western European countries surveyed, less than 40 percent endorse the spread of American ideas and customs, and less than 50 percent like American ideas about democracy.

Such firmly held beliefs in the superiority of American political values and institutions readily find expression in American social, cultural, and political practices. It is almost impossible to miss them: the daily ritual of the Pledge of Allegiance in the nation's schools, the customary performance of the national anthem before sporting events, and the ubiquitous American flags. And in the United States, as in other countries, nationalist sentiments inevitably infuse politics. Candidates rely on hot-button issues such as flag burning and national security to attack their opponents as unpatriotic and worse.

Why does a highly nationalistic society consistently view itself as anything but? The source of this paradox lies in the forces that sustain nationalism in the United States. Achievements in science and technology, military strength, economic wealth, and unrivaled global political influence can no doubt generate strong national pride. But what makes American nationalism truly exceptional are the many ways in which it is naturally expressed in daily life.

One of the most powerful wellsprings of American nationalism is civic voluntarism—the willingness of ordinary citizens to contribute to the public good, either through individual initiatives or civic associations. Outside observers, starting with the French philosopher Alexis de Tocqueville in the early 19th century, have never ceased to be amazed by this font of American dynamism. "Americans of all ages, all stations in life, and all types of dispositions are forever forming associations," noted Tocqueville, who credited Americans for relying on themselves, instead of government, to solve society's problems.

The same grass-roots activism that animates the country's social life also makes American nationalism vibrant and alluring, for most of the institutions and practices that promote and sustain American nationalism are civic, not political; the rituals are voluntary rather than imposed; and the values inculcated are willingly embraced, not artificially indoctrinated. Elsewhere in the world, the state plays an indispensable role in promoting nationalism, which is frequently a product of political manipulation by elites and consequently has a manufactured quality to it. But in the United States, although individual politicians often try to exploit nationalism for political gains, the state is conspicuously absent. . . .

The history of the pledge is an exquisite example of the United States' unique take on nationalism. Francis Bellamy, a socialist Baptist minister, wrote the original text in 1892; three major American civic associations (the National Education Association, the American Legion, and the Daughters of the American Revolution) instituted, refined, and expanded the ceremony of reciting it. The federal government was late getting into the game. Congress didn't officially endorse the pledge until 1942, and it didn't tamper with the language until 1954, when Congress inserted the phrase "under God" after being pressured by a religious organization, the Knights of Columbus.

Indeed, any blunt attempt to use the power of the state to institutionalize U.S. nationalism has been met with strong resistance because of popular suspicion that the government may be encroaching on Americans' individual liberties. In the 1930s, the Jehovah's Witnesses mounted a legal challenge when some school boards tried to make the Pledge of Allegiance mandatory, arguing that the pledge compelled children to worship graven images. The flag-burning amendment has failed twice in the U.S. Congress during the last eight years.

In the United States, promoting nationalism is a private enterprise. In other societies, especially those ruled by authoritarian regimes, the state deploys its resources, from government-controlled media to the police, to propagate "patriotic values." The celebration of national days in such countries features huge government-orchestrated parades that showcase crack troops and the latest weaponry. . . . Yet despite its awesome high-tech arsenal, such orgiastic displays of state-sponsored nationalism are notably absent on Independence Day in the United States. Of course, Americans hold parades and watch fireworks on the Fourth of July, but those events are largely organized by civic associations and partly paid for by local business groups.

Herein lies the secret of the vitality and durability of American nationalism: The dominance of civic voluntarism—and not state coercion—has made nationalist sentiments more genuine, attractive, and legitimate to the general public. These expressions of American nationalism have become so commonplace that they are virtually imperceptible, except to outsiders.

A POLITICAL CREED

American nationalism is hidden in plain sight. But even if Americans saw it, they wouldn't recognize it as nationalism. That's because American nationalism is a different breed from its foreign cousins and exhibits three unique characteristics.

First, American nationalism is based on political ideals, not those of cultural or ethnic superiority. That conception is entirely fitting for a society that still sees itself as a cultural and ethnic melting pot. As President George W. Bush said in his Fourth of July speech last year: "There is no American race; there's only an American creed." And in American eyes, the superiority of that creed is self-evident. American political institutions and ideals, coupled with the practical achievements attributed to them, have firmly convinced Americans that their values ought to be universal. Conversely, when Americans are threatened, they see attacks on them as primarily attacks on their values. Consider how American elites and the public interpreted the September 11 terrorist attacks. Most readily embraced the notion that the attacks embodied an assault on U.S. democratic freedoms and institutions.

Second, American nationalism is triumphant rather than aggrieved. In most societies, nationalism is fueled by past grievances caused by external powers. Countries once subjected to colonial rule, such as India and Egypt, are among the most nationalistic societies. But American nationalism is the polar opposite of such aggrieved nationalism. American nationalism derives its meaning from victories in peace and war since the country's founding. Triumphant nationalists celebrate the positive and have little empathy for the whining of aggrieved nationalists whose formative experience consisted of a succession of national humiliations and defeats.

Finally, American nationalism is forward looking, while nationalism in most other countries is the reverse. Those who believe in the superiority of American values and institutions do not dwell on their historical glories. . . . Instead, they look forward to even better times ahead, not just at home but also abroad. This dynamism imbues American nationalism with a missionary spirit and a short collective memory. Unavoidably, such forward-looking and universalistic perspectives clash with the backward-looking and particularistic perspectives of ethno-nationalism in other countries. Haunted by memories of Western military invasions since the time of the Crusades, the Middle East cannot help but look with suspicion upon U.S. plans to "liberate" the Iraqi people. . . .

INNOCENTS ABROAD

The unique characteristics of American nationalism explain why one of the most nationalist countries in the world is so inept at dealing with nationalism abroad. The best example of this second paradox of American nationalism is the Vietnam War. The combination of the United States' universalistic political values (in this case, anticommunism), triumphalist beliefs in U.S. power, and short national memory led to a disastrous policy that clashed with the nationalism of the Vietnamese, a people whose national experience was defined by resistance against foreign domination (the Chinese and the French) and whose overriding goal was independence and unity, not the spread of communism in Southeast Asia.

In its dealings with several other highly nationalistic societies, the United States has paid little attention to the role nationalism played in legitimizing and sustaining those regimes the country regarded as hostile. U.S. policy toward these nations has either disregarded strong nationalist sentiments . . . or consistently allowed the ideological, free-market bias of American nationalism to exaggerate the antagonism of communist ideologies championed by rival governments (as in China and Cuba). Former Egyptian President Gamal Abdel Nasser's brand of postcolonial Arab nationalism, which rejected a strategic alliance with either the U.S.-led West or the Soviet camp, baffled Washington officials, who could not conceive of any country remaining neutral in the struggle against communist expansionism. Echoes of that mind-set are heard today in the United States' "you're either with us or against us" ultimatum in the war against terrorism.

This ongoing inability to deal with nationalism abroad has three immediate consequences. The first, and relatively minor, is the high level of resentment that U.S. insensitivity generates, both among foreign governments and their people. The second, and definitely more serious, is that such insensitive policies tend to backfire on the United States, especially when it tries to undermine hostile regimes abroad. After all, nationalism is one of the few crude ideologies that can rival the power of democratic liberalism. Look, for example, at the unfolding nuclear drama on the Korean peninsula. The rising nationalism of South Korea's younger generation—which sees its troublesome neighbor to the north as kin, not monsters—hasn't yet figured in Washington's calculations concerning Pyongyang's brinkmanship. In these cases, as in previous similar instances, U.S. policies frequently have the perverse effects of alienating people in allied countries and driving them to support the very regimes targeted by U.S. policy.

Finally, given the nationalism that animates U.S. policies, American behavior abroad inevitably appears hypocritical to others. This hypocrisy is especially glaring when the United States undermines global institutions in the name of defending American sovereignty (such as in the cases of the Kyoto Protocol, the International Criminal Court, and the Comprehensive Test Ban Treaty). The rejection of such multilateral agreements may score points at home, but non-Americans have difficulty reconciling the universalistic rhetoric and ideals Americans espouse with the parochial national interests the U.S. government appears determined to pursue abroad. Over time, such behavior can erode the United States' international credibility and legitimacy.

If American society had been less insulated from the rest of the world by geography and distance, these conflicting perspectives on nationalism might be less severe. To be sure, physical insularity has not diminished Americans' belief in the universalistic appeals of their political ideas. . . .

But the United States' relative isolation, which unavoidably leads to inadequate knowledge about other countries, has created a huge communications barrier between Americans and other societies. According to a recent survey by the Pew Global Attitudes Project, only 22 percent of Americans have traveled to another country in the last five years, compared with 66 percent of Canadians, 73 percent of Britons, 60 percent of the French, and 77 percent of Germans. Lack of direct contact with foreign societies has not been offset by the information revolution. In the years leading up to September 11, 2001, only 30 percent of Americans claimed to be "very interested" in "news about other countries." Even after the September 11, 2001, terrorist attacks, average Americans did not sustain a strong interest in international affairs. According to polls conducted by the Pew Research Center in early 2002, only about 26 percent of the Americans surveyed said they were following foreign news "very closely," and 45 percent of Americans said that international events did not affect them.

An amalgam of political idealism, national pride, and relative insularity, American nationalism evokes mixed feelings abroad. Many admire its idealism, universalism, and optimism and recognize the indispensability of American power and leadership to peace and prosperity around the world. Others reject American nationalism as merely the expression of an overbearing, self-righteous, and misguided bully. In ordinary times, such international ambivalence produces little more than idle chatter. But when American nationalism drives the country's foreign policy, it galvanizes broad-based anti-Americanism. And at such times, it becomes impossible to ignore the inconsistencies and tensions within American nationalism—or the harm they inflict on the United States' legitimacy abroad.

17

Power and Weakness

Robert Kagan

It is time to stop pretending that Europeans and Americans share a common view of the world, or even that they occupy the same world. On the all-important question of power—the efficacy of power, the morality of power, the desirability of power—American and European perspectives are diverging. Europe is turning away from power, or to put it a little differently, it is moving beyond power into a self-contained world of laws and rules and transnational negotiation and cooperation. It is entering a post-historical paradise of peace and relative prosperity, the realization of Kant's "Perpetual Peace." The United States, meanwhile, remains mired in history, exercising power in the anarchic Hobbesian world where international laws and rules are unreliable and where true security and the defense and promotion of a liberal order still depend on the possession and use of military might. That is why on major strategic and international questions today, Americans are from Mars and Europeans are from Venus: They agree on little and understand one another less and less. And this state of affairs is not transitory—the product of one American election or one catastrophic event. The reasons for the transatlantic divide are deep, long in development, and likely to endure. . . .

. . . European intellectuals are nearly unanimous in the conviction that Americans and Europeans no longer share a common "strategic culture." . . . The United States, they argue, resorts to force more quickly and, compared with Europe, is less patient with diplomacy. Americans generally see the world divided between good and evil, between friends and enemies, while Europeans see a more complex picture. When confronting real or potential adversaries, Americans generally favor policies of coercion rather than persuasion, emphasizing punitive sanctions over inducements to better behavior, the stick over the carrot. Americans tend to seek finality in international affairs: They want problems solved, threats eliminated. And, of course, Americans increasingly tend toward unilateralism in international affairs. They are less inclined to act through international institutions such as the United Nations, less inclined to work cooperatively with other nations to pursue common goals, more skeptical about international law, and more willing to operate outside its strictures when they deem it necessary, or even merely useful.

Europeans insist they approach problems with greater nuance and sophistication. They try to influence others through subtlety and indirection. They are more tolerant of failure, more patient when solutions don't come quickly. They generally favor peaceful responses to problems, preferring negotiation, diplomacy, and persuasion to coercion. They are quicker to appeal to international law, international conventions, and international opinion to adjudicate disputes. They try to use commercial and economic ties to bind nations together. They often emphasize process over result, believing that ultimately process can become substance.

This European dual portrait is a caricature, of course, with its share of exaggerations and oversimplifications. . . . Nevertheless, the caricatures do capture an essential truth: The United States and Europe are fundamentally different today. . . . When it comes to the use of force, mainstream American Democrats have more in common with Republicans than they do with most European Socialists and Social Democrats. . . .

What is the source of these differing strategic perspectives? . . . Despite what many Europeans and some Americans believe, these differences in strategic culture do not spring naturally from the national characters of Americans and Europeans. After all, what Europeans now consider their more peaceful strategic culture is, historically speaking, quite new. It represents an evolution away from the very different strategic culture that dominated Europe for hundreds of years and at least until World War I. . . . While the roots of the present European worldview, like the roots of the European Union itself, can be traced back to the Enlightenment, Europe's great-power politics for the past 300 years did not follow the visionary designs of the philosophes and the physiocrats.

As for the United States, there is nothing timeless about the present heavy reliance on force as a tool of international relations, nor about the tilt toward unilateralism and away from a devotion to international law. Americans are children of the Enlightenment, too, and in the early years of the republic were more faithful apostles of its creed. America's eighteenth- and early nineteenth-century statesmen sounded much like the European statesmen of today, extolling the virtues of commerce as the soothing balm of international strife and appealing to international law and international opinion over brute force. The young United States wielded power against weaker peoples on the North American continent, but when it came to dealing with the European giants, it claimed to abjure power and assailed as atavistic the power politics of the eighteenth- and nineteenth-century European empires.

Two centuries later, Americans and Europeans have traded places—and perspectives. Partly this is because in those 200 years, but especially in recent decades, the power equation has shifted dramatically: When the United States was weak, it practiced the strategies of indirection, the strategies of weakness; now that the United States is powerful, it behaves as powerful nations do. When the European great powers were strong, they believed in strength and martial glory. Now, they see the world through the eyes of weaker powers. These very different points of view, weak versus strong, have naturally produced differing strategic judgments, differing assessments of threats and of the proper means of addressing threats, and even differing calculations of interest.

But this is only part of the answer. For along with these natural consequences of the transatlantic power gap, there has also opened a broad ideological gap. Europe, because of its unique historical experience of the past half-century—culminating in the past decade with the creation of the European Union—has developed a set of ideals and principles regarding the utility and morality of power different from the ideals and principles of Americans, who have not shared that experience. If the strategic chasm between the United States and Europe appears greater than ever today, and grows still wider at a worrying pace, it is because these material and ideological differences reinforce one another. The divisive trend they together produce may be impossible to reverse.

THE POWER GAP: PERCEPTION AND REALITY

Europe has been militarily weak for a long time, but until fairly recently its weakness had been obscured. World War II all but destroyed European nations as global powers, and their postwar inability to project sufficient force overseas to maintain colonial empires in Asia, Africa, and the Middle East forced them to retreat on a massive scale after more than five centuries of imperial dominance—perhaps the most significant retrenchment of global influence in human history. For a half-century after World War II, however, this weakness was masked by the unique geopolitical circumstances of the Cold War. Dwarfed by the two superpowers on its flanks, a weakened Europe nevertheless served as the central strategic theater of the worldwide struggle between communism and democratic capitalism. Its sole but vital strategic mission was to defend its own territory against any Soviet offensive, at least until the Americans arrived. Although shorn of most traditional measures of great-power status, Europe remained the geopolitical pivot, and this, along with lingering habits of world leadership, allowed Europeans to retain international influence well beyond what their sheer military capabilities might have afforded.

Europe lost this strategic centrality after the Cold War ended, but it took a few more years for the lingering mirage of European global power to fade. During the 1990s, war in the Balkans kept both Europeans and Americans focused on the strategic importance of the continent and on the continuing relevance of NATO. The enlargement of NATO to include former Warsaw Pact nations and the consolidation of the Cold War victory kept Europe in the forefront of the strategic discussion.

Then there was the early promise of the "new Europe." By bonding together into a single political and economic unit—the historic accomplishment of the Maastricht treaty in 1992—many hoped to recapture Europe's old greatness but in a new political form. "Europe" would be the next superpower, not only economically and politically, but also militarily. . . .

But European pretensions and American apprehensions proved unfounded. The 1990s witnessed not the rise of a European superpower but the decline of Europe into relative weakness. The Balkan conflict at the beginning of the decade revealed European military incapacity and political disarray; the Kosovo conflict at decade's end exposed a transatlantic gap in military technology and the ability to wage modern warfare that would only widen in subsequent years. Outside of Europe, the disparity by the close of the 1990s was even more starkly apparent as it became clear that the ability of European powers, individually or collectively, to project decisive force into regions of conflict beyond the continent was negligible. . . . Under the best of circumstances, the European role was limited to filling out peacekeeping forces after the United States had, largely on its own, carried out the decisive phases of a military mission and stabilized the situation. As some Europeans put it, the real division of labor consisted of the United States "making the dinner" and the Europeans "doing the dishes." . . .

. . . Not only were Europeans unwilling to pay to project force beyond Europe. After the Cold War, they would not pay for sufficient force to conduct even minor military actions on the continent without American help. Nor did it seem to matter whether European publics were being asked to spend money to strengthen NATO or an independent European foreign and defense policy. Their answer was the same. Rather than viewing the collapse of the Soviet Union as an opportunity to flex global muscles, Europeans took it as an opportunity to cash in on a sizable peace dividend. Average European defense budgets gradually fell below 2 percent of GDP. Despite talk of establishing Europe as a global superpower, therefore, European military capabilities steadily fell behind those of the United States throughout the 1990s.

The end of the Cold War had a very different effect on the other side of the Atlantic. For although Americans looked for a peace dividend, too, and defense budgets declined or remained flat during most of the 1990s, defense spending still remained above 3 percent of GDP. Fast on the heels of the Soviet empire's demise came Iraq's invasion of Kuwait and the largest American military action in a quarter-century. Thereafter American administrations cut the Cold War force, but not as dramatically as might have been expected. By historical standards, America's military power and particularly its ability to project that power to all corners of the globe remained unprecedented.

Meanwhile, the very fact of the Soviet empire's collapse vastly increased America's strength relative to the rest of the world. The sizable American military arsenal, once barely sufficient to balance Soviet power, was now deployed in a world without a single formidable adversary. This "unipolar moment" had an entirely natural and predictable consequence: It made the United States more willing to use force abroad. With the check of Soviet power removed, the United States was free to intervene practically wherever and whenever it chose—a fact reflected in the proliferation of overseas military interventions that began during the first Bush administration with the invasion of Panama in 1989, the Persian Gulf War in 1991, and the humanitarian intervention in Somalia in 1992, continuing during the Clinton years with interventions in Haiti, Bosnia, and Kosovo. While American politicians talked of pulling back from the world, the reality was an America intervening abroad more frequently than it had throughout most of the Cold War. . . .

How could this growing transatlantic power gap fail to create a difference in strategic perceptions? Even during the Cold War, American military predominance and Europe's relative weakness had produced important and sometimes serious disagreements. Gaullism, *Ostpolitik*, and the various movements for European independence and unity were manifestations not only of a European desire for honor and freedom of action. They also reflected a European conviction that America's approach to the Cold War was too confrontational, too militaristic, and too dangerous. Europeans believed they knew better how to deal with the Soviets: through engagement and seduction, through commercial and political ties, through patience and forbearance. It was a legitimate view, shared by many Americans. But it also reflected Europe's weakness relative to the United States, the fewer military options at Europe's disposal, and its greater vulnerability to a powerful Soviet Union. It may have reflected, too, Europe's memory of continental war. Americans, when they were not themselves engaged in the subtleties of détente, viewed the European approach as a form of appeasement, a return to the fearful mentality of the 1930s. But appeasement is never a dirty word to those whose genuine weakness offers few appealing alternatives. For them, it is a policy of sophistication.

The end of the Cold War, by widening the power gap, exacerbated the disagreements. Although transatlantic tensions are now widely assumed to have begun with the inauguration of George W. Bush in January 2001, they were already evident during the Clinton administration and may even be traced back to the administration of George H.W. Bush. By 1992, mutual recriminations were rife over Bosnia, where the United States refused to act and Europe could not act. It was during the Clinton years that Europeans began complaining about being lectured by the "hectoring hegemon." This was also the period in which Védrine coined the term *hyperpuissance* to describe an American behemoth too worryingly powerful to be designated merely a superpower. . . .

THE PSYCHOLOGY OF POWER AND WEAKNESS

Today's transatlantic problem, in short, is not a George Bush problem. It is a power problem. American military strength has produced a propensity to use that strength. Europe's military weakness has produced a perfectly un-derstandable aversion to the exercise of military power. Indeed, it has pro-duced a powerful European interest in inhabiting a world where strength doesn't matter, where international law and international institutions pre-dominate, where unilateral action by powerful nations is forbidden, where all nations regardless of their strength have equal rights and are equally protected by commonly agreed-upon international rules of behavior. Euro-peans have a deep interest in devaluing and eventually eradicating the bru-tal laws of an anarchic, Hobbesian world where power is the ultimate de-terminant of national security and success.

This is no reproach. It is what weaker powers have wanted from time immemorial. It was what Americans wanted in the eighteenth and early nineteenth centuries, when the brutality of a European system of power politics run by the global giants of France, Britain, and Russia left Ameri-cans constantly vulnerable to imperial thrashing. It was what the other small powers of Europe wanted in those years, too, only to be sneered at by Bourbon kings and other powerful monarchs, who spoke instead of *rai-son d'état*. The great proponent of international law on the high seas in the eighteenth century was the United States; the great opponent was Britain's navy, the "Mistress of the Seas." In an anarchic world, small powers always fear they will be victims. Great powers, on the other hand, often fear rules that may constrain them more than they fear the anarchy in which their power brings security and prosperity.

This natural and historic disagreement between the stronger and the weaker manifests itself in today's transatlantic dispute over the question of unilateralism. Europeans generally believe their objection to American uni-lateralism is proof of their greater commitment to certain ideals concerning world order. They are less willing to acknowledge that their hostility to unilateralism is also self-interested. Europeans fear American unilateralism. They fear it perpetuates a Hobbesian world in which they may become increasingly vulnerable. The United States may be a relatively benign hegemon, but insofar as its actions delay the arrival of a world order more conducive to the safety of weaker powers, it is objectively dangerous.

This is one reason why in recent years a principal objective of European foreign policy has become, as one European observer puts it, the "multilateralising" of the United States. It is not that Europeans are teaming up against the American hegemon . . . by creating a countervailing power. After all, Europeans are not increasing their power. Their tactics, like their goal, are the tactics of the weak. They hope to constrain American power without wielding power themselves. In what may be the ultimate feat of subtlety and indirection, they want to control the behemoth by appealing to its conscience.

It is a sound strategy, as far as it goes. The United States *is* a behemoth with a conscience. It is not Louis XIV's France or George III's England. Americans do not argue, even to themselves, that their actions may be justified by *raison d'état*. Americans have never accepted the principles of Europe's old order, never embraced the Machiavellian perspective. The United States is a liberal, progressive society through and through, and to the extent that Americans believe in power, they believe it must be a means of advancing the principles of a liberal civilization and a liberal world order. Americans even share Europe's aspirations for a more orderly world system based not on power but on rules—after all, they were striving for such a world when Europeans were still extolling the laws of *machtpolitik*.

But while these common ideals and aspirations shape foreign policies on both sides of the Atlantic, they cannot completely negate the very different perspectives from which Europeans and Americans view the world and the role of power in international affairs. Europeans oppose unilateralism in part because they have no capacity for unilateralism. Polls consistently show that Americans support multilateral action in principle—they even support acting under the rubric of the United Nations—but the fact remains that the United States can act unilaterally, and has done so many times with reasonable success. For Europeans, the appeal to multilateralism and international law has a real practical payoff and little cost. For Americans, who stand to lose at least some freedom of action, support for universal rules of behavior really is a matter of idealism.

Even when Americans and Europeans can agree on the kind of world order they would strive to build, however, they increasingly disagree about what constitutes a threat to that international endeavor. Indeed, Europeans and Americans differ most these days in their evaluation of what constitutes a tolerable versus an intolerable threat. This, too, is consistent with the disparity of power.

Europeans often argue that Americans have an unreasonable demand for "perfect" security, the product of living for centuries shielded behind two oceans. Europeans claim they know what it is like to live with danger, to exist side-by-side with evil, since they've done it for centuries. Hence their greater tolerance for such threats as may be posed by Saddam Hussein's Iraq or the ayatollahs' Iran. Americans, they claim, make far too much of the dangers these regimes pose.

Even before September 11, this argument rang a bit hollow. The United States in its formative decades lived in a state of substantial insecurity, surrounded by hostile European empires, at constant risk of being torn apart by centrifugal forces that were encouraged by threats from without: National insecurity formed the core of Washington's Farewell Address. As for the Europeans' supposed tolerance for insecurity and evil, it can be overstated. For the better part of three centuries, European Catholics and Protestants more often preferred to kill than to tolerate each other; nor have the past two centuries shown all that much mutual tolerance between Frenchmen and Germans.

Some Europeans argue that precisely because Europe has suffered so much, it has a higher tolerance for suffering than America and therefore a higher tolerance for threats. More likely the opposite is true. The memory of their horrendous suffering in World War I made the British and French publics more fearful of Nazi Germany, not more tolerant, and this attitude contributed significantly to the appeasement of the 1930s.

A better explanation of Europe's greater tolerance for threats is, once again, Europe's relative weakness. Tolerance is also very much a realistic response in that Europe, precisely because it is weak, actually faces fewer threats than the far more powerful United States. . . .

. . . Europeans have concluded, reasonably enough, that the threat posed by Saddam Hussein is more tolerable for them than the risk of removing him. But Americans, being stronger, have reasonably enough developed a lower threshold of tolerance for Saddam and his weapons of mass destruction, especially after September 11. Europeans like to say that Americans are obsessed with fixing problems, but it is generally true that those with a greater capacity to fix problems are more likely to try to fix them than those who have no such capability. Americans can imagine successfully invading Iraq and toppling Saddam, and therefore more than 70 percent of Americans apparently favor such action. Europeans, not surprisingly, find the prospect both unimaginable and frightening.

The incapacity to respond to threats leads not only to tolerance but sometimes to denial. It's normal to try to put out of one's mind that which one can do nothing about. . . . Europeans focus on issues—"challenges"— where European strengths come into play but not on those "threats" where European weakness makes solutions elusive. If Europe's strategic culture today places less value on power and military strength and more value on such soft-power tools as economics and trade, isn't it partly because Europe is militarily weak and economically strong? Americans are quicker to acknowledge the existence of threats, even to perceive them where others may not see any, because they can conceive of doing something to meet those threats.

The differing threat perceptions in the United States and Europe are not just matters of psychology, however. They are also grounded in a practical reality that is another product of the disparity of power. For Iraq and other "rogue" states objectively do *not* pose the same level of threat to Europeans as they do to the United States. There is, first of all, the American security guarantee that Europeans enjoy and have enjoyed for six decades, ever since the United States took upon itself the burden of maintaining order in far-flung regions of the world—from the Korean Peninsula to the Persian Gulf—from which European power had largely withdrawn. . . . If during the Cold War Europe by necessity made a major contribution to its own defense, today Europeans enjoy an unparalleled measure of "free security" because most of the likely threats are in regions outside Europe, where only the United States can project effective force. In a very practical sense— that is, when it comes to actual strategic planning—neither Iraq nor Iran nor North Korea nor any other "rogue" state in the world is primarily a European problem. Nor, certainly, is China. Both Europeans and Americans agree that these are primarily American problems.

This is why Saddam Hussein is not as great a threat to Europe as he is to the United States. He would be a greater threat to the United States even were the Americans and Europeans in complete agreement on Iraq policy, because it is the logical consequence of the transatlantic disparity of power. The task of containing Saddam Hussein belongs primarily to the United States, not to Europe, and everyone agrees on this—including Saddam, which is why he considers the United States, not Europe, his principal adversary. In the Persian Gulf, in the Middle East, and in most other regions of the world (including Europe), the United States plays the role of ultimate enforcer. "You are so powerful," Europeans often say to Americans. "So why do you feel so threatened?" But it is precisely America's great power that makes it the primary target, and often the only target. Europeans are understandably content that it should remain so. . . .

When Europeans took to the streets by the millions after September 11, most Americans believed it was out of a sense of shared danger and common interest: The Europeans knew they could be next. But Europeans by and large did not feel that way and still don't. Europeans do not really believe they are next. They may be secondary targets—because they are allied with the U.S.—but they are not the primary target, because they no longer play the imperial role in the Middle East that might have engendered the same antagonism against them as is aimed at the United States. When Europeans wept and waved American flags after September 11, it was out of genuine human sympathy, sorrow, and affection for Americans. For better or for worse, European displays of solidarity were a product more of fellow-feeling than self-interest.

THE ORIGINS OF MODERN EUROPEAN FOREIGN POLICY

Important as the power gap may be in shaping the respective strategic cultures of the United States and Europe, it is only one part of the story. Europe in the past half-century has developed a genuinely different perspective on the role of power in international relations, a perspective that springs directly from its unique historical experience since the end of World War II. It is a perspective that Americans do not share and cannot share, inasmuch as the formative historical experiences on their side of the Atlantic have not been the same.

Consider again the qualities that make up the European strategic culture: the emphasis on negotiation, diplomacy, and commercial ties, on international law over the use of force, on seduction over coercion, on multilateralism over unilateralism. It is true that these are not traditionally European approaches to international relations when viewed from a long historical perspective. But they are a product of more recent European history. The modern European strategic culture represents a conscious rejection of the European past, a rejection of the evils of European *machtpolitik*. It is a reflection of Europeans' ardent and understandable desire never to return to that past. Who knows better than Europeans the dangers that arise from unbridled power politics, from an excessive reliance on military force, from policies produced by national egoism and ambition, even from balance of power and *raison d'état?* As German Foreign Minister Joschka Fischer put it in a speech outlining his vision of the European future at Humboldt University in Berlin (May 12, 2000), "The core of the concept of Europe after 1945 was and still is a rejection of the European balance-of-power principle and the hegemonic ambitions of individual states that had emerged following the Peace of Westphalia in 1648." The European Union is itself the product of an awful century of European warfare.

Of course, it was the "hegemonic ambitions" of one nation in particular that European integration was meant to contain. And it is the integration and taming of Germany that is the great accomplishment of Europe—viewed historically, perhaps the greatest feat of international politics ever achieved. Some Europeans recall, as Fischer does, the central role played by the United States in solving the "German problem." Fewer like to recall that the military destruction of Nazi Germany was the prerequisite for the European peace that followed. Most Europeans believe that it was the transformation of European politics, the deliberate abandonment and rejection of centuries of *machtpolitik,* that in the end made possible the "new order." The Europeans, who invented power politics, turned themselves into born-again idealists by an act of will. . . .

. . . Fischer's principal contention—that Europe has moved beyond the old system of power politics and discovered a new system for preserving peace in international relations—is widely shared across Europe. As senior British diplomat Robert Cooper recently wrote in the *Observer* (April 7, 2002), Europe today lives in a "postmodern system" that does not rest on a balance of power but on "the rejection of force" and on "self-enforced rules of behavior." In the "postmodern world," writes Cooper, "*raison d'état* and the amorality of Machiavelli's theories of statecraft . . . have been replaced by a moral consciousness" in international affairs.

. . . Within the confines of Europe, the age-old laws of international relations have been repealed. Europeans have stepped out of the Hobbesian world of anarchy into the Kantian world of perpetual peace. European life during the more than five decades since the end of World War II has been shaped not by the brutal laws of power politics but by the unfolding of a geopolitical fantasy, a miracle of world-historical importance: The German lion has laid down with the French lamb. The conflict that ravaged Europe ever since the violent birth of Germany in the nineteenth century has been put to rest.

The means by which this miracle has been achieved have understandably acquired something of a sacred mystique for Europeans, especially since the end of the Cold War. Diplomacy, negotiations, patience, the forging of economic ties, political engagement, the use of inducements rather than sanctions, the taking of small steps and tempering ambitions for success—these were the tools of Franco-German rapprochement and hence the tools that made European integration possible. Integration was not to be based on military deterrence or the balance of power. Quite the contrary. The miracle came from the rejection of military power and of its utility as an instrument of international affairs—at least within the confines of Europe. During the Cold War, few Europeans doubted the need for military power to deter the Soviet Union. But within Europe the rules were different.

Collective security was provided from without, meanwhile, by the *deus ex machina* of the United States operating through the military structures of NATO. Within this wall of security, Europeans pursued their new order, freed from the brutal laws and even the mentality of power politics. This evolution from the old to the new began in Europe during the Cold War. But the end of the Cold War, by removing even the external danger of the Soviet Union, allowed Europe's new order, and its new idealism, to blossom fully. Freed from the requirements of any military deterrence, internal or external, Europeans became still more confident that their way of settling international problems now had universal application.

"The genius of the founding fathers," European Commission President Romano Prodi commented in a speech at the Institute d'Etudes Politiques in Paris (May 29, 2001), "lay in translating extremely high political ambitions . . . into a series of more specific, almost technical decisions. This indirect approach made further action possible. Rapprochement took place gradually. From confrontation we moved to willingness to cooperate in the economic sphere and then on to integration." This is what many Europeans believe they have to offer the world: not power, but the transcendence of power. . . . Europe "has a role to play in world 'governance,'" says Prodi, a role based on replicating the European experience on a global scale. In Europe "the rule of law has replaced the crude interplay of power . . . power politics have lost their influence." And by "making a success of integration we are demonstrating to the world that it is possible to create a method for peace." . . .

Thus we arrive at what may be the most important reason for the divergence in views between Europe and the United States. America's power, and its willingness to exercise that power—unilaterally if necessary—represents a threat to Europe's new sense of mission. Perhaps the greatest threat. American policymakers find it hard to believe, but leading officials and politicians in Europe worry more about how the United States might handle or mishandle the problem of Iraq—by undertaking unilateral and extralegal military action—than they worry about Iraq itself and Saddam Hussein's weapons of mass destruction. And while it is true that they fear such action might destabilize the Middle East and lead to the unnecessary loss of life, there is a deeper concern. Such American action represents an assault on the essence of "postmodern" Europe. It is an assault on Europe's new ideals, a denial of their universal validity, much as the monarchies of eighteenth- and nineteenth-century Europe were an assault on American republican ideals. Americans ought to be the first to understand that a threat to one's beliefs can be as frightening as a threat to one's physical security. . . .

Perhaps it is not just coincidence that the amazing progress toward European integration in recent years has been accompanied not by the emergence of a European superpower but, on the contrary, by a diminishing of European military capabilities relative to the United States. Turning Europe into a global superpower capable of balancing the power of the United States may have been one of the original selling points of the European Union—an independent European foreign and defense policy was supposed to be one of the most important byproducts of European integration. But, in truth, the ambition for European "power" is something of an anachronism. It is an atavistic impulse, inconsistent with the ideals of postmodern Europe, whose very existence depends on the rejection of power politics. Whatever its architects may have intended, European integration has proved to be the enemy of European military power and, indeed, of an important European global role.

This phenomenon has manifested itself not only in flat or declining European defense budgets, but in other ways, too, even in the realm of "soft" power. European leaders talk of Europe's essential role in the world. Prodi yearns "to make our voice heard, to make our actions count." And it is true that Europeans spend a great deal of money on foreign aid—more per capita, they like to point out, than does the United States. Europeans engage in overseas military missions, so long as the missions are mostly limited to peacekeeping. But while the EU periodically dips its fingers into troubled international waters in the Middle East or the Korean Peninsula, the truth is that EU foreign policy is probably the most anemic of all the products of European integration. . . . EU foreign policy initiatives tend to be short-lived and are rarely backed by sustained agreement on the part of the various European powers. That is one reason they are so easily rebuffed. . . .

Can Europe change course and assume a larger role on the world stage? There has been no shortage of European leaders urging it to do so. Nor is the weakness of EU foreign policy today necessarily proof that it must be weak tomorrow, given the EU's record of overcoming weaknesses in other areas. And yet the political will to demand more power for Europe appears to be lacking, and for the very good reason that Europe does not see a mission for itself that requires power. Its mission is to oppose power. It is revealing that the argument most often advanced by Europeans for augmenting their military strength these days is not that it will allow Europe to expand its strategic purview. It is merely to rein in and "multilateralize" the United States. . . .

Whether that particular mission is a worthy one or not, it seems unlikely to rouse European passions. Even Védrine has stopped talking about counterbalancing the United States. Now he shrugs and declares there "is no reason for the Europeans to match a country that can fight four wars at once." It was one thing for Europe in the 1990s to increase its collective expenditures on defense from $150 billion per year to $180 billion when the United States was spending $280 billion per year. But now the United States is heading toward spending as much as $500 billion per year, and Europe has not the slightest intention of keeping up. European analysts lament the continent's "strategic irrelevance." NATO Secretary General George Robertson has taken to calling Europe a "military pygmy" in an effort to shame Europeans into spending more and doing so more wisely. . . .

THE U.S. RESPONSE

In thinking about the divergence of their own views and Europeans', Americans must not lose sight of the main point: The new Europe is indeed a blessed miracle and a reason for enormous celebration—on both sides of the Atlantic. For Europeans, it is the realization of a long and improbable dream: a continent free from nationalist strife and blood feuds, from military competition and arms races. War between the major European powers is almost unimaginable. After centuries of misery, not only for Europeans but also for those pulled into their conflicts—as Americans were twice in the past century—the new Europe really has emerged as a paradise. . . .

Nor should we forget that the Europe of today is very much the product of American foreign policy stretching back over six decades. European integration was an American project, too, after World War II. And so, recall, was European weakness. When the Cold War dawned, Americans such as Dean Acheson hoped to create in Europe a powerful partner against the Soviet Union. But that was not the only American vision of Europe underlying U.S. policies during the twentieth century. Predating it was Franklin Delano Roosevelt's vision of a Europe that had been rendered, in effect, strategically irrelevant. As the historian John Lamberton Harper has put it, he wanted "to bring about a radical reduction in the weight of Europe" and thereby make possible "the retirement of Europe from world politics."

. . . Even though the United States pursued Acheson's vision during the Cold War, there was always a part of American policy that reflected Roosevelt's vision, too. . . .

But the more important American contribution to Europe's current world-apart status stemmed not from anti-European but from pro-European impulses. It was a commitment to Europe, not hostility to Europe, that led the United States in the immediate postwar years to keep troops on the continent and to create NATO. The presence of American forces as a security guarantee in Europe was, as it was intended to be, the critical ingredient to begin the process of European integration.

Europe's evolution to its present state occurred under the mantle of the U.S. security guarantee and could not have occurred without it. Not only did the United States for almost half a century supply a shield against such external threats as the Soviet Union and such internal threats as may have been posed by ethnic conflict in places like the Balkans. More important, the United States was the key to the solution of the German problem and perhaps still is. . . .

The United States, in short, solved the Kantian paradox for the Europeans. Kant had argued that the only solution to the immoral horrors of the Hobbesian world was the creation of a world government. But he also feared that the "state of universal peace" made possible by world government would be an even greater threat to human freedom than the Hobbesian international order, inasmuch as such a government, with its monopoly of power, would become "the most horrible despotism." How nations could achieve perpetual peace without destroying human freedom was a problem Kant could not solve. But for Europe the problem was solved by the United States. By providing security from outside, the United States has rendered it unnecessary for Europe's supranational government to provide it.

Europeans did not need power to achieve peace and they do not need power to preserve it.

The current situation abounds in ironies. Europe's rejection of power politics, its devaluing of military force as a tool of international relations, has depended on the presence of American military forces on European soil. Europe's new Kantian order could flourish only under the umbrella of American power exercised according to the rules of the old Hobbesian order. American power made it possible for Europeans to believe that power was no longer important. And now, in the final irony, the fact that United States military power has solved the European problem, especially the "German problem," allows Europeans today to believe that American military power, and the "strategic culture" that has created and sustained it, are outmoded and dangerous.

Most Europeans do not see the great paradox: that their passage into post-history has depended on the United States not making the same passage. Because Europe has neither the will nor the ability to guard its own paradise and keep it from being overrun, spiritually as well as physically, by a world that has yet to accept the rule of "moral consciousness," it has become dependent on America's willingness to use its military might to deter or defeat those around the world who still believe in power politics.

Some Europeans do understand the conundrum. Some Britons, not surprisingly, understand it best. Thus Robert Cooper writes of the need to address the hard truth that although "within the postmodern world [i.e., the Europe of today], there are no security threats in the traditional sense," nevertheless, throughout the rest of the world—what Cooper calls the "modern and pre-modern zones"—threats abound. If the postmodern world does not protect itself, it can be destroyed. But how does Europe protect itself without discarding the very ideals and principles that undergird its pacific system?

"The challenge to the postmodern world," Cooper argues, "is to get used to the idea of double standards." Among themselves, Europeans may "operate on the basis of laws and open cooperative security." But when dealing with the world outside Europe, "we need to revert to the rougher methods of an earlier era—force, preemptive attack, deception, whatever is necessary." . . .

. . . The United States is already operating according to Cooper's double standard, and for the very reasons he suggests. American leaders, too, believe that global security and a liberal order—as well as Europe's "postmodern" paradise—cannot long survive unless the United States does use its power in the dangerous, Hobbesian world that still flourishes outside Europe.

What this means is that although the United States has played the critical role in bringing Europe into this Kantian paradise, and still plays a key role in making that paradise possible, it cannot enter this paradise itself. It mans the walls but cannot walk through the gate. The United States, with all its vast power, remains stuck in history, left to deal with the Saddams and the ayatollahs, the Kim Jong Ils and the Jiang Zemins, leaving the happy benefits to others.

AN ACCEPTABLE DIVISION?

Is this situation tolerable for the United States? In many ways, it is. Contrary to what many believe, the United States can shoulder the burden of maintaining global security without much help from Europe. The United States spends a little over 3 percent of its GDP on defense today. Were Americans to increase that to 4 percent—meaning a defense budget in excess of $500 billion per year—it would still represent a smaller percentage of national wealth than Americans spent on defense throughout most of the past half-century. . . . Can the United States handle the rest of the world without much help from Europe? The answer is that it already does. The United States has maintained strategic stability in Asia with no help from Europe. In the Gulf War, European help was token; so it has been more recently in Afghanistan, where Europeans are once again "doing the dishes"; and so it would be in an invasion of Iraq to unseat Saddam. Europe has had little to offer the United States in strategic military terms since the end of the Cold War—except, of course, that most valuable of strategic assets, a Europe at peace.

The United States can manage, therefore, at least in material terms. Nor can one argue that the American people are unwilling to shoulder this global burden, since they have done so for a decade already. After September 11, they seem willing to continue doing so for a long time to come. . . . Partly because they are so powerful, they take pride in their nation's military power and their nation's special role in the world.

Americans have no experience that would lead them to embrace fully the ideals and principles that now animate Europe. Indeed, Americans derive their understanding of the world from a very different set of experiences. In the first half of the twentieth century, Americans had a flirtation with a certain kind of internationalist idealism. Wilson's "war to end all wars" was followed a decade later by an American secretary of state putting his signature to a treaty outlawing war. . . . But then came Munich and Pearl Harbor, and then, after a fleeting moment of renewed idealism, the plunge into the Cold War. The "lesson of Munich" came to dominate American strategic thought, and although it was supplanted for a time by the "lesson of Vietnam," today it remains the dominant paradigm. While a small segment of the American elite still yearns for "global governance" and eschews military force, Americans from Madeleine Albright to Donald Rumsfeld, from Brent Scowcroft to Anthony Lake, still remember Munich, figuratively if not literally. And for younger generations of Americans who do not remember Munich or Pearl Harbor, there is now September 11. After September 11, even many American globalizers demand blood.

Americans are idealists, but they have no experience of promoting ideals successfully without power. Certainly, they have no experience of successful supranational governance; little to make them place their faith in international law and international institutions, much as they might wish to; and even less to let them travel, with the Europeans, beyond power. Americans, as good children of the Enlightenment, still believe in the perfectibility of man, and they retain hope for the perfectibility of the world. But they remain realists in the limited sense that they still believe in the necessity of power in a world that remains far from perfection. Such law as there may be to regulate international behavior, they believe, exists because a power like the United States defends it by force of arms. . . .

The problem lies neither in American will nor capability, then, but precisely in the inherent moral tension of the current international situation. As is so often the case in human affairs, the real question is one of intangibles—of fears, passions, and beliefs. The problem is that the United States must sometimes play by the rules of a Hobbesian world, even though in doing so it violates European norms. . . . It must live by a double standard. And it must sometimes act unilaterally, not out of a passion for unilateralism but, given a weak Europe that has moved beyond power, because the United States has no choice *but* to act unilaterally.

Few Europeans admit, as Cooper does implicitly, that such American behavior may redound to the greater benefit of the civilized world, that American power, even employed under a double standard, may be the best means of advancing human progress—and perhaps the only means. Instead, many Europeans today have come to consider the United States itself to be the outlaw, a rogue colossus. . . .

Given that the United States is unlikely to reduce its power and that Europe is unlikely to increase more than marginally its own power or the will to use what power it has, the future seems certain to be one of increased transatlantic tension. The danger—if it is a danger—is that the United States and Europe will become positively estranged. Europeans will become more shrill in their attacks on the United States. The United States will become less inclined to listen, or perhaps even to care. The day could come, if it has not already, when Americans will no more heed the pronouncements of the EU than they do the pronouncements of ASEAN or the Andean Pact.

To those of us who came of age in the Cold War, the strategic decoupling of Europe and the United States seems frightening. . . . If Americans were to decide that Europe was no more than an irritating irrelevancy, would American society gradually become unmoored from what we now call the West? It is not a risk to be taken lightly, on either side of the Atlantic. . . .

Americans are powerful enough that they need not fear Europeans, even when bearing gifts. Rather than viewing the United States as a Gulliver tied down by Lilliputian threads, American leaders should realize that they are hardly constrained at all, that Europe is not really capable of constraining the United States. If the United States could move past the anxiety engendered by this inaccurate sense of constraint, it could begin to show more understanding for the sensibilities of others, a little generosity of spirit. It could pay its respects to multilateralism and the rule of law and try to build some international political capital for those moments when multilateralism is impossible and unilateral action unavoidable. It could, in short, take more care to show what the founders called a "decent respect for the opinion of mankind."

These are small steps, and they will not address the deep problems that beset the transatlantic relationship today. But, after all, it is more than a cliché that the United States and Europe share a set of common Western beliefs. Their aspirations for humanity are much the same, even if their vast disparity of power has now put them in very different places. Perhaps it is not too naïvely optimistic to believe that a little common understanding could still go a long way.

18

The Effects of September 11

A Rift between Europe and America?

Todd S. Sechser

A TRANS-ATLANTIC SPLIT?

During the 1990s, beliefs about a growing rift between the United States and Western Europe on issues of national security gained increasing acceptance on both sides of the Atlantic. In 1999, the Brookings Institution published a volume arguing that the disappearance of the Soviet Union, weakening economic ties, and dissimilar international roles were combining to push America and its European allies apart. Likewise, the editor of Germany's influential weekly *Die Zeit* remarked that Europe was beginning to engage in "unconscious" strategic balancing against the United States. Although a common Cold War threat generated parallel American and European interests, he argued, the dissolution of that threat revealed divergent and often competing worldviews.

This view intensified after the September 11, 2001 terrorist attacks in New York and Washington, DC. Initial sentiments of unity (notably, a declaration from the French newspaper *Le Monde* that "We are all Americans") quickly dissipated as commentators . . . asserted that the attacks had caused Americans and Europeans to view international security problems in fundamentally different ways. Polls suggested that after September 11, Europeans and Americans began to diverge sharply in their opinions about American foreign policy (Figure 18.1). When France, Germany, and others

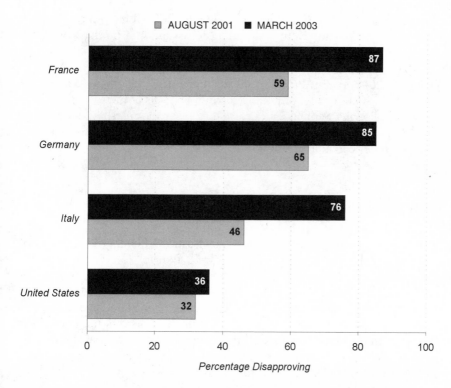

Figure 18.1   Public Disapproval of President Bush's International Policies

Source: Pew Research Center for the People and the Press

refused to support the U.S. invasion of Iraq, it seemed that the western alliance's epitaph had been written.

The "trans-Atlantic split" thesis contained at least four specific claims:

1. After September 11, Americans were more prone than Europeans to favor the use of force as a solution to foreign policy problems. Europeans, on the other hand, preferred to rely on negotiation and diplomacy to resolve conflicts.
2. Americans and Europeans disagreed about the nature and importance of international threats.
3. Having been victimized by terrorism, Americans harbored less patience for international law and international institutions. As a consequence, they tended to favor unilateral action, while Europeans relied on multilateral cooperation to accomplish foreign policy objectives.

4. Americans tended to favor an active international role for themselves, while Europeans were less willing to assume the burdens of global leadership.

Did the 2001 terrorist attacks instigate (or exacerbate) these conditions? What follows is a review of polling records on each of these four issues in the year following September 11. . . . [E]ach section marshals a variety of publicly available data in an effort to paint a broad picture of American and Western European public opinion on national security issues during this period.

THE USE OF FORCE

Europeans widely condemned President Bush's September 2002 National Security Strategy, which endorsed military action to "forestall or prevent" the emergence of threatening adversaries. Newspapers throughout the region urged European leaders to implement counterbalancing initiatives that would suppress the "dangerous" and "arrogant" proposals contained in the document. These reactions reinforced for many observers the conclusion that September 11 had rendered Americans less timorous than Europeans about advocating military force as a solution to foreign policy problems. The following section examines this claim.

Cross-national surveys conducted in June 2002 offer an initial test of the assertion that American citizens had become more prone to favor military action. These surveys, conducted for the Chicago Council on Foreign Relations (CCFR) in six European countries and the United States, asked individuals whether or not they would approve of the use of force to achieve particular foreign policy objectives.

In both Europe and the United States, significant majorities supported the use of force to advance a variety of objectives (Figure 18.2). Over 70% of respondents in both surveys supported military action to destroy terrorist camps, uphold international law, assist famine-struck populations, and liberate hostages. Americans were more willing to use force for only two objectives (to destroy terrorist camps and to ensure the supply of oil); for the other four goals, Europeans supported military action more willingly than did Americans.

Questions about general preferences, of course, offer only limited insight into the nature of public opinion. . . . For this reason, it is useful to compare public opinion regarding the use of force in individual cases. Two recent and highly debated cases (Serbia in 1999 and Iraq in 2002 and 2003) are considered below.

NATO's airstrikes against Serbia in 1999 provoked intense controversy in official circles, but poll data suggest that this debate obscured broad public

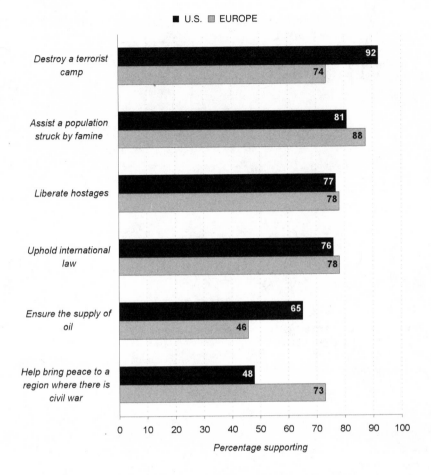

Figure 18.2 Views on the Use of Force for Specific Goals

Source: Reprinted with permission from the Chicago Council on Global Affairs, formerly the Chicago Council on Foreign Relations

support for the decision (Figure 18.3). In France, Germany, and Italy, support for the attacks exceeded 60% a few weeks after the operation began. Surveys conducted at the same time in the United States also revealed well over 50% approval. August 2001 surveys regarding President Bush's decision to keep troops in Bosnia and Kosovo displayed a similar pattern: a majority of European respondents approved of the announcement, while slightly fewer Americans supported it. If anything, Europeans appeared more enthusiastic than Americans about military action in the former Yugoslavia. This observation is consistent with the results in Figure 18.2 that illustrated a greater willingness among Europeans to use force to end civil wars.

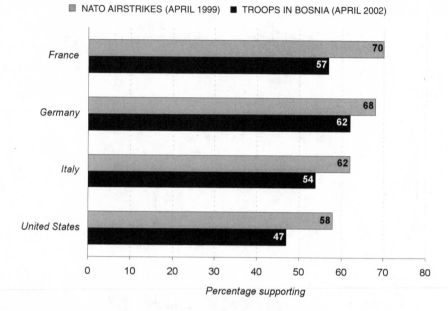

Figure 18.3   Attitudes toward Military Action in the Former Yugoslavia

Sources: Pew Research Center for the People and the Press, U.S. Information Agency, CBS News

Did the September 11 terrorist attacks reverse this pattern? If so, one would expect to find signs of comparative American aggressiveness in the prelude to the 2003 invasion of Iraq. Indeed, Americans initially appeared to be more inclined to support military action against Iraq: an April 2002 survey by the Pew Center reported that 69% of Americans supported "military action" to remove Saddam Hussein from power (as opposed to not supporting it), while European support for an attack was concurrently much lower (46% in France and 34% in both Germany and Italy).

When respondents were given more than a dichotomous choice, however, alternative interpretations emerged. A September 2002 questionnaire by the Pew Center revealed that Americans preferred a diplomatic approach to Iraq over immediate invasion by a wide margin. While 36% of respondents indicated a preference for an immediate invasion, 62% held that the United Nations (U.N.) should first be given the opportunity to disarm Iraq peacefully. CBS News polls as late as February 2003 affirmed these results, although the numbers supporting swift military action jumped in the weeks prior to the war's onset (Figure 18.4). This observation contra-

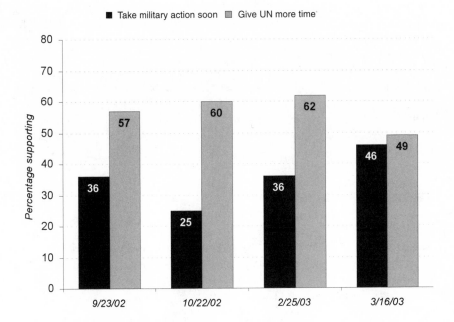

Figure 18.4   U.S. Attitudes about Invading Iraq

Sources: CBS News, CNN/Gallup/*USA Today*

venes the September 11 hypothesis, which would seem to predict high levels of aggressiveness in the months after the attacks but expect this posture to diminish as the memory of the terrorist attacks grew fainter over time.

When presented with the prospect of U.N. weapons inspections (prior to their resumption in November 2002), many supporters of military action turned skeptical. Seventy-seven percent of respondents to a September 14, 2002 ABC News poll agreed that the United States should hold off attacking Iraq if it agreed to allow weapons inspectors into the country. Similarly, although pre-war polls showed widespread support for military action (as opposed to no action) in the event that Iraq did not cooperate with U.N. weapons inspectors, a November 24, 2002 CNN/Gallup/*USA Today* survey showed that only a third of respondents preferred immediate military action over returning to the U.N. for authorization.

The performance of the September 11 hypothesis with respect to the use of force is therefore mixed. On the whole, Americans appeared more willing than Europeans to use force in Iraq, but they retained patience for intermediate diplomatic measures rather than insisting on war. Indeed, the *Washington Post* and ABC News reported on September 26, 2002 that a majority of

Americans were more concerned that the Bush administration was moving too quickly toward military action against Iraq. Even after September 11, the moral legitimacy of military action seems to have been an important consideration for most Americans: when the *New York Times* inquired about defensible reasons for attacking other nations, only 41% of Americans held the view that the United States should be able to attack another country without being attacked first, while 47% disagreed. The Europeans that protested President Bush's National Security Strategy so strongly might thus have more sympathizers in the United States than the editorial pages may have led them to believe.

THREAT PERCEPTION

Shortly after the September 11 attacks, foreign affairs commentator Robert Kagan argued in an influential article that "Europeans and Americans differ most these days in their evaluation of what constitutes a tolerable versus an intolerable threat." Is it the case that threat perceptions differ across the Atlantic, and did September 11 impact these perceptions? Both cross-national and time-series survey data can help answer this question.

The 2002 CCFR survey revealed striking similarities between Americans' and Europeans' views of serious threats (Figure 18.5). On both continents, international terrorism ranked as the threat most often identified as "critical" ("very important" in the European survey). The importance of terrorism was also reflected in the results of an April 2002 Pew Center survey, which reported that 67% of Americans and 61% of Europeans were either "very worried" or "somewhat worried" about the possibility of Islamic terrorism in their country. Problems in the Middle East also ranked highly on both continents: Iraqi weapons of mass destruction placed second in both surveys, while the Israeli-Arab conflict and Islamic fundamentalism claimed the next two spots (albeit in different order).

To be sure, comparable threat rankings coincided with important differences in threat perceptions. Most notably, the intensity of threat perception was significantly greater in the United States: in seven of the eight international issue categories covered by the survey, more Americans than Europeans felt threatened by the problem. For example, although Europeans and Americans appeared to agree that international terrorism constituted the greatest threat to their security, over 90% of Americans saw it as a critical threat, while less than two-thirds of Europeans did. . . . Most striking was the gap in perceptions regarding China: more than three times as many Americans rated China as a critical geopolitical threat.

Differences in the intensity of threat perceptions had important ramifications for policy preferences. For example, although Iraq's development of

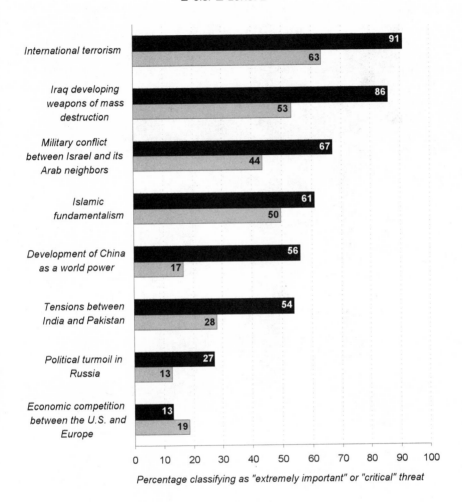

Figure 18.5   **Perceptions of Geopolitical Threats**

Source: Reprinted with permission from the Chicago Council on Global Affairs, formerly the Chicago Council on Foreign Relations

weapons of mass destruction ranked as the second most important threat for both Americans and Europeans, the Pew Center reported that 81% of Americans considered this a "very important" reason to justify attacking Iraq, as opposed to only 53% in Europe. In addition, European reaction to President Bush's 2002 State of the Union address, in which he termed Iraq,

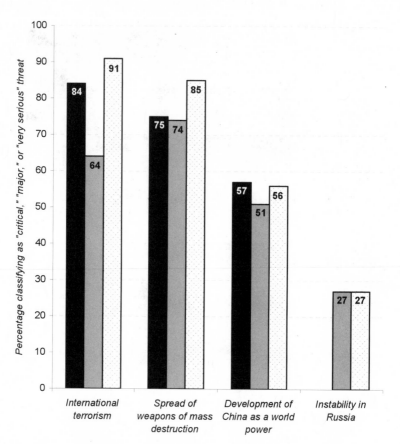

Figure 18.6   Changes in American Threat Perceptions after September 11

Note: Data for 1998 instability in Russia not available.
Sources: Chicago Council on Foreign Relations, Pew Research Center for the People and the Press

Iran, and North Korea an "axis of evil," was sharply negative in comparison to the reaction of Americans. . . .

Consistent with the September 11 hypothesis, American perceptions of terrorist threats appeared to have become comparatively more acute since the attacks (Figure 18.6). In 1998, 84% of Americans saw international terrorism as a critical threat to the United States, but by mid-2001 this figure had dropped to 64% before shooting to 91% nine months after September 11. At the same time, fears of weapons of mass destruction increased slightly, while fears regarding China and Russia both remained stable.

MULTILATERALISM AND
INTERNATIONAL INSTITUTIONS

President Bush's announcement of the country's withdrawal from the Anti-Ballistic Missile (ABM) Treaty in December 2001 suggested to many that September 11 had ushered in a new era of American unilateralism. Such sentiments were bolstered by President Bush's apparent disregard for U.N. authority while considering and conducting the invasion of Iraq. Yet, the data below suggest that September 11 did not persuade the American public that the country must act alone more often. Rather, Americans remained supportive—even insistent—on obtaining international support first.

In 1998, the CCFR reported that 72% of Americans believed that, in general, the United States should not take action in responding to international crises without the support of its allies. By 2002, this figure had dropped to 61%, but those opposing unilateral action remained firmly in the majority. The same percentage of respondents believed the lesson of September 11 was that the U.S. must work more closely with other nations to fight terrorism.

Skepticism about acting unilaterally was apparent in polls regarding U.S. action against Iraq (Figure 18.7). A CNN/Gallup/*USA Today* poll in late

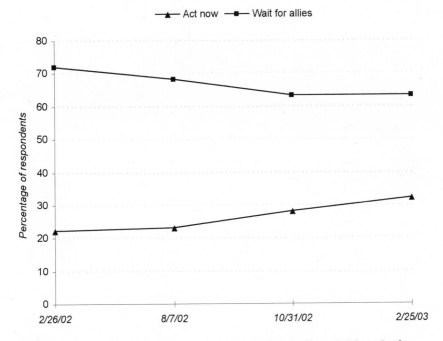

**Figure 18.7   Should the U.S. Wait for Allies before Taking Action
                against Iraq?**

Sources: CBS News, *New York Times*

September 2002 indicated that only 38% of the country would support an invasion of Iraq without allied support; with allied participation, however, this figure jumped to 78%. Concurrent *Newsweek* polls suggested that about 60% of the country believed it was "very important" to obtain allied support before attacking.

Americans' desire to obtain U.N. support for attacking Iraq was similarly strong. The *Newsweek* surveys noted above registered nearly identical numbers regarding the importance of U.N. approval, and CNN reported in September 2002 that 68% believed it was necessary for the Bush administration to obtain a U.N. resolution before attacking Iraq. An August 2002 *Los Angeles Times* poll confirmed that about two-thirds of the nation agreed that the U.S. should attack only with the support of the "international community." Even more striking, a September 23, 2002 poll by the Program on International Policy Attitudes suggested that 64% of Americans believed the U.S. should only invade Iraq if it was able to obtain *both* allied support and U.N. approval.

Surveys regarding general support for the U.N. confirmed that it continues to enjoy broad public support in the United States. Sixty-eight percent of Americans surveyed by Gallup in early 2001 believed that the U.N. should play a "leading" or "major" role in world affairs, and according to the Pew Research Center, 46% viewed strengthening the U.N. as a "top priority" for the United States. The 2002 CCFR poll reported that 77% of Americans supported strengthening the U.N.—a level of support even higher than that in western Europe (75%).

Attitudes toward withdrawal from the ABM Treaty also illustrated American support for multilateralism, albeit less convincingly. While the Bush administration's decision to withdraw from treaty was vehemently opposed in Europe (74% disapproved, according to the Pew Research Center), Americans did not appear to widely support this move. A CBS News/*New York Times* poll showed in March 2001 that support for missile defense dropped from 67% to 33% when respondents were informed that the U.S. would need to break the ABM Treaty in order to build such a system (a comparable poll a year earlier recorded a drop from 58% to 28%). Following President Bush's withdrawal announcement (which occurred after September 11), CNN/Gallup/*USA Today* recorded a higher—but nevertheless sub-majority—44% approval rating of the decision. Notably, however, 26% expressed "no opinion" about the decision, suggesting that missile defense provoked more public opposition in Europe than in the United States, even though outright support was low in both places.

INTERNATIONAL ROLES

A final question is whether the American public preferred a more active international role for itself than the European public as a result of September

11. Public opinion data from 2002 provide solid disconfirming evidence for this claim. The CCFR found that 82% of Americans wanted the U.S. to exert "strong leadership" in world affairs, while 85% of Europeans desired the same role for the European Union (E.U.). Indeed, 72% of Western Europeans took the view that the E.U. should become a superpower like the United States.

Public opinion data thus suggest that claims of a trans-Atlantic divide on national security issues are accurate in some respects but exaggerated in others. First, even after September 11, strong support remained in both the United States and Europe for diplomacy, multilateralism, and international institutions, although Americans were less likely to require these intermediate steps before using military force. Second, Americans and Europeans prioritized threats in similar ways, although Americans tended to perceive those threats more intensely. Finally, publics on both continents firmly backed international activism. Assertions about a widening gap between America and Europe thus appear to be overstated—as the invasion of Iraq illustrated, important differences exist, but too many fundamental similarities remain to speak of an inherent disunity between America and its allies.

19

Views of a Changing World 2003

War with Iraq Further Divides Global Publics

Pew Global Attitudes Project

The Pew Global Attitudes Project surveyed:

- 16,000 people in 20 countries and the Palestinian Authority in May, 2003
- more than 38,000 people in 44 nations in 2002

INTRODUCTION AND SUMMARY

The speed of the war in Iraq and the prevailing belief that the Iraqi people are better off as a result have modestly improved the image of America. But in most countries, opinions of the U.S. are markedly lower than they were a year ago. The war has widened the rift between Americans and Western Europeans, further inflamed the Muslim world, softened support for the war on terrorism, and significantly weakened global public support for the pillars of the post–World War II era—the U.N. and the North Atlantic alliance.

These are the principal findings from the latest survey of the Pew Global Attitudes Project, conducted over the past month in 20 countries and the Palestinian Authority. It is being released together with a broader survey of 44 nations conducted in 2002, which covers attitudes on globalization, democratization and the role of Islam in governance and society.

While the postwar poll paints a mostly negative picture of the image of America, its people and policies, the broader Pew Global Attitudes survey shows wide support for the fundamental economic and political values that the U.S. has long promoted. Globalization, the free market model and democratic ideals are accepted in all corners of the world. Most notably, the 44-nation survey found strong democratic aspirations in most of the Muslim publics surveyed. The postwar update confirms that these aspirations remain intact despite the war and its attendant controversies.

The new survey shows, however, that public confidence in the United Nations is a major victim of the conflict in Iraq. Positive ratings for the world body have tumbled in nearly every country for which benchmark measures are available. Majorities or pluralities in most countries believe that the war in Iraq showed the U.N. to be not so important any more. The idea that the U.N. is less relevant is much more prevalent now than it was just before the war, and is shared by people in countries that backed the war, the U.S. and Great Britain, as well as in nations that opposed it, notably France and Germany.

In addition, majorities in five of seven NATO countries surveyed support a more independent relationship with the U.S. on diplomatic and security affairs. Fully three-quarters in France (76%), and solid majorities in Turkey (62%), Spain (62%), Italy (61%) and Germany (57%) believe Western Europe should take a more independent approach than it has in the past.

The British and Americans disagree—narrow majorities in both countries want the partnership between the U.S. and Western Europe to remain as close as ever. But the percentage of Americans favoring continued close ties with Western Europe has fallen—from 62% before the war to 53% in the current survey. In fact, the American people have cooled on France and Germany as much as the French and Germans have cooled on the U.S.

In Western Europe, negative views of America have declined somewhat since just prior to the war in Iraq, when anti-war sentiment peaked. But since last summer, favorable opinions of the U.S have slipped in nearly every country for which trend measures are available. Views of the American people, while still largely favorable, have fallen as well. The belief that the U.S. pursues a unilateralist foreign policy, which had been extensive last summer, has only grown in the war's aftermath.

In Great Britain and Italy, positive opinions of the U.S. increased considerably since just before the war. Of the 21 publics surveyed in the new poll, overall support for the United States is greatest by far in Israel, where 79% view the U.S. favorably. Israelis also express near-universal support for the U.S.-led war on terrorism, with 85% favoring the fight against terrorism. Majorities in Western Europe and Australia also back the war on terrorism, but support has slipped since last summer in both France and Germany (15 points in France, 10 points in Germany).

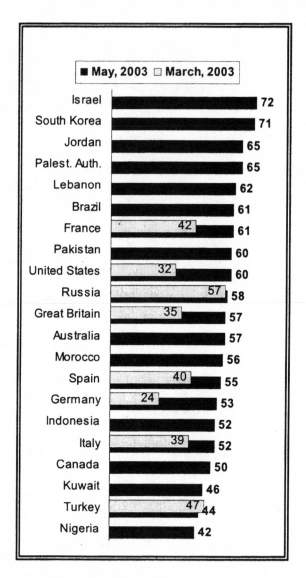

Figure 19.1   U.N. Less Important Now

In addition, the bottom has fallen out of support for America in most of the Muslim world. Negative views of the U.S. among Muslims, which had been largely limited to countries in the Middle East, have spread to Muslim populations in Indonesia and Nigeria. Since last summer, favorable ratings for the U.S. have fallen from 61% to 15% in Indonesia and from 71% to 38% among Muslims in Nigeria.

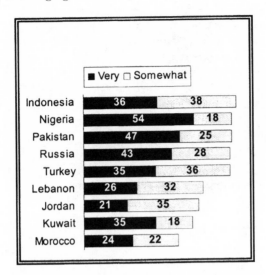

Figure 19.2   Worried about Potential U.S. Military Threat

In the wake of the war, a growing percentage of Muslims see serious threats to Islam. Specifically, majorities in seven of eight Muslim populations surveyed express worries that the U.S. might become a military threat to their countries. Even in Kuwait, where people have a generally favorable view of the United States, 53% voice at least some concern that the U.S. could someday pose a threat.

Support for the U.S.-led war on terrorism also has fallen in most Muslim publics. Equally significant, solid majorities in the Palestinian Authority, Indonesia and Jordan—and nearly half of those in Morocco and Pakistan—

Table 19.1   Confidence in World Figures to Do the Right Thing

	First	Second	Third
Indonesia	Arafat (68%)	Abdallah (66%)	bin Laden (58%)
Jordan	Chirac (61%)	bin Laden (55%)	Abdallah (42%)
Kuwait	Abdallah (84%)	Bush (62%)	Blair (58%)
Lebanon	Chirac (81%)	Annan (38%)	Abdallah (35%)
Morocco	Chirac (65%)	bin Laden (49%)	Arafat (43%)
Nigeria	Annan (52%)	Blair (50%)	Bush (50%)
Pakistan	Abdallah (60%)	bin Laden (45%)	Arafat (42%)
Palest. Auth.	bin Laden (71%)	Arafat (69%)	Chirac (32%)
Turkey	Arafat (32%)	Abdallah (21%)	Annan (18%)

Percent saying they have "a lot" or "some" confidence in each leader's ability to do the right thing regarding world affairs. Three highest rated (of 8 world leaders) shown here.

say they have at least some confidence in Osama bin Laden to "do the right thing regarding world affairs." Fully 71% of Palestinians say they have confidence in bin Laden in this regard.

More generally, the postwar update survey of 16,000 respondents finds, in most countries that are friendly to the United States, only modest percentages have confidence that President Bush will do the right thing in international affairs. People in most countries rate Vladimir Putin, Gerhard Schroeder, Jacques Chirac and Tony Blair more highly than they do Bush. The president also ranks slightly behind Blair in the United States, mostly due to political partisanship. Nearly all Republicans (95%) express confidence in Bush, compared with 64% of Democrats.

WAR VIEWS ENTRENCHED

The war itself did little to change opinions about the merits of using force in Iraq. In countries where there was strong opposition to the war, people overwhelmingly believe their governments made the right decision to stay out of the conflict. In countries that backed the war, with the notable exception of Spain, publics believe their governments made the right decision. In Great Britain, support for the war has grown following its successful outcome. A majority of Turks oppose even the limited help their government offered the U.S. during the war, while Kuwaitis largely approve of their government's support for the military effort.

Opinion about the war is strongly related to perceptions of how the U.S. and its allies conducted the war and are managing its aftermath. In countries opposed to the war, there is a widespread belief the coalition did not try hard enough to avoid civilian casualties. By contrast, solid majorities in most of the coalition countries, as well as Israel, believe the U.S. and its allies did make a serious attempt to spare civilians. Eight in ten Americans (82%) feel that way, the highest percentage of any population surveyed.

A somewhat different pattern is apparent in attitudes toward the postwar reconstruction of Iraq. Americans generally believe the allies are taking the needs of the Iraqi people into account. But there is less support for that point of view elsewhere, even in Great Britain, Australia and Israel. Muslim publics generally believe the United States and its allies are doing only a fair or poor job in addressing the needs of the Iraqi people in the postwar reconstruction.

There also is widespread disappointment among Muslims that Iraq did not put up more of a fight against the U.S. and its allies. Overwhelming majorities in Morocco (93%), Jordan (91%), Lebanon (82%), Turkey (82%), Indonesia (82%), and the Palestinian Authority (81%) say they are disappointed the Iraqi military put up so little resistance. Many others around the

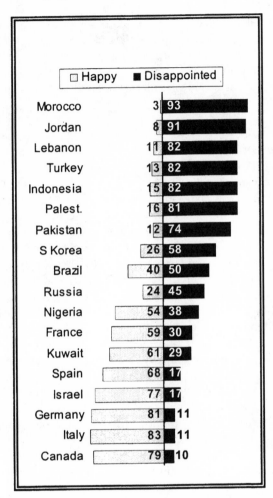

Figure 19.3 Reaction to Lack of Iraqi Military Resistance

world share that view, including people in South Korea (58%), Brazil (50%) and Russia (45%).

Still, even in countries that staunchly opposed the war many people believe that Iraqis will be better off now that Saddam Hussein has been removed from power. Solid majorities in Western Europe believe the Iraqi people will be better off, as do eight in ten Kuwaitis and half of the Lebanese. But substantial majorities elsewhere, notably in Jordan and the Palestinian Authority, say Iraqis will be worse off now that Hussein has been deposed.

The postwar update shows limited optimism for a surge of democratic reform in the Middle East. Substantial minorities of Muslims in many countries say the region will become somewhat more democratic, but only in Kuwait do as many as half predict the Middle East will become much more democratic. Expectations of major political changes in the Middle East are modest in countries that participated in the war. Just 16% in Great Britain, 14% in the U.S. and 10% in Australia think that the Middle East will become much more democratic.

U.S. FAVORS ISRAEL

U.S. policies toward the Middle East come under considerable criticism in the new poll. In 20 of 21 populations surveyed—Americans are the only exception—pluralities or majorities believe the United States favors Israel over the Palestinians too much. This opinion is shared in Israel; 47% of Israelis believe that the U.S. favors Israel too much, while 38% say the policy is fair and 11% think the U.S. favors the Palestinians too much.

But Israel is the only country, aside from the U.S., in which a majority says that U.S. policies lead to more stability in the region. Most Muslim populations think U.S. policies bring less stability to the Middle East, while people elsewhere are divided in their evaluations of the impact of U.S. policies.

More broadly, the postwar survey asked people their views on the conflict between the Israelis and Palestinians. By wide margins, most Muslim populations doubt that a way can be found for the state of Israel to exist so that the rights and needs of the Palestinian people are met. Eight in ten residents of the Palestinian Authority express this opinion. But Arabs in Israel, who voice the same criticisms of U.S. policy in the Middle East as do other Muslims, generally believe that a way can be found for the state of Israel to exist so that Palestinian rights and needs are addressed. In fact, Arabs in Israel are nearly as likely as Jews to hold that opinion (62% of Arabs, 68% of Jews).

Outside of the Muslim world, there is general agreement that there is a way to ensure Israel's existence and meet the needs of Palestinians. This view is widely shared in North America and Western Europe.

As people around the world contemplate emerging security threats, countries in the Middle East—Iran and Syria—are viewed as less of a danger than North Korea. Majorities in most countries see North Korea as at least a moderate threat to Asian stability and world peace, while nearly four in ten in Australia (39%), the U.S. (38%) and Germany (37%) view North Korea as a great danger. However, just 28% of South Koreans agree that North Korea presents a major threat to regional stability. Israelis have a different sense of potential threats than do people elsewhere. More than half of Israelis (54%) say Iran presents a great threat to the Middle East, twice the proportion in the next closest country (U.S. at 26%).

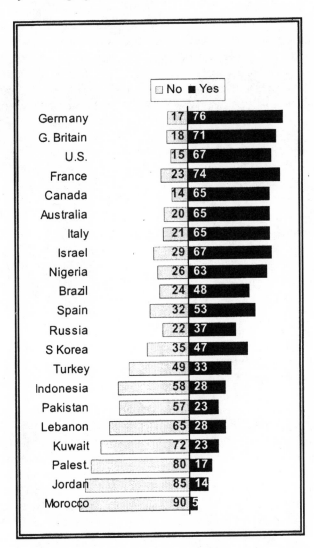

Figure 19.4   A Way for Israeli State and Palestinian Rights to Coexist?

DEMOCRACY CAN WORK HERE

Despite soaring anti-Americanism and substantial support for Osama bin Laden, there is considerable appetite in the Muslim world for democratic freedoms. The broader, 44-nation survey shows that people in Muslim countries place a high value on freedom of expression, freedom of the press, multi-party systems and equal treatment under the law. This includes people living in kingdoms such as Jordan and Kuwait, as well as those in authoritarian states like Uzbekistan and Pakistan. In fact, many of the Muslim publics polled expressed a stronger desire for democratic freedoms than the publics in some nations of Eastern Europe, notably Russia and Bulgaria.

The postwar update finds that in most Muslim populations, large majorities continue to believe that Western-style democracy can work in their countries. This is the case in predominantly Muslim countries like Kuwait (83%) and Bangladesh (57%), but also in religiously diverse countries like Nigeria (75%). There are no substantive differences between Muslims and non-Muslims in Nigeria on this point. Only in Indonesia and Turkey do substantial percentages say democracy is a Western way of doing things that would not work in their countries (53%, 37%).

At the same time, most Muslims also support a prominent—and in some cases expanding—role for Islam and religious leaders in the political life of their countries. Yet that opinion does not diminish Muslim support for a system of governance that ensures the same civil liberties and political rights enjoyed by democracies.

In religiously diverse countries, Muslims generally favor keeping religion a private matter at the same rates as non-Muslims. In Nigeria, for example, six in ten Muslims and the same proportion of non-Muslims completely agree that religion should be kept separate from government policy. In Lebanon, there are only modest differences on this point between Muslims and non-Muslims.

U.S. IDEALS BACKED—MOSTLY

The broad desire for democracy in Muslim countries and elsewhere is but one indication of the global acceptance of ideas and principles espoused by the United States. The major survey also shows that the free market model has been embraced by people almost everywhere, whether in Eastern Europe, sub-Saharan Africa, the Middle East, or Asia. Majorities in 33 of the 44 nations surveyed feel that people are better off in a free market economy, even if that leads to disparities in wealth and income. Despite the protests in recent years against globalization and America's role in fostering it, people are surprisingly accepting of the increased interconnectedness that defines globalization.

This is not to say that they accept democracy and capitalism without qualification, or that they are not concerned about many of the problems of modern life. By and large, however, the people of the world accept the concepts and values that underlie the American approach to governance and business.

Yet there are profound differences in the way Americans and people in other countries—especially Western Europeans—view such fundamental is-

Table 19.2   Western-style Democracy Can Work Well Here

	2002 %	2003 %
Nigeria	79	75
Lebanon	75	71
Jordan	63	69
Pakistan	44	57
Turkey	43	50
Indonesia	64	41
Kuwait	—	83
Morocco	—	64
Palest. Auth.	—	54
Ivory Coast	89	—
Senegal	88	—
Uzbekistan	81	—
Uganda	81	—
Ghana	76	—
Mali	76	—
Tanzania	64	—
Bangladesh	57	—

sues as the limits of personal freedom and the role of government in helping the poor. Americans are more individualistic and favor a less compassionate government than do Europeans and others. Nearly two-thirds of Americans (65%) believe success is not outside of their control. Except for Canadians (63%), most of the world disagrees. Among 44 nations surveyed, the U.S. has one of the highest percentages of people who think that most people who fail in life have themselves to blame, rather than society.

Accordingly, Americans care more about personal freedom than government assurances of social justice. Fully 58% of Americans say it is more important to have the freedom to pursue personal goals without government interference, while just 34% say it is more important for government to guarantee that no one is in need. In most other nations, majorities embrace the opposite view. And while most Americans support a social safety net, they are less strongly committed than other peoples to their government taking care of citizens who cannot take care of themselves.

MANY WANT DEMOCRACY, FEWER HAVE IT

People everywhere are united by their desire for honest multiparty elections, freedom of speech and religion and an impartial judiciary. A fair judiciary is seen as especially important; in most countries it is more highly valued than free elections.

Yet there is a widespread sense that these democratic aspirations are not being fulfilled. In Eastern Europe, only in the Czech Republic does a majority (58%) say they have honest, multiparty elections. In Russia and Ukraine, only small minorities feel they have free elections (15% in Russia, 21% in Ukraine). Skepticism about honest elections and freedom of expression are the norm for almost all of the democratizing countries of the world, but this is especially the case in Muslim countries.

Perceptions of repression in some predominantly Muslim countries—notably Turkey and Lebanon—are as widespread as anywhere in the world. Solid majorities in both Turkey and Lebanon say their nations lack several fundamental rights: freedom of speech, a free press, fair elections and an impartial judiciary.

SOVIET HANGOVER

In much of Eastern Europe, there is now greater acceptance of post-communist political changes compared with Pulse of Europe surveys conducted by the then–Times Mirror Center for the People & the Press in 1991, as the Soviet Union was collapsing. Even so, the legacy of communism is apparent in the attitudes of many Eastern European publics. Only about half of those in Ukraine and Russia approve of the political changes that have occurred since the collapse of the Soviet Union.

More generally, Russians and Ukrainians, as well as most other Eastern European publics, say a leader with a "strong hand" could solve national problems better than a democratic government. Only Czechs and Slovaks favor democracy over a strong leader. In most of Latin America and Africa, there is more of a preference for democracy.

There is, however, a large generation gap on views of democracy in Eastern Europe. In most Eastern European countries surveyed, people age 60 and older are much more likely to disapprove of post-communist political changes than are people under the age of 35.

"YES" TO A SMALLER WORLD

Beyond their common desire for democracy and free markets, people in emerging nations also generally acknowledge and accept globalization. People worldwide have become aware of the impact of increasing interconnectedness on their countries and their own lives. Majorities in 41 of 44 countries surveyed say that international trade and business contacts have increased in the past 5 years.

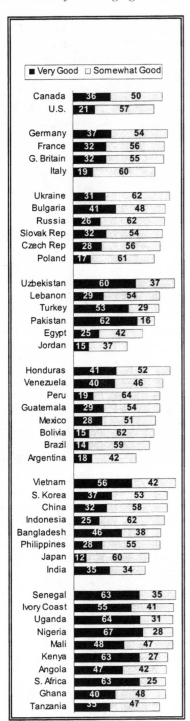

Figure 19.5   Global Trade's Impact on Country

The survey finds broad acceptance of the increasing interconnectedness of the world. Three-quarters or more of those interviewed in almost every country think children need to learn English to succeed in the world today. People generally view the growth in foreign trade, global communication and international popular culture as good for them and their families as well as their countries. For most of the world's people, however, this approval is guarded. Increased trade and business ties and other changes are viewed as somewhat positive, not very positive.

Despite the widespread support for the globalization process, people around the world think many aspects of their lives—including some affected by globalization—are getting worse. Majorities in 34 of 44 countries surveyed say the availability of good-paying jobs has gotten worse compared with five years ago. They also see the gap between rich and poor, the affordability of health care and the ability to save for one's old age as getting worse. But people do not blame a more interconnected world for these problems—they mostly point to domestic factors. This is especially true in economically faltering countries in Africa and Latin America, such as Kenya and Argentina.

People around the world are more inclined to credit globalization for conditions they see as improving, such as increased availability of food in stores and more modern medicines and treatments.

While anti-globalization forces have not convinced the public that globalization is the root cause of their economic struggles, the public does share the critics' concerns about eroding national sovereignty and a loss of cultural identity. Large majorities in 42 of 44 countries believe that their traditional way of life is getting lost and most people feel that their way of life has to be protected against foreign influence. There is less agreement that consumerism and commercialism represent a threat to one's culture. However, that point of view is prevalent in Western Europe and Latin America.

The polling finds, however, that the idea of "global" forces is something of a red flag to people around the world. "Global economy" is seen as more threatening than "trade with other countries." People worry about the impact of global trade on themselves and their families even though they believe that global trade is probably a good thing for their country as a whole. . . .

20

Taming American Power

Stephen M. Walt

THE GREAT DEBATE

U.S. policymakers have spent the past decade debating how best to wield American power. For the rest of the world, the debate is over how best to deal with it. With so much power in the hands of one country—a country that considers itself destined to lead the world—how should other nations respond?

Imagine, for a moment, that you are the president of France. You regard U.S. foreign policy as often naive and overweening, and your ideal world order is one in which no single state is dominant. So what do you do about the United States? Now picture yourself as the president of Russia. The only remnants of your country's former superpower status are an aging nuclear arsenal and membership in the UN Security Council. How do you improve Russia's situation in a world dominated by U.S. power? Or perhaps you are the prime minister of India. You face serious regional challenges—including the rising power of China—but relations with Washington are sometimes prickly, and the United States' global dominance is disquieting. Can you take advantage of parallel U.S. interests to advance those of India?

Leaders throughout the world face similar issues, some more daunting than others. Consider Kim Jong Il. He rules a country that George W. Bush has called part of an "axis of evil," and North Korea's entire GDP is only one-twentieth the size of the U.S. defense budget.

So how can Kim stay in power, much less improve his position, given U.S. opposition and North Korea's Lilliputian status? On the other end of the spectrum, Israeli Prime Minister Ariel Sharon and British Prime Minister Tony Blair have worked hard to establish personal connections with U.S. presidents. Israel and the United Kingdom have long relied on their special relationships with the United States, and the political fortunes of Sharon and Blair depend on keeping these relationships strong.

How do you deal with American power? This question is one for which every world leader must have an answer. And the response of other states to U.S. power is something Americans must care about as well. Basic security is at issue, as the September 11, 2001, terrorist attacks demonstrated. So is the health of the U.S. economy, with the market share of U.S. firms declining in key overseas markets due to anti-American sentiment. The time to worry is now.

To be sure, many governments still value U.S. power and seek to use it to advance their own interests. Yet even Washington's close allies are now looking for ways to tame the United States' might. Many countries fear U.S. influence, and they have devised numerous strategies to manage and limit it. The United States will not and should not exit the world stage anytime soon. But it must make its dominant position acceptable to others—by using military force sparingly, by fostering greater cooperation with key allies, and, most important of all, by rebuilding its crumbling international image.

OF POWER AND POLICY

Americans tend to see U.S. primacy as beneficial to both their country and the rest of the world. In 2002, the Pew Global Attitudes Project found that 79 percent of U.S. citizens believe it is good that "American ideas and customs are spreading around the world," and more than 70 percent think that U.S. foreign policy takes the interests of other states into account either "a great deal" or "a fair amount." Bill Clinton has described the United States as "a beacon of hope to peoples around the world," and Harvard political scientist Samuel Huntington has declared U.S. predominance to be "central to the future of freedom, democracy, open economies, and international order." In other words, without a benign hegemon maintaining a peaceful global order, many countries would not be able to enjoy the prosperity and security they have come to take for granted.

Unfortunately, this rosy view of U.S. power is not shared overseas, where, according to the 2002 Pew survey, overwhelming majorities say that the United States considers the interests of others "not much" or "not at all." Between 40 percent and 60 percent of foreigners polled think the United States is waging its war on terrorism not solely out of security concerns, but also to "control Mideast oil," "protect Israel," "target Muslim governments," or "dominate the world." A January 2005 BBC survey of 21 countries found only five—India, the Philippines, Poland, South Africa, and South Korea—

where a majority of people had "positive" attitudes toward the United States. Although the United States' global standing has rebounded slightly since the invasion of Iraq two years ago, Pew reported in June 2005 that majorities in all 15 countries it surveyed "favor another country challenging America's global military supremacy," and that support for the U.S.-led "war on terror" is declining on every continent. Indeed, citizens in Canada, France, Germany, the Netherlands, Russia, Spain, and the United Kingdom now hold more favorable views of China than of the United States.

The United States' image is especially bleak in the Arab world. Although Arab populations view U.S. popular culture, U.S. science and technology, and the American people somewhat favorably, a 2004 Zogby International poll found that fewer than 10 percent of those surveyed in Egypt, Jordan, Lebanon, Morocco, Saudi Arabia, and the United Arab Emirates approved of U.S. policy on Arabs, Iraq, or the Palestinians. Indeed, when asked to indicate their "first thought" about the United States, the most common response was "unfair foreign policy." . . .

If the United States' primacy is a force for good—as the country's leaders proclaim and its citizens overwhelmingly believe—why do even its allies have concerns about its influence? They have misgivings because they recognize that Washington's power could threaten their own interests. Even those countries that do not fear a U.S. attack are still aware that the United States' position as the world's lone superpower makes it easier for Washington to get its way. And of course, U.S. leaders have sought primacy precisely because they understand that weaker nations have less clout. It should come as no surprise, then, that other states remain wary despite assurances from Washington that U.S. power benefits the entire world. . . . Moreover, even well-intentioned U.S. policies can inadvertently harm other nations, giving them more reason for concern about the long reach of U.S. power. When it supported the Afghan mujahideen in the 1980s, the United States was not trying to create a global terrorist organization. And the United States was not trying to get al Qaeda to bomb the Madrid subway when it courted Spanish support for the war in Iraq. Yet both unfortunate developments were, in part, the unintended consequences of U.S. policy, illustrating why all states must be somewhat concerned about the ways the United States chooses to use its power.

Proponents of a muscular U.S. foreign policy tend to portray anti-Americanism as hostility toward American values or simple resentment of U.S. dominance. President Bush has said that "America was targeted for attack because we're the brightest beacon of freedom . . . in the world." He later explained, "The terrorists who attacked our country on September 11, 2001, were not protesting our policies. They were protesting our existence." And the Pentagon's new National Defense Strategy, issued in March, stated, "Our leading position in the world will continue to breed unease, a degree of resentment, and resistance."

There is a grain of truth in this argument, but foreign opposition to the United States is mostly a reaction to specific U.S. policies. The United States has been the sole great power for nearly 15 years, but its international standing remained fairly high through the late 1990s. Although some foreign leaders expressed concerns about the power imbalance, most nations—their people and their governments—looked favorably on the United States and welcomed Washington's global leadership. Attributing the current unpopularity of the United States solely to its power or values cannot explain the sharp decline in its image that has occurred since 2000, or especially the intense antipathy toward President Bush himself.

Moreover, the United States' main opponents have themselves repeatedly indicated that problematic U.S. policies are their primary concern. For example, bin Laden has made it clear that his hatred is fueled by opposition to what he regards as unjust U.S. actions in the Middle East, not to American values per se. According to the 2002 Pew Global Attitudes survey, "Antipathy toward the United States is shaped more by what it does in the international arena than by what it *stands for* politically and economically" (italics in the original). Similarly, a 2004 study by the Pentagon's Defense Science Board concluded that "Muslims do not 'hate our freedom,' but rather they hate our policies." . . .

Disagreement with U.S. foreign policy does not mean the policy is wrong, but it does mean U.S. actions come with a price. When foreign populations disapprove of U.S. policy and are fearful of U.S. dominance, their governments are less likely to endorse Washington's initiatives and more likely to look for ways to hinder them. Rising anti-Americanism also increases the number of extremists who can be recruited into violent movements such as al Qaeda. The United States may still be able to gain others' compliance and overcome overt resistance, but achieving success will be more difficult and more expensive.

Regardless of whether they disagree with U.S. policy or with the simple fact of U.S. power, can other states do anything to tame the American colossus? Historian Niall Ferguson has argued that the central issue is whether Americans have a "will to power" equal to their global responsibilities. President Bush, for his part, has downplayed the risk of going it alone: "At some point we may be the only ones left. . . . That's okay with me. We are America." Such statements imply that the United States can overcome any international resistance to its agenda so long as its resolve is firm.

But this confidence is unwarranted. Although other states cannot diminish U.S. primacy in the near term, there are still many ways they can rein in U.S. power. Some countries seek to manipulate the United States for their own purposes, using accommodation to gain Washington's trust, support, and protection. Others are more confrontational, attempting to oppose and undercut U.S. interests. In either case, the United States' ability to defend or advance its own foreign policy agenda is impaired.

IF YOU CAN'T BEAT 'EM

Given the reality of U.S. power, some states choose to accommodate it—and in doing so, attempt to ensure that it is used to their benefit. A few countries, wary of coercive measures or even possible military intervention by the United States, may choose to realign their policies to accord with U.S. interests in order to deflect U.S. pressure. More frequently, countries ally themselves with Washington to counter threats posed by their regional adversaries. By developing a close relationship with the United States, as well as with key American constituencies, foreign powers can manipulate U.S. primacy to their own advantage.

Instead of resisting U.S. power, a few states—Libya is the most recent example—"bandwagon" with the United States. To appease Washington, bandwagoners realign their foreign policies according to Washington's dictates. Although the United States has often tried to compel such realignments by pressuring weak and isolated opponents—including Iraq, North Korea, Serbia, and Syria—this strategy rarely works. Even Libya's acquiescence was due as much to prolonged sanctions as to any implied military threat.

More commonly, states choose to ally themselves with the United States out of a desire for U.S. protection from a regional threat. The United States has long been an attractive ally against intimidating neighbors: it is strong enough to shift a regional balance of power, and it generally does so without conquering its allies in the process. Poland, for example, seeks stronger ties with the United States because, as one Polish official explained, Poland "is a country that thinks seriously about security . . . [and] for such a country, it's good to be a close ally of the United States." The specter of China's rising power has created a host of diplomatic opportunities for Washington in Asia: India wants to develop a strategic partnership with the United States, and Malaysia, the Philippines, and Singapore want U.S. forces to remain in the region. Similarly, several smaller Persian Gulf states see the United States as a valuable counterweight to their larger neighbors.

States that do ally themselves with the United States do not do so passively. Indeed, they often go to considerable lengths to ensure that, in return, U.S. power is used in ways that further their own interests. By cultivating personal ties with U.S. officials, especially the president, foreign leaders such as Tony Blair seek to reinforce the United States' commitment to them and to affect how Washington wields its power. Blair's stated goal is to "remain the closest ally of the U.S., and as allies influence [the Americans] to continue broadening their agenda." Not every state can have a special relationship with Washington, of course, and leaders who embrace unpopular U.S. policies sometimes pay a large political price back home. Former Spanish Prime Minister José María Aznar's party fell from power in 2004 in part because he had supported the Iraq war. And Blair's own domestic popularity has

suffered due to his close relationship with President Bush and his unswerv-
ing support for key U.S. policies.

Foreign powers also attempt to take advantage of the unusual openness
of the U.S. political system. After the September 11, 2001, attacks, Saudi
Arabia launched a multimillion-dollar public relations campaign to counter
the perception that the royal family was supporting terrorism. More commonly, foreign governments collaborate with domestic special-interest
groups to encourage the U.S. government to support them. The open, decentralized, and divided U.S. political system is extremely vulnerable to this
sort of manipulation. . . .

The most significant cases of foreign penetration occur when U.S. ethnic groups lobby on behalf of their traditional homelands. Such lobbying
has promoted the causes of Armenia, Greece, Ireland, Israel, and Taiwan,
for example. The efforts of these ethnic lobbies rely on familiar tools of
political pressure, including campaign contributions, direct congressional
lobbying, and extensive letter-writing or media campaigns. Several other
ethnic groups are trying to imitate the well-documented success of organizations such as the Armenian Assembly of America, the American Hellenic
Educational Progressive Association, and the American Israel Public Affairs
Committee. Indian Americans, for example, have formed several political
lobbying organizations in recent years. The groups' potential impact has
not been lost on the Indian government: in 2004, an official Indian government commission concluded that "the Indian community in the United
States constitutes an invaluable asset in strengthening India's relationship
with the world's only superpower."

Apart from occasional attempts by some ethnic lobbies to silence U.S.
domestic opposition to their agendas (attempts that violate the democratic
principle of open debate), these activities are legitimate. But they could
also entice the United States into acting against its best interests. Such influence can lead U.S. foreign policy astray precisely because the United
States' dominant global position gives U.S. leaders so much latitude in making foreign policy decisions.

OPPOSING AMERICAN POWER

Although countries use strategies of accommodation to further their own
ambitions, the United States usually gets something important out of them:
compliance. Many countries, however, are not content to achieve their
goals by accommodating or allying themselves with the United States.
When foreign powers have aims that are incompatible with U.S. policy,
they must develop workable strategies of opposition. Some countries attempt to balance U.S. power by banding together against the United States
or by developing specific military options; others try to bind U.S. power

within the constraints of international institutions. Some resort to blackmail, attempting to extract concessions from Washington by threatening it with undesirable consequences such as the spread of nuclear weapons; others simply ignore or refuse U.S. demands. And many countries are trying to undermine U.S. power by attacking U.S. legitimacy, a strategy that Washington's recent actions have greatly facilitated. Such efforts to balance the power of the United States have thus far been muted, but they are beginning to hamstring U.S. foreign policy.

Although a number of leaders have openly called for a more multipolar world, the global response to U.S. primacy does not resemble the coalitions that defeated Germany in both world wars or the Soviet Union in the Cold War. The reason other nations have not forged a formal anti-U.S. alliance is simple: the United States does not pose the same level of threat. Yet states are beginning to join forces in subtler ways, with the explicit aim of checking U.S. power. Rather than forming an anti-U.S. alliance, countries are "soft balancing": coordinating their diplomatic positions to oppose U.S. policy and obtain more influence together. To name just a few examples: France, Germany, and Russia pursued a unified strategy that helped prevent the United States from obtaining UN Security Council authorization for the invasion of Iraq, and their actions allowed weaker states such as Mexico and Chile to resist U.S. pressure as well. Later, President Bush tried to persuade France, Germany, and the United Kingdom to get tough on Iran's nuclear programs, but he failed to drive a wedge between them and ended up endorsing their diplomatic campaign instead. . . .

Some ways of balancing U.S. power are less benign, such as when countries mobilize their military resources and develop defensive strategies that exploit areas in which U.S. strength is not overwhelming. As the Pentagon's 2005 National Defense Strategy notes, "The U.S. military predominates in the world of traditional forms of warfare. Potential adversaries accordingly shift away from challenging the United States through traditional military actions and adopt asymmetric capabilities and methods."

Weaker states typically rely on some combination of three broad options. First, they develop conventional military capabilities specifically designed to neutralize U.S. strengths. In the 1999 Kosovo war, Serbia used surface-to-air missiles as well as camouflage and other deceptive tactics to blunt NATO'S air offensive. Facing a vastly stronger coalition, the Serbs eventually lost, but they performed far better than NATO expected. Similarly, China is now acquiring military capabilities—including anti-ship cruise missiles, ballistic missiles, and electronic countermeasure technologies—that could hinder U.S. forces if they tried to operate in China's neighborhood.

Second, adversaries sometimes depend on terrorism, the classic "weapon of the weak." Terrorists win by attacking the stronger side's resolve and forcing it to take actions that alienate potential supporters. Al Qaeda and the Iraqi insurgency use terrorism because it allows them to attack vulnerable targets while avoiding direct confrontation with superior U.S. forces. Terrorism can also provoke the United States into overreacting in ways that could increase opposition to the U.S. presence in the Middle East. Sometimes, the strategy works: terrorism helped bin Laden drive much of the U.S. presence out of Saudi Arabia—and it may still defeat the U.S. mission in Iraq.

Third, to balance U.S. primacy, some countries attempt to obtain weapons of mass destruction (WMD), especially nuclear arms. The current nuclear powers developed these weapons to deter their enemies, and that is why Iran and North Korea want them today. As one Iranian reformer stated, "It is basically a matter of equilibrium. If I don't have [nuclear weapons], I don't have security."

Instead of forming such a direct counterpoise to U.S. dominance, many states hope to constrain the United States by binding it within powerful international institutions. Binding works best in areas in which U.S. primacy is not so pronounced, such as international economic affairs. It is not, however, an effective strategy for restraining U.S. action in core areas of national security. The United States failed to obtain Security Council authorization for the wars in Kosovo and Iraq, but that did not stop it from waging them. Nor could Washington keep other states from establishing an International Criminal Court, even though it has refused to acknowledge the court's authority over the United States.

Binding works in economics because the United States is less dominant in that area and because international trade and finance cannot occur without commonly accepted rules. For example, although the rules of the World Trade Organization generally favor U.S. interests, Washington cannot prevent the organization from issuing unfavorable rulings when the United States violates its principles. Nor can Washington ignore these rulings without jeopardizing the trading order on which U.S. prosperity depends. Moreover, the United States cannot simply dictate the terms of multilateral trade agreements—which also helps explain Washington's propensity to negotiate bilateral deals with individual states. The United States can thus be partly bound in this arena, but less easily than other states.

Blackmailing the United States, on the other hand, is an especially effective strategy for states to use—if they can get away with it. Blackmailers must make a credible threat that the United States cannot easily guard against and demands that it can reasonably satisfy. As long as Washington believes that the demands will not be repeated, it may choose to comply. But blackmailing only works in very special circumstances. Threats to use WMD or give them to terrorists are not credible, because blackmailers would thereby trigger their own destruction. Threatening to acquire WMD is, however, another matter. North Korea has been using this threat to great effect, even though the power of the United States dwarfs that of North Korea. Yet Pyongyang was able to extract repeated concessions from Washington and its allies—most obviously in the 1994 Agreed Framework—simply by continuing to develop nuclear weapons. Although North Korea's broken promises have made the Bush administration reluctant to try the same approach again, Pyongyang may still succeed in winning additional concessions, because at this point more attractive options are not available.

Even the United States' allies sometimes use blackmail to gain concessions by threatening their own collapse if they do not receive more U.S. support. Afghan President Hamid Karzai and Pakistan's military leader, Pervez Musharraf, for example, have both won additional benefits by convincing Washington that radicals would seize power if their regimes were to fall.

Another strategy, balking, is a more passive way for states to limit U.S. power: when the United States demands something, they simply refuse. Balking is an especially effective method, too, because even a country as powerful as the United States cannot force every state to do its bidding all of the time. And the more some states balk, the more overextended the United States becomes—making it easier for other states to balk as well. Russia has balked, for example, when asked to end its nuclear collaboration with Iran, just as India and Pakistan balked by resisting U.S. pressure to forgo nuclear testing in 1998.

Balking is sometimes overt—as when Turkey refused to grant the United States use of its territory for the Iraq war—but many countries choose a subtler approach, formally acquiescing to U.S. demands and then doing as little as possible to fulfill them. Thus, Israel has repeatedly pledged to stop building settlements and the Palestinians have promised to crack down on militants, but neither side has actually done much. U.S. leaders are frequently tempted to look the other way when others balk, rather than risk a costly dispute or let others see that they can be openly defied.

Attacking U.S. legitimacy is also a favorite way to erode Washington's international clout. As the world's dominant power, the United States has much to gain from the perception that its power is legitimate. When people around the world believe that U.S. primacy advances broader global interests, Washington finds it easier to rally international support for its policies, leaving its opposition isolated and ineffective. Accordingly, the United States' opponents are currently seeking to convince others that Washington is selfish, hypocritical, immoral, and unsuited for world leadership, and that its dominance harms them. This assault on U.S. legitimacy does not directly challenge U.S. power, but it encourages other people to resent and resist U.S. supremacy.

Unfortunately, the United States has unwittingly given its critics a great deal of ammunition in recent years. Not only did the Bush administration disregard the UN Security Council when it launched its preventive war against Iraq, but its justification for the war turned out to be false, and its bungled occupation has inflicted new suffering on the Iraqi people. President Bush may truly believe that "life [in Iraq] is being improved by liberty," but the rest of the world sees the invasion as a demonstration of the dangers of unchecked U.S. power.

To make matters worse, U.S. policies since September 11 have reinforced the belief that the United States does not abide by its own ideals. The torture and abuse graphically documented at Abu Ghraib prison, the deaths of Muslim prisoners of war in U.S. custody, the desecration of the Koran by U.S. interrogators, the harsh treatment of and denial of due process to prisoners at Guantánamo Bay, and the conspicuous absence of a single high-level resignation in the wake of these revelations have all made it easy for the United States' critics to portray the country as quick to condemn everyone but itself. . . .

Like President Bush, who said that the Abu Ghraib abuses did not reflect "the America I know," Americans may dismiss these accusations as false, misleading, or exaggerated. But the issue is not what Americans think of their nation's conduct; the issue is how that conduct appears to others. Some of these accusations may be unfounded, but many are seen as valid. And they are rapidly draining the reservoir of international goodwill that makes the United States' status as a superpower acceptable to the world.

The United States is in a global struggle for hearts and minds, and it is losing. If anti-Americanism continues to grow, Washington will face greater resistance and find it harder to attract support. Americans will feel increasingly threatened in such a world, but trying to counter these threats alone will merely exacerbate the fear of U.S. power and isolate the United States even more.

A NEW APPROACH

Over the last 15 years, the unipolar era has taught an important lesson: Americans may believe that their dominant position is good for the world, but other countries are far more ambivalent about U.S. supremacy and have developed ways to tame U.S. power. Ironically, then, instead of allowing the United States to act with impunity, primacy requires Washington to work harder to convince the other nations of the world that U.S. power is to be welcomed rather than feared.

A retreat to isolationism should be ruled out immediately. True, efforts to restrict U.S. strength would diminish if the United States withdrew from world affairs, but the benefits would not be worth the costs. Despite what critics may believe, the global community does indeed depend on the United States, to maintain the freedom of the seas, wage the war on terrorism, lead the campaign to control WMD, and underwrite the UN, the International Monetary Fund, and the World Bank, among other things. Washington's overarching influence also helps maintain a stable world order by dampening great-power rivalries in several regions. Few states would be safer or more prosperous if the United States withdrew completely.

Instead, the United States should resume its traditional role as an "offshore balancer." This strategy assumes that only a few parts of the world are of strategic importance to the United States, such as Europe, industrialized Asia, and the Persian Gulf. Instead of controlling these areas directly, the United States would rely on local actors to maintain the regional balance of power. The United States would still stand ready to deploy its power against specific threats to its interests, but it would intervene only when absolutely necessary—when the local balance broke down and vital U.S. interests were clearly threatened by hostile forces. In short, while remaining engaged with its allies, the United States should keep its military presence as small as possible. Reducing the size of the U.S. footprint would diminish the likelihood that foreign terrorists—especially suicide bombers—would target the United States, because such responses are most often triggered by perceived foreign occupation.

Being less directly involved on the ground would also bolster the United States' freedom of action. Washington would be able to play hard to get, making its support for others conditional on broad compliance with U.S. goals. Other states would be less likely to take U.S. protection for granted. By diminishing global concerns about U.S. dominance, this approach would also make it easier for Washington to gain global backing on those rare occasions when it needed to use force. Playing hard to get would not win over a recalcitrant regime such as that in Pyongyang, but it would make it easier for the United States to attract broad assistance for its policies in even those hard cases.

Most important, the United States must defend its international legitimacy. Washington must first recognize how it appears to others and then develop a sustained campaign to shape these perceptions. The United States cannot expect to win over the entire world, but it can surely do better than it has of late. Four years ago, President Bush declared that "we've got to do a better job of making our case," but the administration's advocacy has been flaccid. Voice of America broadcasts in English have been cut nearly in half, and the VOA's Arabic-language news programming has been replaced by politicized, commercial-style broadcasts that attract few listeners and enjoy little credibility in the Middle East. . . . This lackadaisical approach hardly conveys a serious desire to upgrade the United States' image abroad. . . .

To be effective, a public relations campaign needs a good product. If U.S. foreign policy makes global problems worse while U.S. government and military personnel trample on human rights, then no amount of public diplomacy will rescue the nation's image. To restore the moral stature it possessed before the abuses at Abu Ghraib, at Guantánamo, and in Afghanistan,

Washington must sincerely apologize to the victims, and the senior officials responsible should be asked to resign. By failing to hold top officials accountable, the United States demonstrates that it values neither the rights of others nor its own ideals. It is hard to imagine a worse way to rebuild the nation's global image.

U.S. foreign policy must reflect a greater appreciation of what U.S. power can and cannot accomplish. Possessing unmatched strength does not mean the United States can or should impose its values on others, no matter how selfless Americans think their motives are. Instead of telling the world what to do and how to live—a temptation that both neoconservative empire-builders and liberal internationalists find hard to resist—the United States must lead by example. Over time, other nations will see how Americans live and what they stand for, and the rest of the world will want those things too. As Woodrow Wilson once counseled, the United States should "exercise the self-restraint of a really great nation, which realizes its own strength and scorns to misuse it."

In the 2000 presidential campaign, Bush declared that other nations would be attracted to the United States if it were strong but also "humble." They would be repulsed, he warned, if the United States used its power in an "arrogant" fashion. Bush's instincts were correct, but his failure to follow them has led to precisely the results he predicted. The United States' current task is to rebuild the sense of trust, admiration, and legitimacy it once enjoyed, so that the rest of the world can focus not on taming U.S. power but on reaping the benefits that it can bring.

V

Case Studies in U.S. Grand Strategy

The War against Terrorism and the Invasion of Iraq

OVERVIEW

Despite being the son of a former president, George W. Bush entered the White House in January 2001 with relatively little international or foreign policy experience. As a one-term governor of the state of Texas, Bush dealt significantly with border issues related to Mexico and, initially, placed U.S.-Mexican relations near the top of his priority list as president. Like many new presidents before him, however, Bush relied heavily upon more experienced advisers and cabinet appointees for foreign policy advice.

Bush had access to a variety of viewpoints from his principal advisers. Despite his military background, Secretary of State Colin Powell came the closest to representing a liberal institutionalist perspective within the administration. As chair of the Joint Chiefs of Staff under President George H. W. Bush, Powell had initially counseled against the use of military force to oust Iraqi troops from Kuwait prior to the 1991 Persian Gulf War, arguing instead for a policy of vigorous international economic and political sanctions. When the first President Bush rejected Powell's advice, Powell pushed, successfully this time, for Bush to obtain clear backing from the U.S. Congress and the UN Security Council for the use of military force. Powell assisted in assembling a broad international coalition that provided the United States with significant political, financial, and military support prior to and during its attack on Iraqi positions within Kuwait. Powell also counseled against pushing the U.S. offensive to Baghdad itself on the grounds that the overthrow of Saddam Hussein exceeded the boundaries of the mission agreed to by members of the coalition. In general, Powell was, by reputation, a reluctant warrior. When military action was required, however, he advocated overwhelming force combined with maximum international support.

George W. Bush's vice presidential choice, Dick Cheney, offered perhaps the clearest contrast to Powell. Cheney, who served as secretary of defense under George H. W. Bush, could best be described as a democratic nationalist. Cheney took a dim view of international institutions such as the United Nations and believed that international coalitions were valuable only to the extent that they permitted the United States full freedom of action regarding decisions to use military force. Cheney placed greater faith in the efficacy of military options than Powell and tended to prefer regime change rather than diplomacy as the most effective way to deal with adversaries. Cheney's views often dovetailed with those of leading civilian officials in the Department of Defense, including Secretary of Defense Donald Rumsfeld and Deputy Secretary of Defense Paul Wolfowitz.

In the early months of his presidency, however, President George W. Bush looked most often to his national security adviser, Condoleezza Rice, for advice. Rice, who worked for the first President Bush and became a close Bush family friend, served as George W. Bush's principal foreign policy tutor before and during his campaign for the presidency. During this period, Rice could best be described as a realist. Like Cheney, she often took a jaundiced view of multilateralist institutions and treaties, especially in the area of arms control. Rice tended to side with Powell, however, in her skepticism regarding the use of force for humanitarian purposes or to effect regime change in the case of so-called rogue states. Rice often argued that the United States would be unwise to saddle itself with the burdens of "nation building" except in cases where vital national interests were at stake. Rice's influence could be heard in President Bush's early criticisms of the Clinton administration's decision to send U.S. forces to places such as Bosnia and Haiti. As a realist, Rice advocated a strong defense, the purpose of which should be the management of threats from actual or potential great-power foes.

Over the course of Bush's tumultuous first term in office, which was punctuated by the September 11, 2001, terrorist attacks and wars in Afghanistan and Iraq, Colin Powell became increasingly marginalized (ultimately leaving office after Bush's 2004 reelection) while Rice gravitated toward the democratic nationalist camp that came to dominate foreign policy decision making. The new directions that George W. Bush and his advisers brought to U.S. foreign policy proved controversial, both at home and abroad.

The Melding of Unilateralism and Moralism

Bush's foreign policies during his first eight months in office generated considerable friction with other major powers. Relations with Europe were frayed by the U.S. rejection of treaties dealing with global warming and the establishment of a new International Criminal Court. The imposition of high tariffs on European steel exports to U.S. markets also led to conflict. Russian president Vladimir Putin voiced objections to U.S. plans to withdraw from the Anti-Ballistic Missile Treaty and to plans for the expansion of NATO. A midair collision between a U.S. spy plane and a Chinese military jet strained U.S.-Chinese ties. China was also dismayed by a public statement in which President Bush seemingly committed the United States to intervene militarily on behalf of Taiwan should it be attacked by China.[1] In general, Bush's early foreign policy initiatives heightened fears in foreign capitals that the United States might be on its way toward jettisoning multilateral commitments in favor of a unilateralist approach to dealing with international problems.

These strains initially subsided in the wake of the 9/11 terrorist attacks on New York and Washington, D.C. Foreign leaders and publics around the world rallied to express sympathy and support for the United States as well as outrage toward the terrorists who perpetrated the attacks. For the first time in its history, NATO invoked the collective self-defense clause of the treaty. Many nations pledged assistance in combating international terrorism. America's subsequent military campaign to oust the Taliban regime and Al Qaeda from Afghanistan in concert with opposition groups in that country also drew widespread support.

In the months immediately following 9/11, it appeared that U.S. foreign policy might shift toward a more multilateralist track. Bush promised to collaborate with other states in pursuing a "war on terrorism." The U.S. Congress finally passed long-delayed legislation making good a portion of America's accumulated arrears on its dues to the United Nations. U.S. relations with a number of countries, including Russia, China, and Pakistan, showed marked improvement.

Yet while the fight against terrorism united much of the world community, the Bush administration's shift during 2002 and 2003 toward a doctrine of preventive warfare and confrontation with a series of so-called rogue states generated renewed divisions between the United States and a number of its principal allies. In his January 2002 State of the Union address,

---

[1]Since the 1970s, the United States has pursued a policy of ambiguity regarding possible American responses to military conflict between China and Taiwan. Following Bush's statement, White House spokespersons denied that the president's remarks represented a change of policy.

President Bush warned of the dangers posed by an "axis of evil" composed of hostile governments in Iraq, Iran, and North Korea. While most foreign observers also expressed concern about the acquisition of weapons of mass destruction by such states, many felt that Bush's speech generated exaggerated fears and struck an overly hawkish tone. Most troubling were the administration's emphasis on regime change, its apparent preference for military force over diplomacy, and the moralistic frame in which President Bush cast many international problems.

In his June 1, 2002, commencement address at the United States Military Academy at West Point, President Bush commented:

> Some worry that it is somehow undiplomatic or impolite to speak the language of right and wrong. I disagree. Different circumstances require different methods, but not different moralities. Moral truth is the same in every culture, in every time, and in every place. Targeting innocent civilians for murder is always and everywhere wrong. Brutality against women is always and everywhere wrong. There can be no neutrality between justice and cruelty, between the innocent and the guilty. We are in a conflict between good and evil, and America will call evil by its name. By confronting evil and lawless regimes, we do not create a problem, we reveal a problem. And we will lead the world in opposing it.[2]

Critics of the administration wondered whether this black and white view of the world ruled out the possibility of peaceful, diplomatic solutions to many problems. After all, how can one strike a deal with an adversary that has been branded as the embodiment of evil?

Strategic Adjustment

A more formal and comprehensive statement of the administration's new thinking about the requirements of American security and national interests in the post-9/11 era was offered by the 2002 National Security Strategy (NSS) report to the Congress that was released in September of that year.[3]

The 2002 NSS report emphasizes five major themes. First, the report strikes a triumphal note in its claim that victory over the forces of totalitarianism has placed history's stamp on "a single sustainable model for national success: freedom, democracy, and free enterprise." America's cherished freedoms "are right and true for every person, in every society."

---

[2]The text of this speech can be found on the White House Web site at www.whitehouse.gov/news/releases/2002/06/20020601-3.html.

[3]The White House released an updated National Security Strategy (NSS) report in March 2006. Since, however, it was the 2002 document that signaled a number of new departures in U.S. foreign and national security policies and that laid the groundwork for the subsequent invasion of Iraq, we have chosen to reprint the earlier version of the NSS in this volume.

Echoing a commonly expressed sentiment in America's diplomatic history, the Bush administration declared that "we seek . . . to create a balance of power that favors human freedom."

Second, the 2002 NSS identifies terrorism and the spread of weapons of mass destruction as the principal threats to American security and national interests. The United States will "disrupt and destroy terrorist organizations of global reach" while making no distinction between "terrorists and those who knowingly harbor or provide aid to them." The report also warns against rogue states that must be confronted "before they are able to threaten or use weapons of mass destruction against the United States and our allies and friends."

Third, the United States must be ready to "act against such emerging threats before they are fully formed." In contrast with the cold war era, "traditional concepts of deterrence will not work against a terrorist enemy whose avowed tactics are wanton destruction and the targeting of innocents." As a result, the report asserts a U.S. right to "act preemptively" to counter the threats posed by terrorism and the spread of weapons of mass destruction to rogue states.[4]

Fourth, the United States retains the option of unilateral action to protect its international interests. While declaring "we will respect the values, judgments and interests of our friends and partners," the report emphasizes that the United States "will be prepared to act apart when our interests and unique responsibilities require."[5]

Fifth, the United States must maintain a position of military supremacy. Rather than merely seeking to balance the power of rival states, the United States will instead sustain sufficient military strength to "dissuade potential adversaries from pursuing a military build-up in hopes of surpassing, or equaling, the power of the United States."

The Iraq War

Many of the themes found in the 2002 NSS report were evident in the Bush administration's approach to dealing with Iraq. That country had been a

---

[4]Preemption has traditionally been defined as a military response to a clear and immediate threat of attack. As such, preemption is generally viewed as a legitimate right of states under international law. Preventive uses of force, by contrast, target hostile adversaries that may constitute a threat at some undefined point in the future. While invoking the concept of preemptive war, the Bush Doctrine's principles and their application in Iraq are more consistent with the concept of preventive war. Preventive war is generally viewed as more legally and ethically problematic than preemption. We will hereafter use the term *prevention,* rather than *preemption,* in discussing this aspect of the Bush Doctrine.

[5]These quotes appear in sections of the report that were deleted, for reasons of space, from the edited version included in part V of this book.

continuing source of concern for U.S. policymakers since Iraq's 1990 invasion of Kuwait. In 1991, U.S. and allied forces moved into Kuwait from
bases in neighboring Saudi Arabia in an ultimately successful effort to free
Kuwait of Iraqi control. The United States stopped short, however, of overthrowing Saddam Hussein's regime in Iraq.

During much of the following decade, the United States and its international partners focused instead on containing Iraq and weakening its capacity for further aggression. U.S. and British warplanes enforced no-fly zones
designed to inhibit the operation of Iraqi airpower over areas of northern
and southern Iraq. The Kurds of northern Iraq established a self-governing
zone largely free of interference from Baghdad. Tough international sanctions weakened Iraq's economy, although Iraq was permitted to sell limited
quantities of oil in exchange for food and medicine.

Most significantly, UN arms inspectors spread across Iraq in search of
chemical, biological, or nuclear weapons and production sites. Inspectors
discovered and destroyed many banned weapons and production facilities.
In 1998, however, the United Nations pulled out its personnel in protest
over continuing efforts by the Iraqi authorities to limit the movement and
activities of inspectors.

Throughout this period, some voices in the United States advocated
regime change in Iraq rather than containment. Indeed, Congress itself endorsed the removal of Saddam Hussein as an ultimate goal of U.S. foreign
policy in the Iraq Liberation Act, passed in 1998. A number of high officials
in the Bush administration first broached the issue of using force to topple
Saddam Hussein in the early days of the Bush presidency. Serious planning
for such a war began in late 2001 and continued through 2002.

The stated rationales for war included Iraq's alleged pursuit of weapons
of mass destruction, its support for international terrorism, and the regime's
record of human rights abuses. Less publicly, some officials cited broader
geopolitical goals, such as safeguarding Israeli security, establishing a base
for possible U.S. military operations against Syria and Iran, securing continued access to Persian Gulf oil resources, and stimulating a wave of political democratization and economic reform through the Middle East.

As the United States moved toward confrontation with Iraq in the summer
of 2002, the White House considered the possibility of invading Iraq without
consulting other countries through the United Nations. Objections to this
course from Secretary of State Colin Powell, combined with resistance from
domestic and international sources, prompted President Bush to seek UN approval. After vigorous diplomatic efforts, the United States succeeded in securing UN Security Council passage of Resolution 1441 in November 2003,
which demanded Iraqi disarmament of weapons of mass destruction and cooperation with renewed weapons inspections. In the debate leading up to
the passage of this resolution, the Bush administration repeatedly threatened
to move against Iraq without UN approval if the Security Council refused to

act. After inspections failed to find evidence of nuclear, biological, or chemical weapons, the United States, along with Great Britain, nonetheless opted for war. A vote to secure explicit Security Council authorization for the invasion of Iraq was considered but rejected when it became clear that not only would France veto passage of such a resolution but also the United States would fail to obtain the support of a majority on the Security Council. Despite this setback, the United States opted for war with the support of Great Britain and a group of smaller coalition partners.

In an offensive beginning on March 19, 2003, U.S. and British forces quickly crushed Iraqi military resistance and ousted Saddam Hussein's regime. The postinvasion phase, however, proved far more difficult. With Iraqi military and police units disbanded, widespread looting and criminal violence spread across the country. Disruptions to public services, such as clean water, electricity, and health care, created hardships for much of the Iraqi population. An aging infrastructure and frequent sabotage slowed progress toward restoring Iraqi oil production.

Within months, U.S. and British occupying forces confronted a growing insurgency mounted by pro-Baathist elements from the previous regime, disgruntled Sunnis, and foreign terrorists recruited from across the Middle East. This resistance was aided by easy access to weapons looted from the many Iraqi military supply depots left unguarded by occupying forces. Insurgent attacks were aimed not only at U.S. and British troops and Western contractors but also at Iraqis who cooperated with the foreign occupation of Iraq.

Meanwhile, U.S. efforts to win international support and legitimacy for the invasion were undermined by the failure of U.S. investigators to find evidence of Iraqi weapons of mass destruction or of Iraqi ties to Al Qaeda or other terrorist organizations. Many European critics of the invasion felt vindicated by these failures, with the consequence that international support for rebuilding and stabilizing Iraq did not expand much beyond the initial coalition.

In the first year following the invasion, U.S. authorities effectively ruled Iraq, although an unpopular and largely symbolic Iraqi governing council was appointed to rubber-stamp the decisions of the occupation. With UN support, sovereignty was returned to Iraq on June 28, 2004, under a government headed by Prime Minister Iyad Allawi. In January 2005, elections produced a parliament and constitutional assembly dominated by a Shiite political coalition. The Sunni population of Iraq, however, largely boycotted the elections, and postelection bargaining over the allocation of power in the new government delayed the formation of a cabinet for almost two months.

On October 15, 2005, Iraqi voters approved a new, permanent constitution that had been prepared by the National Assembly over the previous summer. Although voter turnout in Sunni regions was much higher than in the previous January, a large majority of Sunnis voted against the constitution, which many of their leaders criticized for weakening Iraq's central government in favor of relatively autonomous regional governments and for distributing oil revenues unfairly.

As specified under the new constitution, elections for Iraq's parliament were held on December 15, 2005. Voter turnout was high in all parts of the country, allowing the Bush administration to hail the elections as a turning point in Iraq's movement toward a stable and democratic political order. However, secular parties and candidates fared poorly in these elections as voters overwhelmingly gravitated toward parties reflecting their own religious and ethnic identities. Moreover, the postelection period was clouded by charges of voting fraud in some parts of the country as well as unabated violence and insurgency.

In short, more than two years after the initial invasion of Iraq, U.S. policymakers faced a daunting list of challenges: a stubborn insurgency that showed no signs of ebbing, factional conflict among and within Iraq's three main religious and ethnic groupings (Sunnis, Shiites, and Kurds), the gargantuan task of rebuilding Iraq's crisis-ridden economy, and the financial burdens associated with a prolonged military presence. As of December 2005, American troops in Iraq had suffered roughly 2200 fatalities and 16,000 wounded. The Iraqi death toll remained uncertain but likely numbered in the tens of thousands.

Evaluating the Bush Doctrine in Theory and Practice

Sympathetic observers of the Bush administration's foreign policy record point to a number of accomplishments. These include Bush's moves to weaken Al Qaeda and to protect the U.S. homeland and the absence of new terrorist attacks on U.S. territory since 9/11. U.S. military operations succeeded in ousting the Taliban from power in Afghanistan and Saddam Hussein from Iraq. Subsequent elections have planted the seeds of democracy in each of these two countries, despite continuing violence and unrest in both. Despite continuing concerns over the nuclear ambitions of Iran and North Korea, Bush's supporters count Libya's abandonment of its nuclear weapons program and Pakistan's dismantlement of an illegal nuclear technology network as examples of progress in the struggle against nuclear proliferation.

For Christopher Hitchens, the war in Iraq is redeemed by the removal from power of Saddam Hussein, a despotic tyrant whose record included gross human rights abuses against his own people, military aggression against his neighbors, and efforts to obtain weapons of mass destruction. Hitchens views both Hussein and the radical supporters of Osama bin Laden, however different they may be in ideology and purpose, as self-evident threats to the principles of peace, freedom, and human rights. Hitchens is critical of fellow liberals who fail to recognize the necessary role that force must sometimes play in opposing violent extremists and rogue states.

Yet the Bush administration's foreign policies and the principles that underlie them also have many detractors. The authors represented in this part offer a number of criticisms of the Bush Doctrine and the administration's approaches to dealing with terrorism and rogue states. In the following paragraphs I summarize the main criticisms contained in these chapters.

First, the Bush administration's unilateralist approach to U.S. foreign policy and, in particular, its decision to invade Iraq without the authorization of the UN Security Council have undermined the legitimacy of U.S. leadership abroad, endangered key alliance relationships, and weakened important international institutions. As a result, the United States may find it difficult to mobilize future international cooperation around issues important to the United States (this criticism is raised in the chapters by G. John Ikenberry and by Robert F. Ellsworth and Dimitri K. Simes).

Second, as Ellsworth and Simes and Jeffrey Record point out, the war in Iraq and its violent aftermath have diverted resources and attention away from more crucial priorities, such as the fight against Al Qaeda and the strengthening of homeland security.

Third, the doctrine of preventive war sets a dangerous precedent. Following the U.S. example, other states may also be tempted to attack adversaries in the absence of international sanction or clear and immediate provocation. Ikenberry and Record both argue that the Bush administration has too quickly dismissed the continuing relevance of deterrence as a means for coping with rogue states and the emergence of new nuclear powers.

Fourth, the administration's use of force against Iraq may prompt states such as Iran and North Korea to accelerate their drive to obtain nuclear weapons out of fear that only the threat of nuclear retaliation may stave off U.S. military action aimed at regime change. Moreover, according to Ellsworth and Simes and Ikenberry, the administration's short-circuiting of the arms inspection process in Iraq may undermine the viability of the existing nuclear nonproliferation regime.

Fifth, some critics express skepticism about the administration's claims that lasting democracy can be produced in Afghanistan, Iraq, or the broader Middle East through force of arms. According to Record, for instance, the United States should aim for political stability rather than the less achievable goal of democracy in managing postwar Iraq.

Sixth, the expansive aims of the Bush Doctrine could lead to a condition of "imperial overstretch." Ikenberry argues that the effectiveness of the U.S. armed forces may erode as U.S. troops are stretched too thinly across the globe while the combined costs of increased defense spending, growing aid budgets, and new expenditures on homeland security bankrupt the U.S. Treasury and sap U.S. economic strength.

In response to some of the real-world complications that have accompanied the "Bush revolution" in U.S. foreign policy, the administration has, in the president's second term of office, made adjustments designed to quell domestic and international criticism. These have included, according to Philip H. Gordon, closer consultation with allies, a greater reliance upon multilateral institutions, positive measures to attack the sources of poverty and violence in poverty-stricken regions of the world, and a more measured and moderate rhetorical tone. Whether these shifts in approach prove lasting, Gordon argues, will depend upon events in the world and how they are perceived by key decision makers.

Conclusion

America's rise to unipolar dominance has coincided with dramatic shifts in the doctrinal underpinnings of U.S. foreign policy, especially in the post-9/11 era. The Bush Doctrine has elevated the principles of unilateralism, preventive war, and regime change to central roles in U.S. grand strategy. The Bush administration has also coupled the war on terrorism with a major push to promote the spread of democracy and free-market economics around the world.

The readings contained in this part and in the volume as a whole provide a rich set of resources for evaluating the sources, wisdom, and consequences of these ambitious and far-reaching adjustments in U.S. foreign and military policy.

DISCUSSION QUESTIONS

1. How great a departure is the "Bush Doctrine" from past traditions and practices in American foreign policy?

2. Will the American experience of war and occupation in Iraq render policymakers more or less willing to undertake similar military ventures in the future?

3. What are the merits of prevention versus deterrence as alternative strategies for coping with the potential threats posed by rogue states seeking weapons of mass destruction?

4. Will regime changes in Afghanistan and Iraq improve the prospects for spreading democracy through the Middle East and Central Asia?

5. Has the invasion of Iraq assisted or undermined the broader war against terrorism?

SUGGESTED READINGS

Art, Robert J. *A Grand Strategy for America*. Ithaca, N.Y.: Cornell University Press, 2003.

Bamford, James. *A Pretext for War: 9/11, Iraq, and the Abuse of America's Intelligence Agencies*. New York: Doubleday, 2004.

Daalder, Ivo H., and James M. Lindsay. *America Unbound: The Bush Revolution in Foreign Policy*, rev. ed. Hoboken, N.J.: Wiley, 2005.

Diamond, Larry. *Squandered Victory: The American Occupation and the Bungled Effort to Bring Democracy to Iraq*. New York: Times Books, 2005.

Gordon, Michael R., and Bernard E. Trainor. *Cobra II: The Inside Story of the Invasion and Occupation of Iraq*. New York: Pantheon, 2006.

Mann, James. *Rise of the Vulcans: The History of Bush's War Cabinet*. New York: Viking, 2004.

National Commission on Terrorist Attacks. *The 9/11 Commission Report: Final Report of the National Commission on Terrorist Attacks upon the United States*. New York: Norton, 2004.

Packer, George. *The Assassins' Gate: America in Iraq*. New York: Farrar, Straus and Giroux, 2005.

Scheuer, Michael. *Imperial Hubris: Why the West Is Losing the War on Terror*. Washington, D.C.: Brassey's, 2004.

Wright, Lawrence. *The Looming Tower: Al-Qaeda and the Road to 9/11*. New York: Knopf, 2006.

21

The National Security Strategy of the United States of America, 2002

The White House

The great struggles of the twentieth century between liberty and totalitarianism ended with a decisive victory for the forces of freedom—and a single sustainable model for national success: freedom, democracy, and free enterprise. In the twenty-first century, only nations that share a commitment to protecting basic human rights and guaranteeing political and economic freedom will be able to unleash the potential of their people and assure their future prosperity. People everywhere want to be able to speak freely; choose who will govern them; worship as they please; educate their children—male and female; own property; and enjoy the benefits of their labor. These values of freedom are right and true for every person, in every society—and the duty of protecting these values against their enemies is the common calling of freedom-loving people across the globe and across the ages.

Today, the United States enjoys a position of unparalleled military strength and great economic and political influence. In keeping with our heritage and principles, we do not use our strength to press for unilateral advantage. We seek instead to create a balance of power that favors human freedom: conditions in which all nations and all societies can choose for themselves the rewards and challenges of political and economic liberty. In a world that is safe, people will be able to make their own lives better. We will defend the peace by fighting terrorists and tyrants. We will preserve the peace by building good relations among the great powers. We will extend the peace by encouraging free and open societies on every continent.

Defending our Nation against its enemies is the first and fundamental commitment of the Federal Government. Today, that task has changed dramatically. Enemies in the past needed great armies and great industrial capabilities to endanger America. Now, shadowy networks of individuals can bring great chaos and suffering to our shores for less than it costs to purchase a single tank. Terrorists are organized to penetrate open societies and to turn the power of modern technologies against us.

To defeat this threat we must make use of every tool in our arsenal— military power, better homeland defenses, law enforcement, intelligence, and vigorous efforts to cut off terrorist financing. The war against terrorists of global reach is a global enterprise of uncertain duration. America will help nations that need our assistance in combating terror. And America will hold to account nations that are compromised by terror, including those who harbor terrorists—because the allies of terror are the enemies of civilization. The United States and countries cooperating with us must not allow the terrorists to develop new home bases. Together, we will seek to deny them sanctuary at every turn.

The gravest danger our Nation faces lies at the crossroads of radicalism and technology. Our enemies have openly declared that they are seeking weapons of mass destruction, and evidence indicates that they are doing so with determination. The United States will not allow these efforts to succeed. We will build defenses against ballistic missiles and other means of delivery. We will cooperate with other nations to deny, contain, and curtail our enemies' efforts to acquire dangerous technologies. And, as a matter of common sense and self-defense, America will act against such emerging threats before they are fully formed. We cannot defend America and our friends by hoping for the best. So we must be prepared to defeat our enemies' plans, using the best intelligence and proceeding with deliberation. History will judge harshly those who saw this coming danger but failed to act. In the new world we have entered, the only path to peace and security is the path of action.

As we defend the peace, we will also take advantage of an historic opportunity to preserve the peace. Today, the international community has the best chance since the rise of the nation-state in the seventeenth century to build a world where great powers compete in peace instead of continually prepare for war. Today, the world's great powers find ourselves on the same side—united by common dangers of terrorist violence and chaos. The United States will build on these common interests to promote global security. We are also increasingly united by common values. Russia is in the midst of a hopeful transition, reaching for its democratic future and a partner in the war on terror. Chinese leaders are discovering that economic freedom is the only source of national wealth. In time, they will find that social and political freedom is the only source of national greatness. America will encourage the advancement of democracy and economic openness in both nations, because these are the best foundations for domestic stability and international order. We will strongly resist aggression from other great powers—even as we welcome their peaceful pursuit of prosperity, trade, and cultural advancement.

Finally, the United States will use this moment of opportunity to extend the benefits of freedom across the globe. We will actively work to bring the hope of democracy, development, free markets, and free trade to every corner of the world. The events of September 11, 2001, taught us that weak states, like Afghanistan, can pose as great a danger to our national interests as strong states. Poverty does not make poor people into terrorists and murderers. Yet poverty, weak institutions, and corruption can make weak states vulnerable to terrorist networks and drug cartels within their borders.

The United States will stand beside any nation determined to build a better future by seeking the rewards of liberty for its people. Free trade and free markets have proven their ability to lift whole societies out of poverty—so the United States will work with individual nations, entire regions, and the entire global trading community to build a world that trades in freedom and therefore grows in prosperity. . . .

We are also guided by the conviction that no nation can build a safer, better world alone. Alliances and multilateral institutions can multiply the strength of freedom-loving nations. The United States is committed to lasting institutions like the United Nations, the World Trade Organization, the Organization of American States, and NATO as well as other long-standing alliances. Coalitions of the willing can augment these permanent institutions. In all cases, international obligations are to be taken seriously. They are not to be undertaken symbolically to rally support for an ideal without furthering its attainment.

Freedom is the non-negotiable demand of human dignity; the birthright of every person—in every civilization. Throughout history, freedom has been threatened by war and terror; it has been challenged by the clashing wills of powerful states and the evil designs of tyrants; and it has been tested by widespread poverty and disease. Today, humanity holds in its hands the opportunity to further freedom's triumph over all these foes. The United States welcomes our responsibility to lead in this great mission.

I. OVERVIEW OF AMERICA'S INTERNATIONAL STRATEGY

The United States possesses unprecedented—and unequaled—strength and influence in the world. Sustained by faith in the principles of liberty, and the value of a free society, this position comes with unparalleled responsibilities, obligations, and opportunity. The great strength of this nation must be used to promote a balance of power that favors freedom.

For most of the twentieth century, the world was divided by a great struggle over ideas: destructive totalitarian visions versus freedom and equality. That great struggle is over. The militant visions of class, nation, and race which promised utopia and delivered misery have been defeated and discredited. America is now threatened less by conquering states than we are by failing ones. We are menaced less by fleets and armies than by catastrophic technologies in the hands of the embittered few. We must defeat these threats to our Nation, allies, and friends.

This is also a time of opportunity for America. We will work to translate this moment of influence into decades of peace, prosperity, and liberty. The U.S. national security strategy will be based on a distinctly American internationalism that reflects the union of our values and our national interests. The aim of this strategy is to help make the world not just safer but better. Our goals on the path to progress are clear: political and economic freedom, peaceful relations with other states, and respect for human dignity. And this path is not America's alone. It is open to all.

To achieve these goals, the United States will:

- champion aspirations for human dignity;
- strengthen alliances to defeat global terrorism and work to prevent attacks against us and our friends;
- work with others to defuse regional conflicts;
- prevent our enemies from threatening us, our allies, and our friends, with weapons of mass destruction;
- ignite a new era of global economic growth through free markets and free trade;
- expand the circle of development by opening societies and building the infrastructure of democracy;
- develop agendas for cooperative action with other main centers of global power; and
- transform America's national security institutions to meet the challenges and opportunities of the twenty-first century.

II. CHAMPION ASPIRATIONS FOR HUMAN DIGNITY

In pursuit of our goals, our first imperative is to clarify what we stand for: the United States must defend liberty and justice because these principles are right and true for all people everywhere. No nation owns these aspirations, and no nation is exempt from them. Fathers and mothers in all societies want their children to be educated and to live free from poverty and violence. No people on earth yearn to be oppressed, aspire to servitude, or eagerly await the midnight knock of the secret police.

America must stand firmly for the non-negotiable demands of human dignity: the rule of law; limits on the absolute power of the state; free speech; freedom of worship; equal justice; respect for women; religious and ethnic tolerance; and respect for private property.

These demands can be met in many ways. America's constitution has served us well. Many other nations, with different histories and cultures, facing different circumstances, have successfully incorporated these core principles into their own systems of governance. History has not been kind to those nations which ignored or flouted the rights and aspirations of their people.

America's experience as a great multi-ethnic democracy affirms our conviction that people of many heritages and faiths can live and prosper in peace. Our own history is a long struggle to live up to our ideals. But even in our worst moments, the principles enshrined in the Declaration of Independence were there to guide us. As a result, America is not just a stronger, but is a freer and more just society.

Today, these ideals are a lifeline to lonely defenders of liberty. And when openings arrive, we can encourage change—as we did in central and eastern Europe between 1989 and 1991; or in Belgrade in 2000. When we see democratic processes take hold among our friends in Taiwan or in the Republic of Korea, and see elected leaders replace generals in Latin America and Africa, we see examples of how authoritarian systems can evolve, marrying local history and traditions with the principles we all cherish.

Embodying lessons from our past and using the opportunity we have today, the national security strategy of the United States must start from these core beliefs and look outward for possibilities to expand liberty.

Our principles will guide our government's decisions about international cooperation, the character of our foreign assistance, and the allocation of resources. They will guide our actions and our words in international bodies.

We will:

- speak out honestly about violations of the non-negotiable demands of human dignity using our voice and vote in international institutions to advance freedom;
- use our foreign aid to promote freedom and support those who struggle non-violently for it, ensuring that nations moving toward democracy are rewarded for the steps they take;
- make freedom and the development of democratic institutions key themes in our bilateral relations, seeking solidarity and cooperation from other democracies while we press governments that deny human rights to move toward a better future; and
- take special efforts to promote freedom of religion and conscience and defend it from encroachment by repressive governments. We will champion the cause of human dignity and oppose those who resist it.

III. STRENGTHEN ALLIANCES TO DEFEAT GLOBAL TERRORISM AND WORK TO PREVENT ATTACKS AGAINST US AND OUR FRIENDS

The United States of America is fighting a war against terrorists of global reach. The enemy is not a single political regime or person or religion or ideology. The enemy is terrorism—premeditated, politically motivated violence perpetrated against innocents.

In many regions, legitimate grievances prevent the emergence of a lasting peace. Such grievances deserve to be, and must be, addressed within a political process. But no cause justifies terror. The United States will make no concessions to terrorist demands and strike no deals with them. We make no distinction between terrorists and those who knowingly harbor or provide aid to them.

The struggle against global terrorism is different from any other war in our history. It will be fought on many fronts against a particularly elusive enemy over an extended period of time. Progress will come through the persistent accumulation of successes—some seen, some unseen.

Today our enemies have seen the results of what civilized nations can, and will, do against regimes that harbor, support, and use terrorism to achieve their political goals. Afghanistan has been liberated; coalition forces continue to hunt down the Taliban and al-Qaida. But it is not only this battlefield on which we will engage terrorists. Thousands of trained terrorists remain at large with cells in North America, South America, Europe, Africa, the Middle East, and across Asia.

Our priority will be first to disrupt and destroy terrorist organizations of global reach and attack their leadership; command, control, and communications; material support; and finances. This will have a disabling effect upon the terrorists' ability to plan and operate.

We will continue to encourage our regional partners to take up a coordinated effort that isolates the terrorists. Once the regional campaign localizes the threat to a particular state, we will help ensure the state has the military, law enforcement, political, and financial tools necessary to finish the task.

The United States will continue to work with our allies to disrupt the financing of terrorism. We will identify and block the sources of funding for terrorism, freeze the assets of terrorists and those who support them, deny terrorists access to the international financial system, protect legitimate charities from being abused by terrorists, and prevent the movement of terrorists' assets through alternative financial networks.

However, this campaign need not be sequential to be effective; the cumulative effect across all regions will help achieve the results we seek.

We will disrupt and destroy terrorist organizations by:

- direct and continuous action using all the elements of national and international power. Our immediate focus will be those terrorist organizations of global reach and any terrorist or state sponsor of terrorism which attempts to gain or use weapons of mass destruction (WMD) or their precursors;
- defending the United States, the American people, and our interests at home and abroad by identifying and destroying the threat before it reaches our borders. While the United States will constantly strive to enlist the support of the international community, we will not hesitate to act alone, if necessary, to exercise our right of self-defense by acting preemptively against such terrorists, to prevent them from doing harm against our people and our country; and
- denying further sponsorship, support, and sanctuary to terrorists by convincing or compelling states to accept their sovereign responsibilities.

We will also wage a war of ideas to win the battle against international terrorism. This includes:

- using the full influence of the United States, and working closely with allies and friends, to make clear that all acts of terrorism are illegitimate so that terrorism will be viewed in the same light as slavery, piracy, or genocide: behavior that no respectable government can condone or support and all must oppose;
- supporting moderate and modern government, especially in the Muslim world, to ensure that the conditions and ideologies that promote terrorism do not find fertile ground in any nation;
- diminishing the underlying conditions that spawn terrorism by enlisting the international community to focus its efforts and resources on areas most at risk; and
- using effective public diplomacy to promote the free flow of information and ideas to kindle the hopes and aspirations of freedom of those in societies ruled by the sponsors of global terrorism.

While we recognize that our best defense is a good offense, we are also strengthening America's homeland security to protect against and deter attack.

This Administration has proposed the largest government reorganization since the Truman Administration created the National Security Council and the Department of Defense. Centered on a new Department of Homeland Security and including a new unified military command and a fundamental reordering of the FBI, our comprehensive plan to secure the homeland encompasses every level of government and the cooperation of the public and the private sector.

This strategy will turn adversity into opportunity. For example, emergency management systems will be better able to cope not just with terrorism but with all hazards. Our medical system will be strengthened to manage not just bioterror, but all infectious diseases and mass-casualty dangers. Our border controls will not just stop terrorists, but improve the efficient movement of legitimate traffic.

While our focus is protecting America, we know that to defeat terrorism in today's globalized world we need support from our allies and friends. Wherever possible, the United States will rely on regional organizations and state powers to meet their obligations to fight terrorism. Where governments find the fight against terrorism beyond their capacities, we will match their willpower and their resources with whatever help we and our allies can provide.

As we pursue the terrorists in Afghanistan, we will continue to work with international organizations such as the United Nations, as well as non-governmental organizations, and other countries to provide the humanitarian, political, economic, and security assistance necessary to rebuild Afghanistan so that it will never again abuse its people, threaten its neighbors, and provide a haven for terrorists.

In the war against global terrorism, we will never forget that we are ultimately fighting for our democratic values and way of life. Freedom and fear are at war, and there will be no quick or easy end to this conflict. In leading the campaign against terrorism, we are forging new, productive international relationships and redefining existing ones in ways that meet the challenges of the twenty-first century. . . .

V. PREVENT OUR ENEMIES FROM THREATENING US, OUR ALLIES, AND OUR FRIENDS WITH WEAPONS OF MASS DESTRUCTION

The nature of the Cold War threat required the United States—with our allies and friends—to emphasize deterrence of the enemy's use of force, producing a grim strategy of mutual assured destruction. With the collapse of the Soviet Union and the end of the Cold War, our security environment has undergone profound transformation.

Having moved from confrontation to cooperation as the hallmark of our relationship with Russia, the dividends are evident: an end to the balance of terror that divided us; an historic reduction in the nuclear arsenals on both sides; and cooperation in areas such as counterterrorism and missile defense that until recently were inconceivable.

But new deadly challenges have emerged from rogue states and terrorists. None of these contemporary threats rival the sheer destructive power that was arrayed against us by the Soviet Union. However, the nature and motivations of these new adversaries, their determination to obtain destructive powers hitherto available only to the world's strongest states, and the greater likelihood that they will use weapons of mass destruction against us, make today's security environment more complex and dangerous.

In the 1990s we witnessed the emergence of a small number of rogue states that, while different in important ways, share a number of attributes. These states:

- brutalize their own people and squander their national resources for the personal gain of the rulers;
- display no regard for international law, threaten their neighbors, and callously violate international treaties to which they are party;
- are determined to acquire weapons of mass destruction, along with other advanced military technology, to be used as threats or offensively to achieve the aggressive designs of these regimes;
- sponsor terrorism around the globe; and
- reject basic human values and hate the United States and everything for which it stands.

At the time of the Gulf War, we acquired irrefutable proof that Iraq's designs were not limited to the chemical weapons it had used against Iran and its own people, but also extended to the acquisition of nuclear weapons and biological agents. In the past decade North Korea has become the world's principal purveyor of ballistic missiles, and has tested increasingly capable missiles while developing its own WMD arsenal. Other rogue regimes seek nuclear, biological, and chemical weapons as well. These states' pursuit of, and global trade in, such weapons has become a looming threat to all nations.

We must be prepared to stop rogue states and their terrorist clients before they are able to threaten or use weapons of mass destruction against the United States and our allies and friends. Our response must take full advantage of strengthened alliances, the establishment of new partnerships with former adversaries, innovation in the use of military forces, modern technologies, including the development of an effective missile defense system, and increased emphasis on intelligence collection and analysis.

Our comprehensive strategy to combat WMD includes:

- *Proactive counterproliferation efforts.* We must deter and defend against the threat before it is unleashed. We must ensure that key capabilities—detection, active and passive defenses, and counterforce capabilities—are integrated into our defense transformation and our homeland security systems. Counterproliferation must also be integrated into the doctrine, training, and equipping of our forces and those of our allies to ensure that we can prevail in any conflict with WMD-armed adversaries.

- *Strengthened nonproliferation efforts to prevent rogue states and terrorists from acquiring the materials, technologies, and expertise necessary for weapons of mass destruction.* We will enhance diplomacy, arms control, multilateral export controls, and threat reduction assistance that impede states and terrorists seeking WMD, and when necessary, interdict enabling technologies and materials. We will continue to build coalitions to support these efforts, encouraging their increased political and financial support for nonproliferation and threat reduction programs. The recent G-8 agreement to commit up to $20 billion to a global partnership against proliferation marks a major step forward.

- *Effective consequence management to respond to the effects of WMD use, whether by terrorists or hostile states.* Minimizing the effects of WMD use against our people will help deter those who possess such weapons and dissuade those who seek to acquire them by persuading enemies that they cannot attain their desired ends. The United States must also be prepared to respond to the effects of WMD use against our forces abroad, and to help friends and allies if they are attacked.

It has taken almost a decade for us to comprehend the true nature of this new threat. Given the goals of rogue states and terrorists, the United States can no longer solely rely on a reactive posture as we have in the past. The inability to deter a potential attacker, the immediacy of today's threats, and the magnitude of potential harm that could be caused by our adversaries' choice of weapons, do not permit that option. We cannot let our enemies strike first.

In the Cold War, especially following the Cuban missile crisis, we faced a generally status quo, risk-averse adversary. Deterrence was an effective defense. But deterrence based only upon the threat of retaliation is less likely to work against leaders of rogue states more willing to take risks, gambling with the lives of their people, and the wealth of their nations.

- In the Cold War, weapons of mass destruction were considered weapons of last resort whose use risked the destruction of those who used them. Today, our enemies see weapons of mass destruction as weapons of choice. For rogue states these weapons are tools of intimidation and military aggression against their neighbors. These weapons may also allow these states to attempt to blackmail the United States and our allies to prevent us from deterring or repelling the aggressive behavior of rogue states. Such states also see these weapons as their best means of overcoming the conventional superiority of the United States.

- Traditional concepts of deterrence will not work against a terrorist enemy whose avowed tactics are wanton destruction and the targeting of innocents; whose so-called soldiers seek martyrdom in death and whose most potent protection is statelessness. The overlap between states that sponsor terror and those that pursue WMD compels us to action.

For centuries, international law recognized that nations need not suffer an attack before they can lawfully take action to defend themselves against forces that present an imminent danger of attack. Legal scholars and international jurists often conditioned the legitimacy of preemption on the existence of an imminent threat—most often a visible mobilization of armies, navies, and air forces preparing to attack.

We must adapt the concept of imminent threat to the capabilities and objectives of today's adversaries. Rogue states and terrorists do not seek to attack us using conventional means. They know such attacks would fail. Instead, they rely on acts of terror and, potentially, the use of weapons of mass destruction—weapons that can be easily concealed, delivered covertly, and used without warning.

The targets of these attacks are our military forces and our civilian population, in direct violation of one of the principal norms of the law of warfare. As was demonstrated by the losses on September 11, 2001, mass civilian casualties are the specific objective of terrorists and these losses would be exponentially more severe if terrorists acquired and used weapons of mass destruction.

The United States has long maintained the option of preemptive actions to counter a sufficient threat to our national security. The greater the threat, the greater is the risk of inaction—and the more compelling the case for taking anticipatory action to defend ourselves, even if uncertainty remains as to the time and place of the enemy's attack. To forestall or prevent such hostile acts by our adversaries, the United States will, if necessary, act preemptively.

The United States will not use force in all cases to preempt emerging threats, nor should nations use preemption as a pretext for aggression. Yet in an age where the enemies of civilization openly and actively seek the world's most destructive technologies, the United States cannot remain idle while dangers gather.

We will always proceed deliberately, weighing the consequences of our actions. To support preemptive options, we will:

- build better, more integrated intelligence capabilities to provide timely, accurate information on threats, wherever they may emerge;
- coordinate closely with allies to form a common assessment of the most dangerous threats; and

- continue to transform our military forces to ensure our ability to conduct rapid and precise operations to achieve decisive results.

The purpose of our actions will always be to eliminate a specific threat to the United States or our allies and friends. The reasons for our actions will be clear, the force measured, and the cause just. . . .

IX. TRANSFORM AMERICA'S NATIONAL SECURITY INSTITUTIONS TO MEET THE CHALLENGES AND OPPORTUNITIES OF THE TWENTY FIRST CENTURY

The major institutions of American national security were designed in a different era to meet different requirements. All of them must be transformed.

It is time to reaffirm the essential role of American military strength. We must build and maintain our defenses beyond challenge. Our military's highest priority is to defend the United States. To do so effectively, our military must:

- assure our allies and friends;
- dissuade future military competition;
- deter threats against U.S. interests, allies, and friends; and
- decisively defeat any adversary if deterrence fails.

The unparalleled strength of the United States armed forces, and their forward presence, have maintained the peace in some of the world's most strategically vital regions. However, the threats and enemies we must confront have changed, and so must our forces. A military structured to deter massive Cold War–era armies must be transformed to focus more on how an adversary might fight rather than where and when a war might occur. We will channel our energies to overcome a host of operational challenges.

The presence of American forces overseas is one of the most profound symbols of the U.S. commitments to allies and friends. Through our willingness to use force in our own defense and in defense of others, the United States demonstrates its resolve to maintain a balance of power that favors freedom. To contend with uncertainty and to meet the many security challenges we face, the United States will require bases and stations within and beyond Western Europe and Northeast Asia, as well as temporary access arrangements for the long-distance deployment of U.S. forces.

Before the war in Afghanistan, that area was low on the list of major planning contingencies. Yet, in a very short time, we had to operate across the length and breadth of that remote nation, using every branch of the armed forces. We must prepare for more such deployments by developing assets such as advanced remote sensing, long-range precision strike capabilities, and transformed maneuver and expeditionary forces. This broad portfolio of military capabilities must also include the ability to defend the homeland, conduct information operations, ensure U.S. access to distant theaters, and protect critical U.S. infrastructure and assets in outer space.

Innovation within the armed forces will rest on experimentation with new approaches to warfare, strengthening joint operations, exploiting U.S. intelligence advantages, and taking full advantage of science and technology. We must also transform the way the Department of Defense is run, especially in financial management and recruitment and retention. Finally, while maintaining near-term readiness and the ability to fight the war on terrorism, the goal must be to provide the President with a wider range of military options to discourage aggression or any form of coercion against the United States, our allies, and our friends.

We know from history that deterrence can fail; and we know from experience that some enemies cannot be deterred. The United States must and will maintain the capability to defeat any attempt by an enemy—whether a state or non-state actor—to impose its will on the United States, our allies, or our friends. We will maintain the forces sufficient to support our obligations, and to defend freedom. Our forces will be strong enough to dissuade potential adversaries from pursuing a military build-up in hopes of surpassing, or equaling, the power of the United States.

22

The Case for Overthrowing Saddam Was Unimpeachable

Christopher Hitchens

Let me begin with a simple sentence that, even as I write it, appears less than Swiftian in the modesty of its proposal: "Prison conditions at Abu Ghraib have improved markedly and dramatically since the arrival of Coalition troops in Baghdad."

I could undertake to defend that statement against any member of Human Rights Watch or Amnesty International, and I know in advance that none of them could challenge it, let alone negate it. Before March 2003, Abu Ghraib was an abattoir, a torture chamber, and a concentration camp. Now, and not without reason, it is an international byword for Yankee imperialism and sadism. Yet the improvement is still, unarguably, the difference between night and day. How is it possible that the advocates of a post-Saddam Iraq have been placed on the defensive in this manner? And where should one begin?

I once tried to calculate how long the post–Cold War liberal Utopia had actually lasted. Whether you chose to date its inception from the fall of the Berlin Wall in November 1989, or the death of Nicolae Ceauşescu in late December of the same year, or the release of Nelson Mandela from prison, or the referendum defeat suffered by Augusto Pinochet (or indeed from the publication of Francis Fukuyama's book about the "end of history" and the unarguable triumph of market liberal pluralism), it was an epoch that in retrospect was over before it began. By the middle of 1990, Saddam Hussein had abolished Kuwait and Slobodan Milošević was attempting to erase the identity and the existence of Bosnia. It turned out that we had not by any means escaped the reach of atavistic, aggressive, expansionist, and totalitarian ideology. Proving the same point in another way, and within approximately the same period, the theocratic dictator of Iran had publicly claimed the right to offer money in his own name for the suborning of the murder of a novelist living in London, and the *génocidaire* faction in Rwanda had decided that it could probably get away with putting its long-fantasized plan of mass murder into operation.

One is not mentioning these apparently discrepant crimes and nightmares as a random or unsorted list. Khomeini, for example, was attempting to compensate for the humiliation of the peace agreement he had been compelled to sign with Saddam Hussein. And Saddam Hussein needed to make up the loss, of prestige and income, that he had himself suffered in the very same war. Milosevic . . . was riding a mutation of socialist nationalism into national socialism. It was to be noticed in all cases that the aggressors, whether they were killing Muslims, or exalting Islam, or just killing their neighbors, shared a deep and abiding hatred of the United States.

The balance sheet of the Iraq war, if it is to be seriously drawn up, must also involve a confrontation with at least this much of recent history. Was the Bush administration right to leave—actually to confirm—Saddam Hussein in power after his eviction from Kuwait in 1991? Was James Baker correct to say, in his delightfully folksy manner, that the United States did not "have a dog in the fight" that involved ethnic cleansing for the mad dream of a Greater Serbia? Was the Clinton administration prudent in its retreat from Somalia, or wise in its opposition to the U.N. resolution that called for a preemptive strengthening of the U.N. forces in Rwanda? . . .

The only speech by any statesman that can bear reprinting from that low, dishonest decade came from Tony Blair when he spoke in Chicago in 1999. Welcoming the defeat and overthrow of Milošević after the Kosovo intervention, he warned against any self-satisfaction and drew attention to an inescapable confrontation that was coming with Saddam Hussein. So far from being an American "poodle," as his taunting and ignorant foes like to sneer, Blair had in fact leaned on Clinton over Kosovo and was insisting on the importance of Iraq while George Bush was still an isolationist governor of Texas.

Notwithstanding this prescience and principle on his part, one still cannot read the journals of the 2000/2001 millennium without the feeling that one is revisiting a hopelessly somnambulist relative in a neglected home. I am one of those who believe, uncynically, that Osama bin Laden did us all a service (and holy war a great disservice) by his mad decision to assault the American homeland four years ago. Had he not made this world-historical mistake, we would have been able to add a Talibanized and nuclear-armed Pakistan to our list of the threats we failed to recognize in time. . . .

The subsequent liberation of Pakistan's theocratic colony in Afghanistan, and the so-far decisive eviction and defeat of its bin Ladenist guests, were only a reprisal. It took care of the last attack. But what about the next one? For anyone with eyes to see, there was only one other state that combined the latent and the blatant definitions of both "rogue" and "failed." This state—Saddam's ruined and tortured and collapsing Iraq—had also met all the conditions under which a country may be deemed to have sacrificed its own legal sovereignty. To recapitulate: It had invaded its neighbors, committed genocide on its own soil, harbored and nurtured international thugs and killers, and flouted every provision of the Non-Proliferation Treaty. The United Nations, in this crisis, faced with regular insult to its own resolutions and its own character, had managed to set up a system of sanctions-based mutual corruption. In May 2003, had things gone on as they had been going, Saddam Hussein would have been due to fill Iraq's slot as chair of the U.N. Conference on Disarmament. Meanwhile, every species of gangster from the hero of the *Achille Lauro* hijacking to Abu Musab al Zarqawi was finding hospitality under Saddam's crumbling roof.

One might have thought, therefore, that Bush and Blair's decision to put an end at last to this intolerable state of affairs would be hailed, not just as a belated vindication of long-ignored U.N. resolutions but as some corrective to the decade of shame and inaction that had just passed in Bosnia and Rwanda. But such is not the case. An apparent consensus exists, among millions of people in Europe and America, that the whole operation for the demilitarization of Iraq, and the salvage of its traumatized society, was at best a false pretense and at worst an unprovoked aggression. How can this possibly be?

There is, first, the problem of humorless and pseudo-legalistic literalism. In Saki's short story *The Lumber Room*, the naughty but clever child Nicholas, who has actually placed a frog in his morning bread-and-milk, rejoices in his triumph over the adults who don't credit this excuse for not eating his healthful dish:

> *"You said there couldn't possibly be a frog in my bread-and-milk; there was a frog in my bread-and-milk," he repeated, with the insistence of a skilled tactician who does not intend to shift from favorable ground.*

Childishness is one thing—those of us who grew up on this wonderful Edwardian author were always happy to see the grown-ups and governesses discomfited. But puerility in adults is quite another thing, and considerably less charming. "You said there were WMDs in Iraq and that Saddam had friends in al Qaeda. . . . Blah, blah, pants on fire." I have had many opportunities to tire of this mantra. It takes ten seconds to intone the said mantra. It would take me, on my most eloquent C-SPAN day, at the very least five minutes to say that Abdul Rahman Yasin, who mixed the chemicals for the World Trade Center attack in 1993, subsequently sought and found refuge in Baghdad; that Dr. Mahdi Obeidi, Saddam's senior physicist, was able to lead American soldiers to nuclear centrifuge parts and a blueprint for a complete centrifuge (the crown jewel of nuclear physics) buried on the orders of Qusay Hussein; that Saddam's agents were in Damascus as late as February 2003, negotiating to purchase missiles off the shelf from North Korea; or that Rolf Ekeus, the great Swedish socialist who founded the inspection process in Iraq after 1991, has told me for the record that he was offered a $2 million bribe in a face-to-face meeting with Tariq Aziz. And these eye-catching examples would by no means exhaust my repertoire, or empty my quiver. Yes, it must be admitted that Bush and Blair made a hash of a good case, largely because they preferred to scare people rather than enlighten them or reason with them. Still, the only real strategy of deception has come from those who believe, or pretend, that Saddam Hussein was no problem. . . .

Antaeus was able to draw strength from the earth every time an antagonist wrestled him to the ground. A reverse mythology has been permitted to take hold in the present case, where bad news is deemed to be bad news only for regime-change. Anyone with the smallest knowledge of Iraq knows that its society and infrastructure and institutions have been appallingly maimed and beggared by three decades of war and fascism (and the "divide-and-rule" tactics by which Saddam maintained his own tribal minority of the Sunni minority in power). In logic and morality, one must therefore compare the current state of the country with the likely or probable state of it had Saddam and his sons been allowed to go on ruling.

At once, one sees that all the alternatives would have been infinitely worse, and would most likely have led to an implosion—as well as opportunistic invasions from Iran and Turkey and Saudi Arabia, on behalf of their respective interests or confessional clienteles. This would in turn have necessitated a more costly and bloody intervention by some kind of coalition, much too late and on even worse terms and conditions. This is the lesson of Bosnia and Rwanda yesterday, and of Darfur today. When I have made this point in public, I have never had anyone offer an answer to it. A broken Iraq was in our future no matter what, and was a responsibility (somewhat conditioned by our past blunders) that no decent person could shirk. The only unthinkable policy was one of abstention. . . .

[There] is a certain fiber displayed by a huge number of anonymous Americans. Faced with a constant drizzle of bad news and purposely demoralizing commentary, millions of people stick out their jaws and hang tight. I am no fan of populism, but I surmise that these citizens are clear on the main point: It is out of the question—plainly and absolutely out of the question—that we should surrender the keystone state of the Middle East to a rotten, murderous alliance between Baathists and bin Ladenists. When they hear the fatuous insinuation that this alliance has only been created by the resistance to it, voters know in their intestines that those who say so are soft on crime and soft on fascism. The more temperate anti-warriors, such as Mark Danner and Harold Meyerson, like to employ the term "a war of choice." One should have no problem in accepting this concept. As they cannot and do not deny, there was going to be another round with Saddam Hussein no matter what. To whom, then, should the "choice" of time and place have fallen? The clear implication of the antichoice faction—if I may so dub them—is that this decision should have been left up to Saddam Hussein. . . .

Does the President deserve the benefit of the reserve of fortitude that I just mentioned? Only just, if at all. We need not argue about the failures and the mistakes and even the crimes, because these in some ways argue themselves. But a positive accounting could be offered without braggartry, and would include:

(1)   The overthrow of Talibanism and Baathism, and the exposure of many highly suggestive links between the two elements of this Hitler-Stalin pact. Abu Musab al Zarqawi, who moved from Afghanistan to Iraq before the coalition intervention, has even gone to the trouble of naming his organization al Qaeda in Mesopotamia.

(2)   The subsequent capitulation of Qaddafi's Libya in point of weapons of mass destruction—a capitulation that was offered not to Kofi Annan or the E.U. but to Blair and Bush.

(3)   The consequent unmasking of the A.Q. Khan network for the illicit transfer of nuclear technology to Libya, Iran, and North Korea.

(4)   The agreement by the United Nations that its own reform is necessary and overdue, and the unmasking of a quasi-criminal network within its elite.

(5)   The craven admission by President Chirac and Chancellor Schröder, when confronted with irrefutable evidence of cheating and concealment, respecting solemn treaties, on the part of Iran, that not even this will alter their commitment to neutralism. . . .

(6)   The ability to certify Iraq as actually disarmed, rather than accept the word of a psychopathic autocrat.

(7)   The immense gains made by the largest stateless minority in the region—the Kurds—and the spread of this example to other states.

(8)   The related encouragement of democratic and civil society movements in Egypt, Syria, and most notably Lebanon, which has regained a version of its autonomy.

(9)   The violent and ignominious death of thousands of bin Ladenist infiltrators into Iraq and Afghanistan, and the real prospect of greatly enlarging this number.

(10) The training and hardening of many thousands of American servicemen and women in a battle against the forces of nihilism and

absolutism, which training and hardening will surely be of great use in future combat.

It would be admirable if the president could manage to make such a presentation. It would also be welcome if he and his deputies adopted a clear attitude toward the war within the war: in other words, stated plainly, that the secular and pluralist forces within Afghan and Iraqi society, while they are not our clients, can in no circumstance be allowed to wonder which outcome we favor.

The great point about Blair's 1999 speech was that it asserted the obvious. Coexistence with aggressive regimes or expansionist, theocratic, and totalitarian ideologies is not in fact possible. One should welcome this conclusion for the additional reason that such coexistence is not desirable, either. If the great effort to remake Iraq as a demilitarized federal and secular democracy should fail or be defeated, I shall lose sleep for the rest of my life in reproaching myself for doing too little. But at least I shall have the comfort of not having offered, so far as I can recall, any word or deed that contributed to a defeat.

23

America's Imperial Ambition

G. John Ikenberry

THE LURES OF PREEMPTION

In the shadows of the Bush administration's war on terrorism, sweeping new ideas are circulating about U.S. grand strategy and the restructuring of today's unipolar world. They call for American unilateral and preemptive, even preventive, use of force, facilitated if possible by coalitions of the willing—but ultimately unconstrained by the rules and norms of the international community. At the extreme, these notions form a neoimperial vision in which the United States arrogates to itself the global role of setting standards, determining threats, using force, and meting out justice. It is a vision in which sovereignty becomes more absolute for America even as it becomes more conditional for countries that challenge Washington's standards of internal and external behavior. It is a vision made necessary—at least in the eyes of its advocates—by the new and apocalyptic character of contemporary terrorist threats and by America's unprecedented global dominance. . . .

America's nascent neoimperial grand strategy threatens to rend the fabric of the international community and political partnerships precisely at a time when that community and those partnerships are urgently needed. It is an approach fraught with peril and likely to fail. It is not only politically unsustainable but diplomatically harmful. And if history is a guide, it will trigger antagonism and resistance that will leave America in a more hostile and divided world.

246

PROVEN LEGACIES

The mainstream of American foreign policy has been defined since the 1940s by two grand strategies that have built the modern international order. One is realist in orientation, organized around containment, deterrence, and the maintenance of the global balance of power. Facing a dangerous and expansive Soviet Union after 1945, the United States stepped forward to fill the vacuum left by a waning British Empire and a collapsing European order to provide a counter-weight to Stalin and his Red Army.

The touchstone of this strategy was containment, which sought to deny the Soviet Union the ability to expand its sphere of influence. Order was maintained by managing the bipolar balance between the American and Soviet camps. Stability was achieved through nuclear deterrence. . . . But containment and global power-balancing ended with the collapse of the Soviet Union in 1991. . . .

This strategy has yielded a bounty of institutions and partnerships for America. The most important have been the NATO and U.S.-Japan alliances, American-led security partnerships that have survived the end of the Cold War by providing a bulwark for stability through commitment and reassurance. . . .

The other grand strategy, forged during World War II as the United States planned the reconstruction of the world economy, is liberal in orientation. It seeks to build order around institutionalized political relations among integrated market democracies, supported by an opening of economies. This agenda was not simply an inspiration of American businessmen and economists, however. There have always been geopolitical goals as well. Whereas America's realist grand strategy was aimed at countering Soviet power, its liberal grand strategy was aimed at avoiding a return to the 1930s, an era of regional blocs, trade conflict, and strategic rivalry. Open trade, democracy, and multilateral institutional relations went together. Underlying this strategy was the view that a rule-based international order, especially one in which the United States uses its political weight to derive congenial rules, will most fully protect American interests, conserve its power, and extend its influence.

This grand strategy has been pursued through an array of postwar initiatives that look disarmingly like "low politics": the Bretton Woods institutions, the World Trade Organization (WTO), and the Organization for Economic Cooperation and Development are just a few examples. Together, they form a complex layer cake of integrative initiatives that bind the democratic industrialized world together. During the 1990s, the United States continued to pursue this liberal grand strategy. Both the first Bush and the Clinton administrations attempted to articulate a vision of world order that was not dependent on an external threat or an explicit policy of balance of power. Bush the elder talked about the importance of the transatlantic community and articulated ideas about a more fully integrated Asia-Pacific region. In both cases, the strategy offered a positive vision of alliance and partnership built around common values, tradition, mutual self-interest, and the preservation of stability. The Clinton administration likewise attempted to describe the post–Cold War order in terms of the expansion of democracy and open markets. In this vision, democracy provided the foundation for global and regional community, and trade and capital flows were forces for political reform and integration. . . .

AMERICA'S HISTORIC BARGAINS

These two grand strategies are rooted in divergent, even antagonistic, intellectual traditions. But over the last 50 years they have worked remarkably well together. The realist grand strategy created a political rationale for establishing major security commitments around the world. The liberal strategy created a positive agenda for American leadership. The United States could exercise its power and achieve its national interests, but it did so in a way that helped deepen the fabric of international community. American power did not destabilize world order; it helped create it. The development of rule-based agreements and political-security partnerships was good both for the United States and for much of the world. By the end of the 1990s, the result was an international political order of unprecedented size and success: a global coalition of democratic states tied together through markets, institutions, and security partnerships.

This international order was built on two historic bargains. One was the U.S. commitment to provide its European and Asian partners with security protection and access to American markets, technology, and supplies within an open world economy. In return, these countries agreed to be reliable partners providing diplomatic, economic, and logistical support for the United States as it led the wider Western postwar order. The other is the liberal bargain that addressed the uncertainties of American power. East Asian and European states agreed to accept American leadership and operate within an agreed-upon political-economic system. The United States, in response, opened itself up and bound itself to its partners. In effect, the United States built an institutionalized coalition of partners and reinforced the stability of these mutually beneficial relations by making itself more "user-friendly"—that is, by playing by the rules and creating ongoing political processes that facilitated consultation and joint decision-making. The United States made its power safe for the world, and in return the world agreed to live within the U.S. system. These bargains date from the 1940s, but they continue to shore up the post–Cold War order. The result has been the most stable and prosperous international system in world history. But new ideas within the Bush administration—crystallized by September 11 and U.S. dominance—are unsettling this order and the political bargains behind it.

A NEW GRAND STRATEGY

For the first time since the dawn of the Cold War, a new grand strategy is taking shape in Washington. It is advanced most directly as a response to terrorism, but it also constitutes a broader view about how the United States should wield power and organize world order. According to this new paradigm, America is to be less bound to its partners and to global rules and institutions while it steps forward to play a more unilateral and anticipatory role in attacking terrorist threats and confronting rogue states seeking WMD. The United States will use its unrivaled military power to manage the global order.

This new grand strategy has seven elements. It begins with a fundamental commitment to maintaining a unipolar world in which the United States has no peer competitor. No coalition of great powers without the United States will be allowed to achieve hegemony. Bush made this point the centerpiece of American security policy in his West Point commencement address in June: "America has, and intends to keep, military strengths beyond challenges—thereby making the destabilizing arms races of other eras pointless, and limiting rivalries to trade and other pursuits of peace." The United States will not seek security through the more modest realist strategy of operating within a global system of power balancing, nor will it pursue a liberal strategy in which institutions, democracy, and integrated markets reduce the importance of power politics altogether. America will be so much more powerful than other major states that strategic rivalries and security competition among the great powers will disappear, leaving everyone—not just the United States—better off. . . .

Some thinkers have described the strategy as "breakout," in which the United States moves so quickly to develop technological advantages (in robotics, lasers, satellites, precision munitions, etc.) that no state or coalition could ever challenge it as global leader, protector, and enforcer.

The second element is a dramatic new analysis of global threats and how they must be attacked. The grim new reality is that small groups of terrorists—perhaps aided by outlaw states—may soon acquire highly destructive nuclear, chemical, and biological weapons that can inflict catastrophic destruction. These terrorist groups cannot be appeased or deterred, the administration believes, so they must be eliminated. . . . They are not nation-states, and they do not play by the accepted rules of the game.

The third element of the new strategy maintains that the Cold War concept of deterrence is outdated. Deterrence, sovereignty, and the balance of power work together. When deterrence is no longer viable, the larger realist edifice starts to crumble. The threat today is not other great powers that must be managed through second-strike nuclear capacity but the transnational terrorist networks that have no home address. They cannot be deterred because they are either willing to die for their cause or able to escape retaliation. The old defensive strategy of building missiles and other weapons that can survive a first strike and be used in a retaliatory strike to punish the attacker will no longer ensure security. The only option, then, is offense.

The use of force, this camp argues, will therefore need to be preemptive and perhaps even preventive—taking on potential threats before they can present a major problem. But this premise plays havoc with the old international rules of self-defense and United Nations norms about the proper use of force. . . .

At West Point, Bush put it succinctly when he stated that "the military must be ready to strike at a moment's notice in any dark corner of the world. All nations that decide for aggression and terror will pay a price." The administration defends this new doctrine as a necessary adjustment to a more uncertain and shifting threat environment. This policy of no regrets errs on the side of action—but it can also easily become national security by hunch or inference, leaving the world without clear-cut norms for justifying force.

As a result, the fourth element of this emerging grand strategy involves a recasting of the terms of sovereignty. Because these terrorist groups cannot be deterred, the United States must be prepared to intervene anywhere, anytime to preemptively destroy the threat. Terrorists do not respect borders, so neither can the United States. Moreover, countries that harbor terrorists, either by consent or because they are unable to enforce their laws within their territory, effectively forfeit their rights of sovereignty. . . .

Here the war on terrorism and the problem of the proliferation of WMD get entangled. The worry is that a few despotic states—Iraq in particular, but also Iran and North Korea—will develop capabilities to produce weapons of mass destruction and put these weapons in the hands of terrorists. The regimes themselves may be deterred from using such capabilities, but they might pass along these weapons to terrorist networks that are not deterred. Thus another emerging principle within the Bush administration: the possession of WMD by unaccountable, unfriendly, despotic governments is itself a threat that must be countered. In the old era, despotic regimes were to be lamented but ultimately tolerated. With the rise of terrorism and weapons of mass destruction, they are now unacceptable threats. Thus states that are not technically in violation of any existing international laws could nevertheless be targets of American force—if Washington determines that they have a prospective capacity to do harm. . . .

The fifth element of this new grand strategy is a general depreciation of international rules, treaties, and security partnerships. This point relates to the new threats themselves: if the stakes are rising and the margins of error are shrinking in the war on terrorism, multilateral norms and agreements that sanction and limit the use of force are just annoying distractions. The critical task is to eliminate the threat. But the emerging unilateral strategy is also informed by a deeper suspicion about the value of international agreements themselves. Part of this view arises from a deeply felt and authentically American belief that the United States should not get entangled in the corrupting and constraining world of multilateral rules and institutions. For some Americans, the belief that American sovereignty is politically sacred leads to a preference for isolationism. But the more influential view—particularly after September 11—is not that the United States should withdraw from the world but that it should operate in the world on its own terms. The Bush administration's repudiation of a remarkable array of treaties and institutions—from the Kyoto Protocol on global warming to the International Criminal Court to the Biological Weapons Convention—reflects this new bias. . . . In other words, the United States has decided it is big enough, powerful enough, and remote enough to go it alone.

Sixth, the new grand strategy argues that the United States will need to play a direct and unconstrained role in responding to threats. This conviction is partially based on a judgment that no other country or coalition—even the European Union—has the force-projection capabilities to respond to terrorist and rogue states around the world. . . . This view is also based on the judgment that joint operations and the use of force through coalitions tend to hinder effective operations. . . . Rumsfeld explained this point earlier this year, when he said, "The mission must determine the coalition; the coalition must not determine the mission. If it does, the mission will be dumbed down to the lowest common denominator, and we can't afford that." . . . America's allies become merely strategic assets that are useful depending on the circumstance. The United States still finds attractive the logistical reach that its global alliance system provides, but the pacts with countries in Asia and Europe become more contingent and less premised on a vision of a common security community.

Finally, the new grand strategy attaches little value to international stability. There is an unsentimental view in the unilateralist camp that the traditions of the past must be shed. Whether it is withdrawal from the Anti-Ballistic Missile Treaty or the resistance to signing other formal arms-control treaties, policymakers are convinced that the United States needs to move beyond outmoded Cold War thinking. . . .

In this brave new world, neoimperial thinkers contend that the older realist and liberal grand strategies are not very helpful. American security will not be ensured, as realist grand strategy assumes, by the preservation of deterrence and stable relations among the major powers. In a world of asymmetrical threats, the global balance of power is not the linchpin of war and peace. Likewise, liberal strategies of building order around open trade and democratic institutions might have some long-term impact on terrorism, but they do not address the immediacy of the threats. Apocalyptic violence is at our doorstep, so efforts at strengthening the rules and institutions of the international community are of little practical value. If we accept the worst-case imagining of "we don't know what we don't know," everything else is secondary: international rules, traditions of partnership, and standards of legitimacy. It is a war. And as Clausewitz famously remarked, "War is such a dangerous business that the mistakes which come from kindness are the very worst."

IMPERIAL DANGERS

Pitfalls accompany this neoimperial grand strategy, however. Unchecked U.S. power, shorn of legitimacy and disentangled from the postwar norms and institutions of the international order, will usher in a more hostile international system, making it far harder to achieve American interests. The secret of the United States' long brilliant run as the world's leading state was its ability and willingness to exercise power within alliance and multinational frameworks, which made its power and agenda more acceptable to allies and other key states around the world. This achievement has now been put at risk by the administration's new thinking.

The most immediate problem is that the neoimperialist approach is unsustainable. Going it alone might well succeed in removing Saddam Hussein from power, but it is far less certain that a strategy of counterproliferation, based on American willingness to use unilateral force to confront dangerous dictators, can work over the long term. An American policy that leaves the United States alone to decide which states are threats and how best to deny them weapons of mass destruction will lead to a diminishment of multilateral mechanisms—most important of which is the nonproliferation regime.

The Bush administration has elevated the threat of WMD to the top of its security agenda without investing its power or prestige in fostering, monitoring, and enforcing nonproliferation commitments. The tragedy of September 11 has given the Bush administration the authority and willingness to confront the Iraqs of the world. But that will not be enough when even more complicated cases come along—when it is not the use of force that is needed but concerted multilateral action to provide sanctions and inspections. . . . America's well-meaning imperial strategy could undermine the principled multilateral agreements, institutional infrastructure, and cooperative spirit needed for the long-term success of nonproliferation goals.

The specific doctrine of preemptive action poses a related problem: once the United States feels it can take such a course, nothing will stop other countries from doing the same. Does the United States want this doctrine in the hands of Pakistan, or even China or Russia? After all, it would not require the intervening state to first provide evidence for its actions. The United States argues that to wait until all the evidence is in, or until authoritative international bodies support action, is to wait too long. Yet that approach is the only basis that the United States can use if it needs to appeal for restraint in the actions of others. Moreover, and quite paradoxically, overwhelming American conventional military might, combined with a policy of preemptive strikes, could lead hostile states to accelerate programs to acquire their only possible deterrent to the United States: WMD. This is another version of the security dilemma, but one made worse by a neoimperial grand strategy.

Another problem follows. The use of force to eliminate WMD capabilities or overturn dangerous regimes is never simple, whether it is pursued unilaterally or by a concert of major states. After the military intervention is over, the target country has to be put back together. Peacekeeping and state building are inevitably required, as are long-term strategies that bring the UN, the World Bank, and the major powers together to orchestrate aid and other forms of assistance. This is not heroic work, but it is utterly necessary. Peacekeeping troops may be required for many years, even after a new regime is built. Regional conflicts inflamed by outside military intervention must also be calmed. This is the "long tail" of burdens and commitments that comes with every major military action.

When these costs and obligations are added to America's imperial military role, it becomes even more doubtful that the neoimperial strategy can be sustained at home over the long haul—the classic problem of imperial overstretch. The United States could keep its military predominance for decades if it is supported by a growing and increasingly productive economy. But the indirect burdens of cleaning up the political mess in terrorist-prone failed states levy a hidden cost. . . .

A third problem with an imperial grand strategy is that it cannot generate the cooperation needed to solve practical problems at the heart of the U.S. foreign policy agenda. In the fight on terrorism, the United States needs cooperation from European and Asian countries in intelligence, law enforcement, and logistics. Outside the security sphere, realizing U.S. objectives depends even more on a continuous stream of amicable working relations with major states around the world. It needs partners for trade liberalization, global financial stabilization, environmental protection, deterring transnational organized crime, managing the rise of China, and a host of other thorny challenges. But it is impossible to expect would-be partners to acquiesce to America's self-appointed global security protectorate and then pursue business as usual in all other domains.

The key policy tool for states confronting a unipolar and unilateral America is to withhold cooperation in day-to-day relations with the United States. . . . The United States may be a unipolar military power, but economic and political power is more evenly distributed across the globe. The major states may not have much leverage in directly restraining American military policy, but they can make the United States pay a price in other areas.

Finally, the neoimperial grand strategy poses a wider problem for the maintenance of American unipolar power. It steps into the oldest trap of powerful imperial states: self-encirclement. When the most powerful state in the world throws its weight around, unconstrained by rules or norms of legitimacy, it risks a backlash. Other countries will bridle at an international order in which the United States plays only by its own rules. The proponents of the new grand strategy have assumed that the United States can single-handedly deploy military power abroad and not suffer untoward consequences; relations will be coarser with friends and allies, they believe, but such are the costs of leadership. But history shows that powerful states tend to trigger self-encirclement by their own overestimation of their power. Charles V, Louis XIV, Napoleon, and the leaders of post-Bismarck Germany sought to expand their imperial domains and impose a coercive order on others. Their imperial orders were all brought down when other countries decided they were not prepared to live in a world dominated by an overweening coercive state. America's imperial goals and modus operandi are much more limited and benign than were those of age-old emperors. But a hard-line imperial grand strategy runs the risk that history will repeat itself.

BRING IN THE OLD

Wars change world politics, and so too will America's war on terrorism. How great states fight wars, how they define the stakes, how they make the peace in its aftermath—all give lasting shape to the international system that emerges after the guns fall silent. In mobilizing their societies for battle, wartime leaders have tended to describe the military struggle as more than simply the defeat of an enemy. Woodrow Wilson sent U.S. troops to Europe not only to stop the Kaiser's army but to destroy militarism and usher in a worldwide democratic revolution. Franklin Roosevelt saw the war with Germany and Japan as a struggle to secure the "four great freedoms." . . . To advance these visions, Wilson and Roosevelt proposed new international rules and mechanisms of cooperation. Their message was clear: If you bear the burdens of war, we, your leaders, will use this dreadful conflict to usher in a more peaceful and decent order among states. Fighting the war had as much to do with building global relations as it did with vanquishing an enemy.

Bush has not fully articulated a vision of postwar international order, aside from defining the struggle as one between freedom and evil. The world has seen Washington take determined steps to fight terrorism, but it does not yet have a sense of Bush's larger, positive agenda for a strengthened and more decent international order.

This failure explains why the sympathy and goodwill generated around the world for the United States after September 11 quickly disappeared. Newspapers that once proclaimed, "We are all Americans," now express distrust toward America. The prevailing view is that the United States seems prepared to use its power to go after terrorists and evil regimes, but not to use it to help build a more stable and peaceful world order. The United States appears to be degrading the rules and institutions of international community, not enhancing them. To the rest of the world, neoimperial thinking has more to do with exercising power than with exercising leadership.

In contrast, America's older strategic orientations—balance-of-power realism and liberal multilateralism—suggest a mature world power that seeks stability and pursues its interests in ways that do not fundamentally threaten the positions of other states. They are strategies of co-option and reassurance. The new imperial grand strategy presents the United States very differently: a revisionist state seeking to parlay its momentary power advantages into a world order in which it runs the show. Unlike the hegemonic states of the past, the United States does not seek territory or outright political domination in Europe or Asia; "America has no empire to extend or utopia to establish," Bush noted in his West Point address. But the sheer power advantages that the United States possesses and the doctrines of preemption and counterterrorism that it is articulating do unsettle governments and people around the world. The costs could be high. The last thing the United States wants is for foreign diplomats and government leaders to ask, How can we work around, undermine, contain, and retaliate against U.S. power?

Rather than invent a new grand strategy, the United States should reinvigorate its older strategies, those based on the view that America's security partnerships are not simply instrumental tools but critical components of an American-led world political order that should be preserved. U.S. power is both leveraged and made more legitimate and user-friendly by these partnerships. The neoimperial thinkers are haunted by the specter of catastrophic terrorism and seek a radical reordering of America's role in the world. America's commanding unipolar power and the advent of frightening new terrorist threats feed this imperial temptation. But it is a grand strategic vision that, taken to the extreme, will leave the world more dangerous and divided—and the United States less secure.

24

Realism's Shining Morality

Robert F. Ellsworth
and Dimitri K. Simes

. . . The second Bush Administration will have to deal with two fundamental dilemmas: first, how to reconcile the war against terror with a commitment to make the world safe for democracy; and second, how to assure that unchallenged U.S. military supremacy is used to enhance America's ability to shape the world rather than provoke global opposition to the United States, making us more isolated and accordingly less secure. The neoconservative vision for conducting American foreign policy is fraught with risks. And continuing to follow the prescriptions of the neoconservative faction in the Republican party may damage President Bush's legacy, imperil the country's fiscal stability and complicate America's ability to exercise global leadership.

It has become an article of faith for the increasingly influential alliance of liberal interventionists and neoconservatives that the United States, as the world's democratic hegemonic power, is both entitled and even morally bound to use whatever tools are necessary to save the world from brutality and oppression and to promote democratization around the globe. Up to a point, the War on Terror and encouraging democracy worldwide are mutually reinforcing. President Bush is quite right that democracy, particularly if we are talking about democracy in a stable society coupled with a rule of law and with adequate protection of minority rights, is not only morally preferable to authoritarian rule, but also is the best prescription against the emergence of deeply alienated radical groups prone to terrorism. The "democracy project" also appeals to the highest aspirations of the American people. After all, the Cold War was never driven solely by the need to contain Soviet power, but by the moral conviction that defending freedom in the United States and in the world in general was something worth fighting and dying for—even, in the Berlin Crisis, risking nuclear war itself.

High-minded realists do not disagree with the self-appointed champions of global democracy (the neoconservatives and the liberal interventionists) that a strong preference for liberty and justice should be an integral part of U.S. foreign policy. But they realize that there are tradeoffs between pushing for democracy and working with other sovereign states—some not always quite democratic—to combat global terror. Realists also, following the advice of General Charles Boyd, understand the need to "separate reality from image" and "to tell the truth, if only to ourselves"—not to play fast and loose with facts to create the appearance of acting morally. And they are aware that there are important differences in how the United States helps the world achieve freedom. Indeed, in his first press conference after his triumph at the polls, President Bush used three different terms in talking about America's global pro-democracy effort. He discussed the need "to encourage freedom and democracy," to "promote free societies," and to "spread freedom and democracy."

"Encouraging" democracy is not a controversial position. Nearly everyone in the world accepts that the sole superpower is entitled and indeed expected to be true to its core beliefs. "Promoting" democracy is vaguer and potentially more costly. Still, if the United States does so without resorting to military force and takes into account the circumstances and perspectives of other nations, then it is likely not to run into too much international opposition. "Spreading" democracy, however, particularly spreading it by force, coercion and violent regime change, is a different thing altogether. Those who suspect they may be on the receiving end of such treatment are unlikely to accept American moral superiority, are bound to feel threatened, and cannot reasonably be expected to cooperate with the United States on other important American priorities, including the War on Terror and nuclear proliferation.

Worse still, they may decide that acquiring nuclear weapons is the last—perhaps their only—option to deter an American attempt to overthrow their governments. This already appears to be the dynamic in the case of Iran and North Korea. Also, in dealing with the likes of Tehran and Pyongyang, there can be no certainty with whom they may share nuclear technology. Accordingly, there is a clear and present danger that pro-democracy zeal may enhance the greatest possible threat to U.S. security and the American way of life—the threat of nuclear terrorism.

We have already seen how overzealousness in the cause of democracy (along with a corresponding underestimation of the costs and dangers) has led to a dangerous overstretch in Iraq. As Shlomo Avineri, a professor at

Hebrew University in Jerusalem, has observed, what is currently going on in Iraq is not "the war the U.S.-led coalition had in mind when the decision was taken to topple Saddam Hussein." The United States could have rid Iraq of Saddam and his most notorious associates without turning the whole country upside down. America could have made it clear from the start that Washington had no ambitions in Iraq beyond removing the threat from Saddam's regime and co-opted the United Nations and the Arab League to create a provisional post-Saddam government. It would have been possible to communicate to less-discredited members of the old regime—first and foremost the military command—that in return for coming clean on Iraq's programs to develop weapons of mass destruction, co-operating with coalition forces, introducing the rule of law and accepting a broad-based transitional government that would incorporate Iraqi exiles . . . they could retain some degree of influence in the new Iraq. Additionally, Iraq's neighbors, none of them friends of Saddam, could have been assured that they had nothing to worry about from the American military presence on their borders, as long as they did not attempt to obstruct a U.S. occupation which their benign attitude could help to make shorter.

Instead, we opted to dismantle the Ba'ath party government altogether without having anything with which to replace it, dissolved the Iraqi army and proudly pronounced that the liberation of Iraq was just a beginning of a grand democratic transformation of the Greater Middle East. It required an inordinate degree of naivete and, frankly, ignorance about the real conditions in Iraq and in the Middle East in general to believe that this overly ambitious scheme could work—especially when pursued without any visible effort to promote the Arab-Israeli settlement and from the position of being the sole sponsor of the Sharon government. An effort to reshape the Middle East according to American specifications was bound to face opposition on the ground in Iraq, from Iraq's neighbors such as Iran and Syria, and to say the least, dampen enthusiasm for helping the United States in Iraq even on the part of the most friendly Arab regimes such as Egypt, Saudi Arabia and Jordan, all of which had cause for concern that they could become targets of the American master plan for restructuring the region.

America has had to pay for these errors with blood, treasure, diminished international prestige and a weakened ability to focus adequately on and get much needed international cooperation on other urgent priorities, such as the emerging nuclear capabilities of North Korea and now of Iran. Reactions from other major powers strongly suggest that the Iraqi experience, for example, has made it considerably harder for the United States to get European, Russian and Chinese cooperation on tough measures against Iran. . . . There is a reluctance to pass UN Security Council resolutions that would include a threat of force—a threat that would be quite useful in pressuring the Iranian government, but which many nations, including some of

America's long-standing partners, are afraid would be used by the United States to justify unilateral military action. . . .

Nothing short of a midcourse adjustment can allow America to reassert true world leadership—enjoying the concrete support of other major powers, not (with the notable exception of Great Britain) token contributions made by insufficient "coalitions of the willing."

We suggest an adjustment, rather than a wholesale course correction. In its first term, the Bush Administration showed it was capable of pursuing a realist foreign policy grounded in vital interests. After an initially rough start with China and Russia, the Bush team came to accept the importance of building partnerships with these major powers.

And after the tragedies of 9/11, President Bush was absolutely right in his call for a relentless and ruthless pursuit of terrorists wherever they may be, and, unlike many neoconservatives and liberal interventionists, he rejected double standards in dealing with the terrorist threat. He did not reclassify certain terrorists as "freedom fighters," even in the face of sometimes considerable pressure from special interests. Thus, he refused to criticize Russian President Vladimir Putin for his tough (even if not always effective) measures against terrorists acting in the name of the Chechen cause. President Bush has made it clear that groups that perpetrate horrific violence specifically directed against civilian targets are terrorists. No matter how noble the cause they espouse, and even if there are legitimate grievances at play, sympathy must never become a means to aid and abet terrorism.

After an initial bout of euphoria following the fall of Baghdad, the Bush Administration has come to realize that, as a practical matter, with the United States being preoccupied with Iraq, it is unlikely that force should be used to remove other repressive regimes as long as they do not threaten the United States. And in Iraq itself, once National Security Advisor Condoleezza Rice became responsible for guiding that country's political reconstruction, the focus changed from starry-eyed democratic experimentation to establishing stability and ensuring a quick transfer of authority to the new Iraqi government. This is a policy not only less threatening to Iraq's neighbors, but also one which has a better chance of success among Iraqis who are tired of disorder.

Of course, in the post–September 11 world, the leading superpower has no choice but to remain assertive, and that includes rare instances when America has to act unilaterally and to use military force pre-emptively. The question is, under which circumstances and in the name of what? No responsible American president . . . can surrender the right to do whatever is required to defend American security, even when the UN, NATO and other international bodies refuse to give consent. Realistically, other nations would not expect that much from us—even those who cherish their ability to use international law as a straightjacket on U.S. freedom of action.

As far as pre-emption is concerned, there is a growing consensus in the world that traditional notions of deterrence, appropriate against nation-states (which were in control of their territory and were vulnerable to massive retaliation in response to irresponsible behavior), simply cannot work in the age of sub-national terrorist coalitions and with the apocalyptic consequences of weapons of mass destruction increasingly available to non-state actors. The issue is not with pre-emption itself, but rather with the notion, now widespread in the world, that the United States may use pre-emption arbitrarily—not against genuine enemies threatening America, but against those whom the American political consensus at the moment decides to label as brutal and undemocratic. With their historic reluctance to have authority without the consent of the governed, Americans should be the first to understand why the rest of the world would not be prepared to surrender such overwhelming power to any one nation. After all, there is no such thing as a benign tyranny. The ability of one power to act freely without constraints, short of those it is willing to impose upon itself, would look like a tyranny even to those countries that, as a result of their democratic credentials, have little reason to fear American punishment themselves.

The president of the United States proudly proclaims that he is a man of faith, and so were the American Founding Fathers. However, the genius of the American experiment was based on the fact that great ideals were combined with an equally great pragmatism and that strong belief in one's cause was also measured by a decent respect for the passions of others. That is what makes the neoconservative creed such a departure from the American political tradition. President Bush will enhance his legacy and do a lot of good for U.S. foreign policy effectiveness if he makes high-minded realism his foreign policy motto. Such high-minded realism should be based on five important principles.

First, the War on Terror should be made the true organizing principle of U.S. foreign policy. That does not mean neglecting other important preferences such as U.S. economic interests, environmental issues and human rights. But none of them should be pursued at the expense of the struggle against terror. After all, success or failure in the War on Terror could very well determine the fate of America.

Second, the Bush Administration should work hard in its second term to re-establish American leadership. This is not about allowing anyone else to checkmate the exercise of U.S. power. Rather, it requires a serious evaluation of tradeoffs between compromises in the name of greater international support and the freedom of action associated with acting alone when no multilateral solution is available. . . . In that context it should be made clear that pre-emption is a last resort, applicable only when there is credible evidence of a real threat to vital U.S. interests.

Third, as a pre-eminent military power, whose capabilities no one disputes, we should follow the guidance of President Theodore Roosevelt to speak softly while carrying a big stick. America should not be timid in protecting and promoting its interests, but a modicum of humility when talking about our exceptional goodness would help others reconcile themselves to American preponderance and make it easier for them to accommodate our preferences. . . .

Fourth, we should abandon the demonstrably false pretense that all nations and cultures share essentially the same values. Every country, every region, every civilization has its own cycle, circumstances and path of development. We have disagreements over values and policies even with our democratic European allies and with Canada and Mexico just across the border—so we should not expect that the peoples of the Middle East would share our attitudes. One key passion in the Middle East is the rights of the Palestinians. This passion may seem exaggerated to us and manipulated by undemocratic Arab leaders. But the fact remains that it is strongly felt among the Muslim elites and masses alike. If we want our good intentions to be trusted in the Islamic world, and if we want to be able to encourage moderation and positive attitudes towards Western civilization among Muslims, a sympathetic attention to the Palestinian problem, obviously without abandoning the security of Israel, is a must. Yasir Arafat's departure may provide an important opening in that regard.

Finally, our focus on democracy should not be presented to others as an imperial command. Over the centuries we have been advised by leaders from John Adams to George Kennan to Ronald Reagan to be unto the world as a shining city on a hill, appealing to the better instincts of mankind—not to become a military empire demanding subservience. We certainly would not object to other countries emulating us, but it is more important that we have shared interests and work to address and promote them.

For President Bush to use his second term to enhance his legacy and to build—as he clearly wants—a lasting Republican majority, the United States needs to pursue a foreign policy based on thoughtful evaluation, dealing with the world as it is, rather than embracing polemical cliches passed off as ideas. And such a policy needs as its moral lodestone the traditional American value of prudence, not a neo-Trotskyite belief in a permanent revolution (even if it is a democratic rather than proletarian one). The neo-conservative insistence that the United States can be made safe only by making other nations accept American values is a recipe for provoking a clash of civilizations rather than a way to enhance and promote America's global leadership.

In 1999, then-candidate Bush said, "Let us have an American foreign policy that reflects American character. The modesty of true strength, the humility of real greatness." September 11 has made this realistic and honorable approach even more essential for U.S. international conduct.

25

Bounding the Global War on Terrorism

Jeffrey Record

BOUNDING THE GWOT

The central conclusion of this study is that *the global war on terrorism as currently defined and waged is dangerously indiscriminate and ambitious, and accordingly that its parameters should be readjusted to conform to concrete U.S. security interests and the limits of American power.* Such a readjustment requires movement from unrealistic to realistic war aims and from unnecessarily provocative to traditional uses of military force. Specifically, a realistically bounded GWOT [Global War on Terrorism] requires the following measures:

(1) Deconflate the threat. This means, in both thought and policy, treating rogue states separately from terrorist organizations, and separating terrorist organizations at war with the United States from those that are not. Approaching rogue states and terrorist organizations as an undifferentiated threat ignores critical differences in character, threat level, and vulnerability to U.S. military action. Al-Qaeda is an undeterrable transnational organization in a war with the United States that has claimed the lives of thousands of Americans. North Korea is a (so far) deterrable (and destroyable) state that is not in a hot war with the United States. Similarly, lumping together all terrorist organizations into a generic threat of terrorism gratuitously makes the United States an enemy of groups that do not threaten U.S. security interests. Terrorism may be a horrendous means to any end,

but do the Basque E.T.A. and the Tamil Tigers really threaten the United States? Strategy involves choice within a framework of scarce resources; as such, it requires threat discrimination and prioritization of effort.

(2) Substitute credible deterrence for preventive war as the primary policy for dealing with rogue states seeking to acquire WMD. This means shifting the focus of U.S. policy from rogue state acquisition of WMD to rogue state use of WMD. There is no evidence that rogue state use of WMD is undeterrable via credible threats of unacceptable retaliation or that rogue states seek WMD solely for purposes of blackmail and aggression. There is evidence, however, of failed deterrence of rogue state acquisition of WMD; indeed, there is evidence that a declared policy of preventive war encourages acquisition. Preventive war in any case alienates friends and allies, leaving the United States isolated and unnecessarily burdened (as in Iraq). A policy of first reliance on deterrence moreover does not foreclose the option of preemption; striking first is an inherent policy option in any crisis, and preemption, as opposed to preventive war, has legal sanction under strict criteria. Colin Gray persuasively argues against making preventive war "*the* master strategic idea for [the post-9/11 era]" because its "demands on America's political, intelligence, and military resources are too exacting." The United States:

> has no practical choice other than to make of deterrence all that it can be. . . . If this view is rejected, the grim implication is that the United States, as the sheriff of world order, will require heroic performances from those policy instruments charged with cutting-edge duties on behalf of preemptive or preventive operations. Preemption and prevention have their obvious attractions as contrasted with deterrence, at least when they work. But they carry the risk of encouraging a hopeless quest for total security.

Dr. Condoleezza Rice got it right in 2000: "[T]he first line of defense [in dealing with rogue states] should be a clear and classical statement of deterrence—if they do acquire WMD, their weapons will be unusable because any attempt to use them will bring national obliteration."

(3) Refocus the GWOT first and foremost on al-Qaeda, its allies, and homeland security. This may be difficult, given the current preoccupation with Iraq. But it was, after all, al-Qaeda, not a rogue state, that conducted the 9/11 attacks, and it is al-Qaeda, not a rogue state, that continues to conduct terrorist attacks against U.S. and Western interests worldwide. The war against Iraq was a detour from, not an integral component of, the war on terrorism; in fact, Operation IRAQI FREEDOM may have expanded the terrorist threat by establishing a large new American target set in an Arab heartland. The unexpectedly large costs incurred by Operation IRAQI FREEDOM and its continuing aftermath probably will not affect funding of the relatively cheap counterterrorist campaign against al-Qaeda. But those costs most assuredly impede funding of woefully underfunded homeland security requirements. . . .

(4) Seek rogue-state regime change via measures short of war. Forcible regime change of the kind undertaken in Iraq is an enterprise fraught with unexpected costs and unintended consequences. Even if destroying the old regime entails little military risk, as was the case in Iraq, the task of creating a new regime can be costly, protracted, and strategically exhausting. Indeed, it is probably fair to say that the combination of U.S. preoccupation in postwar Iraq and the more formidable resistance a U.S. attack on Iran or North Korea almost certainly would encounter effectively removes both of those states as realistic targets of forcible regime change. The United States has in any event considerable experience in engineering regime change by measures short of war (e.g., covert action); and even absent regime change there are means, such as coercive diplomacy and trade/aid concessions, for altering undesirable regime behavior. Additionally, even the most hostile regimes can change over time. Gorbachev's Russia would have been unrecognizable to Stalin's, as would Jiang Zemin's China to Mao's.

(5) Be prepared to settle for stability rather than democracy in Iraq, and international rather than U.S. responsibility for Iraq. The United States may be compelled to lower its political expectations in Iraq and by extension the Middle East. Establishing democracy in Iraq is clearly a desirable objective, and the United States should do whatever it can to accomplish that goal. But if the road to democracy proves chaotic and violent or if it is seen to presage the establishment of a theocracy via "one man, one vote, one time," the United States might have to settle for stability in the form of a friendly autocracy of the kind with which it enjoys working relationships in Cairo, Riyadh, and Islamabad. This is certainly not the preferred choice, but it may turn out to be the only one consistent with at least the overriding near-term U.S. security interest of stability. Similarly, the United States may have to accept a genuine internationalization of its position in Iraq. A UN-authorized multinational force encompassing contingents from major states that opposed the U.S. war against Iraq would both legitimize the American presence in Iraq as well as share the blood and treasure burden of occupation/reconstruction, which the United States is bearing almost single-handedly.

(6) Reassess U.S. force levels, especially ground force levels. Operation IRAQI FREEDOM and its aftermath argue strongly for an across-the-board reassessment of U.S. force levels. Though defense transformation stresses (among other things) substitution of technology for manpower, postwar tasks of pacification and nation-building are inherently manpower-intensive. Indeed, defense transformation may be counterproductive to the tasks that face the United States in Iraq and potentially in other states the United States may choose to subdue and attempt to re-create. Frederick A. Kagan argues that the reason why "the United States [has] been so successful in recent wars [but] encountered so much difficulty in securing its political aims after the shooting stopped" lies partly in "a vision of war" that "see[s] the enemy as a target set and believe[s] that when all or most

of the targets have been hit, he will inevitably surrender and American goals will be achieved." This vision ignores the importance of "how, exactly, one defeats the enemy and what the enemy's country looks like at the moment the bullets stop flying." For Kagan, the "entire thrust of the current program of military transformation of the U.S. armed forces . . . aims at the implementation and perfection of this sort of target-set mentality." More to the point:

> If the most difficult task facing a state that desires to change the regime in another state is securing the support of the defeated populace for the new government, then the armed forces of that state must do more than break things and kill people. They must secure critical population centers and state infrastructure. They have to maintain order and prevent the development of humanitarian catastrophes likely to undermine American efforts to establish a stable new regime.

These tasks require not only many "boots on the ground" for long periods of time, but also recognition that:

> If the U.S. is to undertake wars that aim at regime change and maintain its current critical role in controlling and directing world affairs, then it must fundamentally change its views of war. It is not enough to consider simply how to pound the enemy into submission with stand-off forces. War plans must also consider how to make the transition from that defeated government to a new one. A doctrine based on the notion that superpowers don't do windows will fail in this task. Regime change is inextricably intertwined with nation-building and peacekeeping. Those elements must be factored into any such plan from the outset. . . .
> To effect regime change, U.S. forces must be positively in control of the enemy's territory and population as rapidly and continuously as possible. That control cannot be achieved by machines, still less by bombs. Only human beings interacting with other human beings can achieve it. The only hope for success in the extension of politics that is war is to restore the human element to the transformation equation.

Americans have historically displayed a view of war as a substitute for politics, and the U.S. military has seemed congenitally averse to performing operations other than war. But the Kagan thesis does underscore the importance of not quantitatively disinvesting in ground forces for the sake of a transformational vision. Indeed, under present and foreseeable circumstances the possibility of increasing ground force end-strengths should be examined.

The global war on terrorism as presently defined and conducted is strategically unfocused, promises much more than it can deliver, and threatens to dissipate U.S. military and other resources in an endless and hopeless search for absolute security. The United States may be able to defeat, even destroy, al-Qaeda, but it cannot rid the world of terrorism, much less evil.

26

The End of the Bush Revolution

Philip H. Gordon

A RETURN TO REALISM

Reading over President George W. Bush's March 2006 National Security Strategy, one would be hard-pressed to find much evidence that the president has backed away from what has become known as the Bush doctrine. "America is at war," says the document; we will "fight our enemies abroad instead of waiting for them to arrive in our country" and "support democratic movements and institutions in every nation and culture," with the ultimate goal of "ending tyranny in our world."

Talk to any senior administration official, and he or she will tell you that the president is as committed as ever to the "revolutionary" foreign policy principles he spelled out after 9/11: the United States is fighting a war on terror and must remain on the offensive and ready to act alone, U.S. power is the foundation of global order, and the spread of democracy and freedom is the key to a safer and more peaceful world. Bush reiterated such thinking in his 2006 State of the Union address, insisting that the United States will "act boldly in freedom's cause" and "never surrender to evil."

But if the rhetoric of the Bush revolution lives on, the revolution itself is over. The question is not whether the president and most of his team still hold to the basic tenets of the Bush doctrine—they do—but whether they can sustain it. They cannot. Although the administration does not like to admit it, U.S. foreign policy is already on a very different trajectory than it was in Bush's first term. The budgetary, political, and diplomatic realities that the first Bush team tried to ignore have begun to set in.

The reversal of the Bush revolution is a good thing. By overreaching in Iraq, alienating important allies, and allowing the war on terrorism to overshadow all other national priorities, Bush has gotten the United States bogged down in an unsuccessful war, overstretched the military, and broken the domestic bank. Washington now lacks the reservoir of international legitimacy, resources, and domestic support necessary to pursue other key national interests.

It is not too late to put U.S. foreign policy back on a more sustainable course, and Bush has already begun to do so. But these new, mostly positive trends are no less reversible than the old ones were. Another terrorist attack on the United States, a major challenge from Iran, or a fresh burst of misplaced optimism about Iraq could entice the administration to return to its revolutionary course—with potentially disastrous consequences.

THE ACCIDENTAL REVOLUTION

It is no small irony that Bush's foreign policy ended up on the idealistic end of the U.S. foreign policy spectrum. Contrary to the notion, common on the left and overseas, that the Bush team was hawkish and interventionist from the start, the administration was in fact deeply divided in its first months. If anything, it leaned toward the realist view that the United States should avoid meddling in the domestic affairs of other nations. In his campaign, Bush famously called for a "humble" foreign policy, meant to contrast with the interventionism of Bill Clinton's presidency, and promised to focus on "enduring national interests" rather than idealistic humanitarian goals. Candidate Bush warned against the notion that "our military is the answer to every difficult foreign policy situation—a substitute for strategy."

To be sure, the administration included major players from the neoconservative camp—including Deputy Secretary of Defense Paul Wolfowitz, Undersecretary of Defense Douglas Feith, and Undersecretary of State John Bolton—who believed in the forceful promotion of democracy in other countries. But the more central players appeared to be closer to the realism of Bush's father. Vice President Dick Cheney, a key player in the George H. W. Bush administration, had opposed using U.S. forces to overthrow Saddam Hussein during the first Gulf War ("How long would we have had to stay in Baghdad?") and had lobbied against sanctions on Iran as CEO of Halliburton in the late 1990s. Secretary of State Colin Powell was famously cautious about the use of force to pursue foreign policy goals and emphasized the value of allies. National Security Adviser Condoleezza Rice—who insisted that the role of the 82nd Airborne was not to "escort kids to kindergarten"—was a protégé of the realist icon Brent Scowcroft. In her Republican Party foreign policy manifesto, published in *Foreign Affairs* in January/February 2000, Rice wrote that regimes such as those in Iraq and North Korea were "living on borrowed time, so there need be no sense of panic about them." She called for the first line of defense to be "a clear and classical statement of deterrence—if they do acquire WMD [weapons of mass destruction], their weapons will be unusable because any attempt to use them will bring national obliteration." Powell had also questioned whether Iraq posed a serious threat and had suggested in his January 2001 confirmation hearings that U.S. policy would be to "keep [the Iraqis] in the rather broken condition they are in now."

How, then, did the United States go from this cautious realism to the invasion of Iraq and a foreign policy focused on ending tyranny throughout the world? The answer is to be found in the unique combination of two factors.

The first was the sudden sense of vulnerability Americans felt following 9/11. The attacks profoundly altered the American worldview—not only because they took place on U.S. soil, but also because of Americans' low tolerance, born of their country's relatively blessed history, for insecurity. Not since the Cuban missile crisis had Americans felt anything remotely as threatening to their homeland as this, which made the public highly receptive to calls to "do something" about terrorism. When anthrax attacks killed five Americans and terrorized the general population later that fall, many concluded that only a dramatic change in U.S. foreign policy—even if it meant military action to transform the world, starting with the Middle East—could make the homeland safe again. . . .

The second factor that led to the revolution in U.S. foreign policy was a feeling of tremendous power. It may have been a sense of vulnerability that convinced Americans that they had to do something to transform the world, but it was a sense of unprecedented power that convinced them that they could. After the preoccupation with national "decline" in the deficit-ridden late 1980s, a decade of fantastic economic growth, technological progress, and military successes led Americans to conclude by 2001 that transformation was possible, if only the country's leaders committed to that goal. Naysayers at home and abroad might warn about overreach, but that was because they did not appreciate what a determined United States could accomplish. . . .

The combination of these two factors—a feeling of vulnerability and a feeling of power—tipped the balance within the administration in favor of the idealists and put the president and the vice president firmly in that camp. Gone was the aversion to interventionism and gone was caution; in their place was an unwavering determination to make the homeland safe, first by using U.S. military power to eliminate threats such as Saddam Hussein and then by spreading freedom and democracy around the world.

Whether Washington's European allies, or anyone else, for that matter, accepted the administration's logic was thought largely immaterial. According to the administration, success in Iraq, which few top officials doubted, would have a positive spillover effect elsewhere in the Middle East, at which point U.S. allies would start to come on board. U.S. leadership, the thinking went, consisted not of endlessly consulting pessimistic allies to see what they had to say, but of setting out a bold course, decisively following it, and winning over allies through victory rather than persuasion.

REVOLUTION MEETS REALITY

Needless to say, everything has not turned out as planned. Far from producing the rapid liberation, stabilization, and democratization of Iraq, the U.S. invasion has led to a protracted insurgency, significant Iraqi civilian and U.S. military casualties, and a high risk of civil war. At the time of the fall of Baghdad, in the spring of 2003, polls showed that more than 70 percent of Americans supported the war; by early 2006, polls indicated that a majority had concluded that the war was a mistake. The allied support that success was supposed to bring also failed to materialize. The absence of the WMD that had provided the official pretext for the war—and the widespread impression that the administration had exaggerated the threat in order to sell the war and had violated international law by waging it—raised serious questions about the legitimacy of U.S. foreign policy in Iraq and elsewhere.

The consequences of the war in Iraq—and of other U.S. policies on issues ranging from the Middle East to climate change, prisoner treatment, and the International Criminal Court (ICC)—have taken their toll on the United States' popularity in the world and thus on its ability to win over allies. Far from producing the expected "bandwagoning," the exercise of unilateral U.S. power has led to widespread hostility toward the Bush administration and, in many cases, the United States itself. . . .

On top of failure in Iraq and a decline in legitimacy and popularity abroad, the feeling and the reality of U.S. power needed for a foreign policy of transforming the world have also been evaporating. When Bush took office in 2001, he inherited an annual budgetary surplus of over $200 billion and many additional years' worth of projected surpluses. Under those circumstances, it was not surprising that Americans regained confidence in their ability to change the world for the better, even if that meant supporting military interventions abroad and vastly expanding the defense budget. But after the terrorist attacks, a recession, two wars, and several massive tax cuts, the sense that the United States can afford "whatever it takes" is gone. By the start of 2006, the $200 billion annual surplus had turned into a more than $400 billion annual deficit, and the national debt that Washington had started paying off in 1999 was up to more than $8 trillion and was rising.

Domestic support for the administration . . . is also on the wane. . . . Bush's approval rating has fallen to under 35 percent and Cheney's to just 20 percent. By early 2006, 55 percent of Americans surveyed said that the invasion of Iraq had not been "worth it," and more Americans thought the United States should "mind [its] own business" than at any time since Vietnam. In a 2006 Public Agenda poll, only 20 percent of respondents agreed that spreading democracy to other countries was a "very important goal" for U.S. foreign policy, representing the lowest support for any goal asked about in the survey. A blind spot in the neoconservative case for democracy promotion and unilateral military action has always been that it overlooks the limits on the American public's willingness to tolerate the costs.

These developments have inevitably had a major impact on the administration's ability to pursue the transformative foreign policy that was its hallmark in Bush's first term. Although the president's rhetoric and core beliefs may not have changed, the realities of a difficult world are clearly sinking in.

THE COUNTERREVOLUTION

The modified approach to foreign policy was immediately apparent in the new tone and style adopted at the start of Bush's second term. Newly appointed Secretary of State Rice stated in her confirmation hearing that "the time for diplomacy is now" and immediately set off on a fence-mending trip to Europe, where the costs of U.S. unilateralism had become most apparent. A few weeks later, the president himself went to Europe, where he reached out to allies in a way that sharply contrasted with the unilateralism of his first term. . . .

The new tone and style were also reflected in the foreign policy team Bush and Rice put together. The president, the vice president, and the secretary of defense were obviously still in place and in charge, but many of those most closely associated with the ideology of the first term were not. Gone from the halls of power were the neoconservatives Wolfowitz, Feith, and Bolton (the last was sent to the United Nations, an important post but not a policymaking job). The new team instead featured pragmatists such as Deputy Secretary of State Robert Zoellick, Undersecretary of State Nicholas Burns, and North Korea negotiator Christopher Hill.

What is more important than the new tone or new personnel, policies have also started to shift during the Bush administration's second term. After criticizing European engagement with Iran for years and insisting that the United States would not "reward bad behavior," the president returned from his February 2005 trip and announced that the United States would support the "EU-3" negotiations being conducted by France, Germany, and the United Kingdom and even throw some of its own "carrots"—airplane spare parts and support for World Trade Organization accession negotiations—into the mix. When, in late 2005, Iran threatened to break off negotiations with the Europeans and resume nuclear enrichment, the United States insisted there was plenty of time to take the issue to the UN Security Council, leaving some of its European partners wondering if it was going "wobbly." In March 2006, the administration announced that it had offered to open up a dialogue with Tehran about Iraq, a dramatic departure from its earlier insistence that such a step would legitimize the Iranian regime, and it bowed to Russia's refusal to accept anything stronger than a critical "presidential statement" when the nuclear issue was reported to the Security Council. Bush's declaration, in his 2006 State of the Union speech, that the United States would "continue to rally the world" to confront the Iranian threat was a far cry from earlier suggestions of how the United States might deal with a charter member of "the axis of evil."

There was also a significant change in policy toward the other outstanding member of that club, North Korea. Having denounced the Clinton administration's 1994 Agreed Framework and having insisted it would never agree to anything similar, the Bush administration accepted an arrangement with Pyongyang in September 2005 that would have provided North Korea with energy aid, security guarantees, and the gradual normalization of relations in exchange for North Korea's abandoning its nuclear weapons programs. Such an agreement could almost certainly have been reached years before, but it was anathema to the first Bush team. . . .

The second Bush team has also made modest changes in its stances on foreign aid and climate change, in an effort to reverse the United States' negative image in the world. In the run-up to the G-8 summit in Gleneagles, Scotland, Bush announced his intention to double U.S. aid to Africa by 2010 and to commit $1.2 billion for a five-year plan to combat malaria in sub-Saharan Africa. At the summit itself, Bush acknowledged that global climate change was a "serious, urgent, and largely man-made problem" and agreed to join other countries in discussions of what to do about it. . . .

The new Bush team has even modified its stance toward certain international organizations. In Bush's first term, the administration displayed unmitigated hostility toward the ICC—to the point of cutting off financial aid to anyone, even key allies, who refused to grant U.S. citizens a blanket exemption from its provisions. During Bush's second term, in contrast, the administration has supported a UN resolution that would refer war crimes suspects from Sudan's Darfur region to the ICC and has agreed to the use of ICC facilities in The Hague for the war crimes trial of former Liberian President Charles Taylor. In February 2006, Bush pledged support for a UN mission to help end the killing in Darfur, something the administration resisted throughout its first term. And when, in March 2006, UN members agreed to set up a Human Rights Council (to replace the UN Commission on Human Rights) that was not to Washington's liking, the administration did not vote for it but at the same time pledged to support it and work with it—instead of delegitimizing it, as Washington initially had the ICC.

Finally, the administration has shown signs of backing away from a core tenet of the foreign policy of its first term by deciding, in the summer of 2005, that the "global war on terror" (GWOT) would henceforth be known as the "global struggle against violent extremism" (GSAVE). The president himself let it be known that he still believed the United States was fighting a "war" and repudiated the new rhetoric, but the fact that the administration was even pondering such a change . . . was a sure sign that it had acknowledged some of the excesses of Bush's first term. The administration now goes out of its way to emphasize that it knows it is in a "generational" struggle and that it must do more to win global hearts, minds, and sympathy—a task recently put under the control of one of Bush's most trusted advisers, Karen Hughes.

THE RISK OF RELAPSE

The stalling of the Bush revolution is not really surprising. U.S. foreign policy has historically been marked by regular and sometimes wild swings between internationalism and isolationism, and those swings have been influenced by changes in threat perceptions, the amount of available resources, and the level of domestic political support, just as they are today.

Accordingly, the new direction of Bush's foreign policy is far from irreversible. Although the Bush team has been forced by reality to work more closely with allies and to set aside the doctrine of regime change by military intervention, many in the administration still believe that the threat of terrorism allows—or even requires—the United States to operate under different international rules from everyone else, limiting the degree to which the administration can continue to adapt. Moreover, powerful figures within the administration—not least the vice president—will continue to argue against the new pragmatism. Indeed, part of the "revolutionary" premise of the foreign policy of Bush's first term was the notion, harking back to the Reagan administration, that determination, optimism, and U.S. power would eventually prevail, regardless of what Democrats and foreign critics might assert. It is a convenient thesis, but one that does not allow for self-correction; it paints any lack of domestic or international support as a badge of honor and apparent failures as only temporary setbacks rather than as reasons to change course.

What could cause Bush to reconsider his new approach and put U.S. foreign policy back on a more revolutionary path? Certainly, another major terrorist attack on the United States, which remains possible, could do so.

If a U.S. city were hit by a chemical or biological terrorist attack leading to mass casualties, more Americans might come around to the view that the United States is in fact "at war" and that the administration's aggressive efforts to "change the world" are "worth it." Bombing Iran in order to prevent it from acquiring nuclear weapons would probably seem rash and counterproductive to most Americans today, but in the wake of a nuclear or even a "dirty bomb" attack that killed large numbers of Americans, the calculation about the risks of nuclear proliferation might look very different. A WMD attack might even provide retrospective justification for the Iraq war, reinforcing the notion that the United States cannot risk not acting in the face of a potential threat of proliferation.

Even in the absence of another terrorist attack, Iran—which the new National Security Strategy says poses the greatest challenge to the United States of any single country—could provoke a reversion to the original Bush doctrine. For the past two years, the trend in the administration has been to emphasize diplomacy and international consensus, the opposite of the approach that characterized the administration's Iraq policy in 2002–3. But if that approach manifestly fails—for example, if evidence emerges that Iran is actually closer to a nuclear weapons capability than previously thought—Bush may be faced sooner rather than later with a choice between acquiescing to a nuclear Iran and resorting to the unilateral use of force. For now, the administration's clear preference is to avoid a confrontation and keep the international community on its side. But what if that requires direct engagement with the radical regime of President Mahmoud Ahmadinejad and an end to U.S. efforts to promote regime change? That might be a bridge too far for this team, and Bush might conclude that military force—or accelerated efforts to destabilize the Iranian regime—is the only way to uphold his 2002 State of the Union pledge not to allow "the world's most dangerous regimes to threaten us with the world's most destructive weapons."

Finally, it is always possible that new developments will be taken as evidence that the Bush doctrine has actually been working. For example, the formation of a viable Iraqi government followed by an ebbing of the insurgency and progress toward democratization elsewhere in the Middle East could lead the administration back in the direction of foreign policy assertiveness. After all, it was not that long ago that successful elections in Iraq and Afghanistan, a revolution in Lebanon followed by Syrian withdrawal, nuclear disarmament in Libya, and steps toward democracy elsewhere in the Arab world were leading administration enthusiasts to crow about their success; even some skeptical observers were concluding that Bush might actually be right. Renewed progress in these areas, especially if it allows for a military withdrawal from Iraq and coincides with a burst of growth in the U.S. economy, could give new force to the idea that a determined United States can transform the world and new arguments to those who believe that Bush should not waver in the promotion of his doctrine.

The more likely course is that global realities and resource constraints will continue to force the administration toward pragmatism, modesty, and cooperation with allies. Even serious new challenges and threats would be unlikely to persuade chastened Americans to get back on board for the types of policies they have been coming to doubt; the scenario whereby dictatorships start falling like dominoes and the United States feels rich, powerful, and right is highly desirable but unlikely to unfold anytime soon.

Still, it would be rash to exclude a return to a more radical approach, especially from a president who believes he is on a mission and who has time and again proved willing to take massive risks and surprise his critics. If such a return happens, brace yourself—because there is no reason to believe that round two of the Bush revolution would be more successful than round one. Indeed, without the resources, international legitimacy, and degree of political support Bush had the first time around, it might be considerably worse.

Conclusion

This collection of essays offers a diverse range of perspectives on the opportunities and challenges that confront U.S. foreign policymakers under conditions of change. A number of key questions stand out from the preceding chapters. In this brief conclusion, I highlight some of the issues that are likely to shape policy debates and choices over the coming years.

CAN AMERICAN DOMINANCE LAST?

In the past, the prospect that a single state might achieve a position of international supremacy has often stimulated other states to coalesce in an effort to balance the power of the prospective hegemon. In the case of the United States, this balancing response is not evident so far, although the unilateral uses of American power in recent years have generated heightened international criticism and instances of noncooperation. The unprecedented power advantages that the United States enjoys over other states and the absence of coordinated efforts to balance U.S. strengths provide American policymakers with considerable freedom of action. Nevertheless, the long-term prospects for continued American dominance appear less sure. Some argue that the economic foundations of U.S. power will be eroded by the combination of a low rate of domestic savings, uncontrolled budget and trade deficits, and growing U.S. indebtedness to foreign investors. Meanwhile, the rapid economic growth of China and India, both large, populous countries possessing nuclear arsenals, suggests that the United States may eventually face growing rivalry with one or both of these rising powers. How rapidly American power erodes and the terms under which it is challenged are key questions.

WHAT ARE THE LIMITS OF AMERICAN POWER?

If we define power in terms of relative military and economic resources, American strength appears unchallenged by any single competitor. Yet if we think of power as the ability to dictate international outcomes, then it becomes easier to grasp the real limits that constrain American influence. In head-to-head conventional warfare, the military advantages enjoyed by U.S. forces quickly become evident. It took less than three weeks for the U.S. military to thoroughly defeat Saddam Hussein's military machine. Yet when it comes to more complex tasks, such as locating and destroying terrorists, combating a guerrilla-style insurgency in Iraq, or producing stable and orderly governing institutions in place of failed or defeated regimes, even the orchestrated combination of American military, economic, and political resources appears to be inadequate. Figuring out where the limits of U.S. control over outcomes lie is an important task for American policymakers.

WHEN SHOULD THE UNITED STATES USE MILITARY FORCE IN SUPPORT OF ITS FOREIGN POLICY OBJECTIVES?

The traditional realist response to this question is that military force should be employed only when vital national interests are at stake. This leaves considerable room, however, for debate over how such interests are to be defined and whether American security could be better served through nonmilitary options, such as diplomacy or economic sanctions. Moreover, some argue that the United States has a responsibility to intervene militarily on behalf of humanitarian objectives, as in several recent cases, including Somalia, Kosovo, Haiti, and Liberia. The Iraq war raised both sets of issues. Deep disagreements arose over whether Iraq posed an immanent threat to the United States or its allies. Divisions also appeared over whether the brutal nature of Saddam Hussein's rule in Iraq offered a sufficient humanitarian rationale for intervention. In general, a lack of consensus remains within the United States over the criteria that should govern the uses of military force.

HOW IMPORTANT IS INTERNATIONAL LEGITIMACY?

Under what conditions will the international community accord legitimacy to the exercise of power by a dominant state? Two possible sources of legitimacy exist. The actions of a great power might be viewed as legitimate if they conform to the rules and norms of existing international institutions, including procedures for consultation and consensus building. Alternatively, the behavior of a dominant state may be viewed as legitimate if other actors are convinced that its power is employed on behalf of the general interests of the international community as a whole rather than a narrower, self-serving set of interests. The first is a procedural conception of legitimacy while the second is a substantive conception. In either case, some argue that hegemony is more stable and the costs of maintaining order are lower to the extent that the exercise of power by the dominant state is viewed as legitimate by other actors. In this view, the United States is best served by a foreign policy that is firmly grounded in international consensus. Others, by contrast, argue that international consensus is either too difficult to achieve or places too many constraints on the pursuit of American interests abroad. From this perspective, it is power, rather than legitimacy, that should serve as the underlying determinant of U.S. foreign policy.

SHOULD THE UNITED STATES ACT UNILATERALLY OR THROUGH MULTILATERAL INSTITUTIONS?

Closely related to the issue of international legitimacy is the question of whether the United States should work within the constraints of multilateral institutions or reserve the freedom to act independently of those constraints. Multilateralism allows states to make mutually beneficial tradeoffs, to share burdens, and to address collective problems that cannot be managed by individual states acting alone. Advocates insist that multilateralism holds out the promise of a more cooperative, rule-bound, and predictable international system. Critics, on the other hand, view multilateralist institutions as unnecessary constraints on American freedom of action. Multilateral institutions work slowly and often produce agreements that reflect the lowest common denominator among participating states. While weaker states gain a voice and influence through multilateral institutions, American critics argue that multilateralism serves only to encumber U.S. power. In a changing world, the United States is best served by maximizing its freedom to deploy its power advantages without constraint. The debate over multilateralism versus unilateralism has risen in prominence since the end of the cold war and will likely produce continued disagreement over the modalities of U.S. foreign policy.

IS DETERRENCE OUTDATED?

Even the most powerful states face serious challenges in protecting their citizens from the potential threats posed by weapons of mass destruction (nuclear, biological, and chemical). During the cold war, the United States sought security along two tracks. First, the United States relied upon the threat of massive retaliation to deter the Soviet Union from launching a nuclear attack against the United States or its allies. Second, the Nuclear Non-Proliferation Treaty and similar international agreements dealing with biological and chemical weapons sought to prevent the spread of weapons of mass destruction to new states. In recent years, however, the Bush administration has called into question the adequacy of deterrence as a mechanism for preventing the use of weapons of mass destruction by rogue states or terrorist groups. Meanwhile, multilateral agreements have appeared less effective in halting nuclear proliferation among both signatory (e.g., Iran and North Korea) and nonsignatory (e.g., India and Pakistan) states. In response to these developments, the Bush administration has endorsed the principle of preventive warfare against hostile states that appear intent upon acquiring weapons of mass destruction. This rationale was employed in support of the war in Iraq. However, the failure of subsequent inspections to find any weapons of mass destruction in postwar Iraq has raised questions about the reliability of U.S. intelligence and the wisdom of preventive war as a response to the risks of proliferation. As of this writing, the viability of the military option as a means to halt the proliferation of weapons of mass destruction in cases such as Iran and North Korea remains a matter of continued debate.

BY WHAT MEANS SHOULD THE UNITED STATES SEEK TO PROMOTE THE SPREAD OF DEMOCRACY ABROAD?

The U.S. invasion of Iraq was initially justified as a response to Iraq's suspected ambitions to develop weapons of mass destruction. Given the subsequent failure to discover such weapons, however, the rationale for America's continued political and military presence in Iraq shifted to the promotion of democracy there and, potentially, elsewhere in the Middle East. This redefinition of mission has once again raised the recurring question of whether it is desirable or feasible for the United States to seek the spread of democracy through military intervention. Less coercive methods for promoting democracy abroad—political support, aid, education, and election monitoring—generate little controversy in the United States. The wisdom of more forceful means for bringing about democratic regime change, however, remains a matter of keen dispute. The success or failure of U.S. intervention in Iraq will likely shape U.S. policies on this issue for years to come.

WILL THE WAR ON TERROR SERVE AS A LASTING FOCAL POINT FOR U.S. FOREIGN POLICY?

For the United States, the decades following World War II were defined by the struggle against communism. Will U.S. foreign policy be similarly marked by a war on terrorism in the coming era? The comparison is in some ways apt. Like the cold war, the post-9/11 fight against terrorism involves political, military, and ideological dimensions. Also similar is the expansive geographic scope of the conflict. In other ways, however, the present conflict differs from the cold war. Communism represented an all-encompassing political and economic order with universal pretensions and was sponsored by a great rival power, the Soviet Union. Terrorism, by contrast, is a political tactic that has been employed by varied states and nonstate actors. The principal terrorist threats directed against the United States today arise from militant Islamic groups such Al Qaeda and allied organizations. With the fall of the Taliban in Afghanistan, Al Qaeda lacks any explicit state sponsor. While Al Qaeda claims to act upon the basis of Islamic principles, most Muslims reject terrorism and the United States has sought to disavow charges that the struggle against terrorism is targeted at the Islamic world as a whole. In general, the stakes, the nature of the threat, and the ideological character of the present conflict differ in numerous respects from those of the cold war. Nevertheless, it remains to be seen whether the war on terror proves as protracted and deep-seated as the preceding war on communism.

CONCLUSION

The questions posed here are likely to prove of enduring relevance as the United States struggles to define its international role in a changing world. The varied perspectives on these and other issues addressed in the chapters of this volume provide a valuable roadmap to the complex debates that surround U.S. foreign policy in the present era.

Credits

The readings included in this volume have been used with permission from the following sources. They appear in condensed form, and all footnotes, endnotes, and references have been omitted.

"American Primacy in Perspective" by Stephen G. Brooks and William C. Wohlforth reprinted from *Foreign Affairs* 81, no. 4 (July/August 2002). Reprinted by permission of FOREIGN AFFAIRS (Volume 81, 2002). Copyright 2002 by the Council on Foreign Relations, Inc.

"The Decline of America's Soft Power" by Joseph S. Nye Jr. reprinted from *Foreign Affairs* 83, no. 3 (May/June 2004). Reprinted by permission of FOREIGN AFFAIRS (Volume 83, 2004). Copyright 2004 by the Council on Foreign Relations, Inc.

"The Inadequacy of American Power" by Michael Mandelbaum reprinted from *Foreign Affairs* 81, no. 5 (September/October 2002). Reprinted with the permission of Perseus Books Group.

"America as a European Hegemon" by Christopher Layne reprinted from *The National Interest* (Summer 2003), 17–29. Reprinted with the permission of *The National Interest*.

"A Global Power Shift in the Making" by James F. Hoge Jr. reprinted from *Foreign Affairs* 83, no. 4 (July/August 2004). Reprinted by permission of FOREIGN AFFAIRS (Volume 83, 2004). Copyright 2004 by the Council on Foreign Relations, Inc.

"History Lesson: What Woodrow Wilson Can Teach Today's Imperialists" by John B. Judis reprinted from *The New Republic*, June 9, 2003. Reprinted with the permission of The New Republic.

About the Editor and Contributors

EDITOR

David Skidmore is a professor in the Department of Politics and International Relations at Drake University. Skidmore currently serves as director of the Drake University Center for Global Citizenship. He is coauthor (with Thomas D. Lairson) of *International Political Economy: The Struggle for Power and Wealth* (Thomson/Wadsworth 2003) and editor of *Contested Social Orders and International Politics* (Vanderbilt University Press 1997).

CONTRIBUTORS

Andrew J. Bacevich is professor of international relations and history at Boston University. He is author of *The New American Militarism: How Americans Are Seduced by War* (Oxford University Press 2005) and *American Empire: The Realities and Consequences of American Diplomacy* (Harvard University Press 2002).

Max Boot is an Olin senior fellow at the Council on Foreign Relations. He is author of *War Made New: Technology, Warfare, and the Course of History* (Gotham 2006) and *The Savage Wars of Peace: Small Wars and the Rise of American Power* (Basic 2003).

Stephen G. Brooks is an assistant professor in the Department of Government at Dartmouth College. He is the author of *Producing Security: Multinational Corporations, Globalization, and the Changing Calculus of Conflict* (Princeton University Press 2005).

Ralph G. Carter is a professor of political science at Texas Christian University. He is editor of *Contemporary Cases in U.S. Foreign Policy: From Terrorism to Trade* (CQ Press 2005).

Robert F. Ellsworth is a former U.S. congressional representative, U.S. ambassador, and assistant secretary of defense.

Niall Ferguson is the Lawrence A. Tisch professor of history at Harvard University. He is author of *The War of the World: Twentieth Century Conflict and the Descent of the West* (Penguin 2006) and *Colossus: The Price of America's Empire* (Penguin 2004).

Francis Fukuyama is Bernard L. Schwartz Professor of International Political Economy at the School of Advanced International Studies, Johns Hopkins University. He is author of *America at the Crossroads: Democracy, Power, and the Neoconservative Legacy* (Yale University Press 2006).

Philip H. Gordon is a senior fellow for U.S. foreign policy at the Brookings Institution. He is coeditor and coauthor (with Ivo H. Daalder and Nicole Gnesotto) of *Crescent of Crisis: U.S.-European Strategy for the Greater Middle East* (Brookings Institution Press 2006).

Christopher Hitchens is a columnist for *Vanity Fair*. He is author of *Blood, Class, and Empire: The Enduring Anglo-American Relationship* (Nation Books 2004) and *A Long, Short War: The Postponed Liberation of Iraq* (Plume 2003).

James F. Hoge Jr. is the editor and Peter G. Peterson chair of *Foreign Affairs* magazine. He is coeditor (with Gideon Rose) of *How Did This Happen? Terrorism and the New War* (Public Affairs 2001).

Michael Ignatieff is director of the Carr Center at the Kennedy School of Government. He is author of *The Lesser Evil: Political Ethics in an Age of Terror* (Princeton University Press 2004).

G. John Ikenberry is Peter F. Krogh Professor of Geopolitics and Global Justice at Georgetown University. He is author of *After Victory: Institutions, Strategic Restraint, and the Rebuilding of Order after Major Wars* (Princeton

University Press 2001) and *Liberal Order and Imperial Ambition: Essays on American Power and International Order* (Polity Press 2006).

John B. Judis is senior editor at *The New Republic*. He is author of *The Folly of Empire: What George W. Bush Could Learn from Theodore Roosevelt and Woodrow Wilson* (Scribner 2004) and *The Paradox of American Democracy: Elites, Special Interests, and the Betrayal of the Public Trust* (Pantheon 2000).

Robert Kagan is a senior associate at the Carnegie Endowment of International Peace. He is author of *Dangerous Nation: America's Role in the World from Its Earliest Days to the Dawn of the Twentieth Century* (Knopf 2006) and *Of Paradise and Power: America and Europe in the New World Order* (Knopf 2003).

Charles Krauthammer, winner of the Pulitzer Prize for commentary, is a syndicated columnist for the *Washington Post* and an essayist for *Time*.

Christopher Layne is a research fellow at the Center on Peace and Liberty at the Independent Institute. He is author of *The Peace of Illusions: American Grand Strategy from 1940 to the Present* (Cornell University Press 2006) and coauthor (with Bradley A. Thayer) of *American Empire: A Debate* (Routledge 2006).

Michael Mandelbaum is Christian A. Herter Professor of American Foreign Policy at the Johns Hopkins School of Advanced International Studies and senior fellow at the Council on Foreign Relations. He is author of *The Ideas That Conquered the World: Peace, Democracy, and Free Markets in the Twenty-first Century* (Public Affairs 2002).

Joseph S. Nye Jr. is dean of Harvard University's Kennedy School of Government. He is author of *Soft Power: The Means to Success in World Politics* (Public Affairs 2004) and *The Paradox of American Power: Why the World's Only Superpower Can't Go It Alone* (Oxford University Press 2002).

Minxin Pei is a senior associate and director of the China Program at the Carnegie Endowment for International Peace in Washington, D.C. He is author of *China's Trapped Transition: The Limits of Developmental Autocracy* (Harvard University Press 2006).

Pew Global Attitudes Project is a project of the Pew Research Center for the People and the Press, an independent opinion research group based in Washington, D.C., that studies attitudes toward the press, politics, and public policy issues.

Jeffrey Record is a professor in the Department of Strategy and International Security at the U.S. Air Force's Air War College. He is author of *Dark Victory: America's Second War against Iraq* (Naval Institute Press 2004) and *Making War, Thinking History: Munich, Vietnam, and Presidential Uses of Force from Korea to Kosovo* (Naval Institute Press 2002).

Paul W. Schroeder is professor emeritus in history at the University of Illinois, Urbana-Champaign. He is author of *The Transformation of European Politics, 1763–1848* (Oxford University Press 1994).

Todd S. Sechser is an assistant professor of politics at the University of Virginia. He has written a number of journal articles and book chapters, including "Are Soldiers Less War-Prone Than Statesmen?" (*Journal of Conflict Resolution* 48, no. 5, 2004).

Dimitri K. Simes is founding president of the Nixon Center. He is author of *After the Collapse: Russia Seeks Its Place as a Great Power* (Simon & Schuster 1999).

Stephen M. Walt is the Robert and Renee Belfer Professor of International Affairs at the John F. Kennedy School of Government at Harvard University. He is author of *Taming American Power: The Global Response to U.S. Primacy* (Norton 2005).

The White House issued the National Security Strategy statement of September 20, 2002, in accordance with the Goldwater-Nichols Department of Defense Reorganization Act, which mandated an annual report to the Congress on U.S. national security strategy. The 2002 edition of the National Security Strategy is reprinted in edited form here due to its groundbreaking policy departures.

William C. Wohlforth is professor and chair of the Department of Government at Dartmouth University. He is author of *The Elusive Balance: Power and Perceptions during the Cold War* (Cornell University Press 1993).